Jaguar
AT LE MANS

Jaguar
AT LE MANS

EVERY RACE, CAR AND DRIVER, 1950–1995

Paul Parker Foreword by Tony Southgate

Dedication

To 'Tiger', wherever he may be.

First published in 2001

A catalogue record for this book is
available from the British Library

ISBN 1 85960 632 6

Library of Congress catalog card no. 2001131345

Published by Haynes Publishing, Sparkford,
Nr Yeovil, Somerset BA22 7JJ, UK.
Tel: 01963 442030 Fax: 01963 440001
Int.tel: +44 1963 442030 Fax: +44 1963 440001
E-mail: sales@haynes-manuals.co.uk
Web site: www.haynes.co.uk

Haynes North America Inc., 861 Lawrence Drive,
Newbury Park, California 91320, USA.

Designed and typeset by G&M,
Raunds, Wellingborough, Northamptonshire

Printed and bound in Britain by
J. H. Haynes & Co. Ltd, Sparkford

Contents

Foreword by Tony Southgate

For a car manufacturer there are few sporting events in this world which can compare with the Le Mans 24-hour motor race for prestige, glamour and engineering excellence. To win this famous event is a great achievement for the team and the manufacturer. To win this event seven times, as Jaguar has done, is simply a supreme achievement. Jaguar has now gained immortal association with this race. All these victories were established through the use of new technologies and designs in the chassis, while using racing versions of their road-going car engines.

The 1950s, a very exciting period in British motor racing history, produced five Le Mans victories for Jaguar. Two were with the C-type, whose revolutionary use of disc brakes helped to change the world of motoring. This was followed by three victories with the beautiful D-type, whose aerodynamics and monocoque chassis structure set the standards for others to aim at.

When Jaguar returned to racing at Le Mans with the V12-engined cars of the 1980s and 1990s, I was delighted to accept the offer from TWR to design the new cars. The XJR6 to XJR12 were all state-of-the-art sports race cars with advanced aerodynamics, suspension systems, carbon-fibre chassis structures and bodywork. TWR developed the engines from 6 litres in 1985 to 7.4 litres in 1991 with up to 750bhp available for 24 hours – an impressive record for a production-based two valves per cylinder, single camshaft per head engine. Aerodynamically the XJRs were in a class of their own when compared with the formerly all-conquering Porsches, and even the later Jaguar lookalike Mercedes. Inevitably, the turbo Porsches and later the Mercedes, due to their ability to temporarily increase their engine boost pressure, were able to out-qualify the naturally aspirated Jaguars. However, this advantage was short-lived and the Jaguars would overwhelm them under true race conditions.

Two of the most satisfying moments from Le Mans have been from seeing the Jaguars cruise past the Porsches and Mercedes on the long Mulsanne Straight, thus justifying all my long hours of work in the wind tunnel. Then, after Win Percy's huge accident in 1987 when he barrel rolled at maximum speed on the Mulsanne Straight due to a rear tyre delamination, scattering debris for hundreds of yards, hearing with great relief that he had walked away from it unharmed, proving the massive structural strength and protection provided by the Jaguar's carbon-fibre monocoque.

I can honestly say that of all the racing cars that I have designed and of all the teams that I have worked for over 38 years in motor racing, TWR Jaguar was the most enjoyable. With Le Mans the result is so great, like winning the F1 World Championship in one race, that you have time to savour it and recall magic moments for 12 months before doing it all again.

I feel privileged to have been in a position to have helped Jaguar add to their Le Mans heritage and hope to see them return in the not-too-distant future.

Tony Southgate
May 2001

Preface and acknowledgements

Although it was my original suggestion to write this book, I did so with some reservations. My other life as historic racing correspondent for *Classic Jaguar World* and association with the fabulous photographic archive of Karl Ludvigsen was crucial to the project. A life-long interest in the subject helps of course, as did the family ownership of an XK140 FHC s/e in the 1950s and the original 'HWM 1' HWM Jaguar and the 1958 Le Mans ENB Lister-Jaguar during the 1960s, these last two purchased for £800 and £1,250 respectively! Subsequently I bought two Jaguar XK120 FHCs, the first when I was 18, the second when I was old enough to know better.

I was fully aware that Jaguar books abounded and much of the story surrounding their racing activities had been chronicled in one form or another over the years. Hopefully you will find the assembled facts and figures about Jaguar at Le Mans of fresh interest, as no dedicated book on this specific area of Jaguar's racing history has been published before under one cover. Additionally I have included some of the background and a brief summary of Jaguar's other racing endeavours. This is essentially two books, the first being the Lyons/Heynes XK era, the second, the Egan/Group 44/TWR period.

Inevitably I had to draw on the research of others, particularly Andrew Whyte's two wonderful tomes. Many of the original cast of characters have now departed, as sadly, he did also at a tragically early age. Nevertheless some hitherto obscure facts of Jaguar's racing past plus the first-hand reminiscences of some of those involved, stretching back to the early 1950s, have emerged. A source of concern was the seemingly endless variations of the average speeds, numbers of laps and distances covered, calculated in imperial and metric form. Contemporary reports, Le Mans records and assorted books all seemed to have their own slightly different calculations, so my apologies for any apparent disparities. Later race results lacked the average speed and distance details for the placemen.

No book like this can be written in isolation and many people have given generously of their time and knowledge. Firstly Karl Ludvigsen provided the encouragement, advice and experience plus his superb photographic archive that made this project possible. Secondly I must thank Darryl Reach, Mark Hughes and the editorial staff of Haynes Publishing for their patience and faith in my abilities. I am grateful to all the others who contributed to this work:

Hugh Chamberlain, Michael Cooper, Claude Dubois, Geoff Goddard, Penny Graham, Mrs Angela Hamilton, Peter Higham, Chris Keith-Lucas, Terry Larson, Kevin Lee, Peter Lumsden, Ian Marshall (LAT), John Mayston-Taylor, Doug Nye, Keith Partridge, John Pearson, Win Percy, Brian Playford, Brian Redman, Maurice Rowe, Peter Sargent, Paul Skilleter, Tony Southgate, Stan Sproat, Gary Watkins and Jeff Wilson.

Introduction

The names Jaguar and Le Mans are almost synonymous. Located in the department of Sarthe in north-western France, Le Mans is, together with Indianapolis, the most famous motor racing venue in the world. Le Mans was first used for motor racing in 1906 for the *Grand Prix de l'A.C.F.,* better known as the French Grand Prix. This was organised by the *Automobile Club de la Sarthe*, the forerunner of the *Automobile Club de l'Ouest.* After the First World War, a new permanent circuit was established using the public roads to the south of Le Mans 10.726 miles (17.262km) in length. Three men were responsible for the Le Mans 24 hour race. Georges Durand of the *Automobile Club de l'Ouest*, Charles Faroux, editor of *La Vie Automobile* and Emile Coquille, the French agent for Rudge-Whitworth detachable wire wheels. The original layout hosted the first *Le Grand Prix d'Endurance de Vingt-Quatre Heures du Mans* in 1923. Six years later the circuit was slightly reduced in length and retained this form for just three races before adopting the now familiar 8.383-mile (13.492km) pattern which was used from 1931 to 1955.

Track alterations following the 1955 disaster reduced the circuit to 8.364 miles (13.461km) in 1956 and this remained until 1968 when a chicane, called the Virage Ford was built after White House to slow down the cars as they passed the pits area. Thereafter various chicanes and safety driven changes were made to try to control the burgeoning speeds, but the essential nature of the track retained much of its original character until the early 1980s.

Perhaps the biggest changes however reside with the cars, the original concept of road-equipped touring machines gradually evolving into out-and-out racing cars. Nevertheless, as late as the 1970s, some Le Mans devices could still have been driven on the road, albeit not legally. Jaguar's five victories during the 1950s had an historic precedent, W. O. Bentley's magnificent 3, 4.5 and 6.5-litre automobiles winning five such races between 1924 and 1930. Overall, only Porsche and Ferrari have won more races at Le Mans, and both these marques had a much longer and more consistent racing participation than Jaguar.

As Formula One developed and grew during the 1970s with the advent of serious commercial sponsorship, so sports car racing began to lose its cast of grand prix drivers. Ferrari, Maserati, Mercedes-Benz, Porsche, Aston Martin, Jaguar, Ford *et al* employed the top F1 drivers of the day, but gradually their numbers dwindled, although there were exceptions. Instead, sports car racing attracted its own brand of specialists as touring cars had, some of whom were just as quick in this category as any F1 driver. TWR bucked the trend in the 1980s, but even then they had no regular F1 winners or champions. Ironically Schumacher (and Frentzen) were part of the Sauber-Mercedes set-up in 1990, but this was during their formative years and they were soon lost to F1.

Like all the truly classic events Le Mans has continuity. Jaguar has now entered F1, and it too remains a tribute to its origins and the wonderful racing heritage that made the Coventry marque so famous.

Chapter 1

1950 – And in the beginning

The origins of Jaguar emanated from the Swallow Sidecar Company in Blackpool started by William Walmsley and officially incorporated on 4 September 1922 with William Lyons as his partner.

The production of these small, streamlined units was a great success and they were used far and wide in both touring and motorcycle combination racing. As the business evolved through a change of premises which allowed the birth of the Austin Seven-based Swallow saloon and two-seater in 1927, Lyons's entrepreneurial skills were coming to the fore. North London motor dealers Henlys placed a very large order for the dapper looking little car – the ability to produce something aesthetically attractive was already apparent and remained with Lyons all his life – and as a result, further premises were sought in the Midlands to handle the production demands.

Thereafter came the SS cars, mainly mechanical derivatives of Standard cars with long, low bonnets and racey lines which resulted in them being regarded by the 'carriage trade' as cad's cars. Nevertheless a healthy competition life was enjoyed, mainly in rallies, and in 1935 the SS90 two-seater appeared which was quickly superseded by the SS100 in 2.7 and 3.5-litre form using an OHV version of a Standard engine engineered by Harry Weslake. There were also saloon variants, but inevitably, it was the sports car models which attracted most of the attention and attendant glamour. By now William Heynes had arrived and the name Jaguar had been adopted. The SS100 became the most popular large engined sports car of its day and enjoyed many successes in rallies and amateur racing, although sometimes it had to give best to the more sophisticated and much more expensive BMW 328. (Even after the war the SS100 was still winning its class in major rallies driven by future Alpine Rally star Ian Appleyard.)

Then, in 1939, a difference of opinion about territory erupted with our future trading partners, and Lyons found himself in the aircraft manufacturing business. So it was that during the war, Lyons, Heynes (who had begun research into chassis and suspension designs for a new Jaguar car in 1938), Claude Baily (who had recently joined the drawing office), and Walter Hassan (ex-Bentley and renowned designer of the Barnato Hassan Brooklands special) honed their ideas for a genuine twin-cam production engine. With the war over Hassan contacted his old friend F. R. W. 'Lofty' England, who had come to Alvis via Whitney Straight, ERA and Siamese racing ace Prince Bira before the hostilities, to inform him that a position was available as service manager at Jaguar. England was appointed on 11 September 1946 and a further piece of the jigsaw was in place.

After various stages and variations including a four-cylinder version successfully used by Major 'Goldie' Gardner in one of his special MG record breakers, the concept metamorphosed into the now legendary XK engine with its highly polished cam covers, but as yet there was no car to put it in. More than anything else it was this beautiful powerplant, 3,442cc in the original production

Shepperton garage owner John Marshall and Peter Whitehead in their XK120 (660042) that finished 15th after serious brake problems. Note the early style quick-release fuel filler cap and the windscreen wiper spindles sticking out of the scuttle. The Brooklands aero screen afforded very little protection and the buffeting at speed must have been horrendous. The small children and the scarred wall offer a typical French backdrop of the period. (Collection Bernard Viart/Paul Skilleter)

form, rated at 160bhp at 5,000rpm with almost vintage dimensions of 83mm bore and 106mm stroke giving longevity and reliability as well as adequate power, that made possible the future victories and worldwide success. Ironically William Lyons was intent on making luxury saloon cars, his commercial instincts ever to the fore, but circumstances dictated that a sports car (needed in any case to replace the obsolete SS100) would be ideal for the necessary development before large scale production could commence. So it was that a Mk V saloon chassis was shortened by 18in (457mm), narrowed slightly and using the existing suspension and brakes, was married to the sensational two-seater roadster body with its long bonnet, elegant sweeping lines, long tail and rounded flanks.

With the benefit of hindsight similarities can be seen with some pre-war designs, most notably certain special-bodied BMW 328s, but the impact this car made in the drab and austere period of post-war Great Britain at the 1948 Earl's Court Motor Show cannot be overstated. It was and remains a thing of beauty, and even more so when

compared with most of its contemporaries, many of which were warmed-over pre-war designs. More remarkable still the body was designed and built by eye in less than two weeks, using aluminium which was light, cheap and plentiful, and fitted straight on to the rolling chassis! (All the early XKs were aluminium bodied, some 240 in total.) The shape of course was a testament to William Lyons's unique eye for form and function. Despite the exciting specification and performance potential of this new machine, there were no plans for racing as such, but a demonstration of the XK120 was to be given to the press on the Jabbeke road near Ostend in Belgium on 18 May 1949.

Driven by Ron 'Soapy' Sutton of Jaguar's experimental department, the repainted white XK120 (Reg No. HKV 500, chassis No. 670002) achieved 132.596mph (213.347kph) over one mile with the screen removed and full length undertray fitted, and 126.448mph (203.455kph) with hood and sidescreens in situ. These were massive speeds in 1949 for what was essentially a production car and when the *Daily Express* sponsored a major meeting at Silverstone for August of that year, the newspaper told the organising club (the BRDC) that they wanted a one-hour production car race. This was something that Jaguar ignored at their peril. They could not afford to stay away; but worse, they could not enter and lose. So Messrs Hassan and England with Lyons in attendance spent three hours thrashing an XK120 prototype around Silverstone in a secret session to find out whether it was good enough. The ensuing technical report highlighted brakes, temperature problems, traction problems, gearing and other fundamental shortcomings typical of production cars of the time.

However, the potential was there and three cars were specially modified to suit and entered in red (chassis No. 670001) driven by Peter Walker, white (chassis No. 670002) driven by Leslie Johnson and blue (chassis No. 660001) driven by Prince B. Bira. Patriotism is not always the last resort of scoundrels! Bira led until a tyre blew due to rubbing on a wheel arch (they raced with rear spats in place), which left Johnson and Walker to finish first and second after a spirited challenge from Culpan's Frazer Nash which was only 14.2 seconds behind Walker in third. Now Jaguar was top dog, at least in England, and much was expected of them, but for the rest of the year the pressure was off in the competitions department at least. *Motor* borrowed Bira's Silverstone car for a road test, and Walter Hassan went to Montlhéry near Paris where he lapped at over 117mph (188kph) before a tyre threw a tread causing the end of play. He then went on to Jabbeke and recorded 126.8mph (204.02kph) without the undertray to further prove the car's capabilities for *Motor* magazine's technical editor Laurence Pomeroy.

Leslie Johnson started 1950 by racing 670001 at Palm Beach in Florida, finishing fourth after fading brakes dropped him from second behind an ex-Indianapolis Duesenberg. Pre-race publicity was handled by Austrian Max Hoffman who was Jaguar's American importer in New York, and destined to become an important figure in Jaguar's transatlantic business. After the race, mechanic John Lea delivered the XK to Jack Rutherford who, having bought the car, became the first person ever to have purchased an ex-works Jaguar 'racer'.

Back in the UK six new cars were being assembled for competition use, one of them being

John Marshall backs Jaguar XK120 (660042) into the echelon prior to the start of Le Mans 1950. Car No. 14 is the Nash-Healey of future Jaguar team-mates Tony Rolt and Duncan Hamilton who will finish fourth in the race. (Maurice-Louis Rosenthal/ Adrian Hamilton)

Ian Appleyard's now world famous NUB 120 (chassis No. 660044) with which he was to gain so much rallying success. The other five were all intended for racing and were allocated to: Leslie Johnson (660040), Nick Haines (660041), Peter Walker (660042), Clemente Biondetti (660043), and Tommy Wisdom (660057). Of these only Biondetti's car remained the property of Jaguar. The provision of a car for Biondetti gave Jaguar some much needed Continental road racing exposure and experience. The veteran Italian was rather disenchanted with his countrymen and wanted to teach the Italian manufacturers a lesson.

Despite his advancing years he was a real road racing ace having won the Mille Miglia four times! To begin with he was going to race the XK in the Targa Florio, which he duly did, holding second place behind Ascari in a Ferrari, before the Jaguar broke its No. 3 connecting rod. This failure led to all Jaguar conrods being crack-tested thereafter.

Three weeks later, on 23 April 1950, the 17th Mille Miglia was won by Giannino Marzotto/ Crosara in a Ferrari from the similar car of Serafini/Salami with Leslie Johnson and John Lea finishing fifth in 660040. However, had not Biondetti suffered a broken rear spring just beyond

Nick Haines in his Jaguar XK120 (660041) that he shared with Peter Clark to finish 12th. It is interesting how much less attractive the car is bereft of its road windscreen and the later more popular wire wheels. The prominent RAF roundel on the scuttle lends an authentic Second World War touch. (Paul Skilleter)

Ancona, which was patched up and had subsequent overheating problems, which cost him over an hour, a win or second place was very much on the cards. Ultimately he came in eighth. The other two cars of Wisdom and Haines both retired after good runs, Wisdom with a jammed gearbox and Haines losing too much time to be classified after co-driver Rudi Haller got lost! Perhaps the most noteworthy comment on Jaguar's first Mille Miglia attempt was that Leslie Johnson's fifth place was to remain their best result despite subsequent and very serious assaults with C-types, as noted elsewhere. Biondetti meanwhile came third in the revived Parma-Poggio di Berceto hill-climb on 14 May and then crashed and bent the chassis in the Giro dell'Umbria. Subsequently he wanted to build an XK-based special which he was sure could win the Mille Miglia. He did in 1951, but it did not.

The next big race was Le Mans on 24/25 June for which three cars were entered, but one week earlier Tommy Wisdom, who was not going to France, raced at Oporto where he finished third behind the winning 4.5-litre Alfa Romeo and an Osca. He had been running second until the

achilles heel of the XK, worn out brakes, lost him a place.

Le Mans 1950

The entries were:

No. 15 Nick Haines/Peter Clark XK120 (660041). Engine W1145-8. Reg MGJ 79.
No. 16 Peter Whitehead/John Marshall XK120 (660042). Engine W1146-8. Reg JWK 977.
No. 17 Leslie Johnson/Bert Hadley XK120 (660040). Engine W1144-8. Reg JWK 651.

Peter Walker was unable to participate due to commitments at his Herefordshire farm, so his place was taken by Peter Whitehead, whose cars Walker often raced. Whitehead was an experienced and fast all-rounder who had raced ERAs before the war and had latterly campaigned one of the early Ferrari grand prix cars. Co-driver John Marshall was a garage owner from Shepperton, while Bert Hadley was a pre-war Austin works driver of considerable ability who had to be

Leslie Johnson, who shared with Bert Hadley, looks thoroughly fed up as well he might, having lost a certain third place and possibly even second when the clutch failed after 21 hours, possibly as a result of his over-enthusiastic practice starts prior to the race. Note how the XK120 (660040) has a pronounced nose-up stance even while stationary, and the original curved exhaust exiting from under the left-hand rear wing. (LAT Photographic)

persuaded to race again after so long. Of these, the Johnson/Hadley pairing was the most evenly matched. Leslie Johnson was another driver who had raced pre-war and was very quick and experienced in all kinds of cars, as well as owning the ERA company name. He was to be a future 'works' Jaguar driver briefly and was the first person to win a race with the XK120 and to race one abroad. Sadly his career was compromised by ill health due to an unusual medical condition, and despite a robust build and appearance, his stamina was failing. He also suffered badly from pre-race nerves which caused some friction between himself and Hadley. Both Haines and Clark had raced at Le Mans before, so given the quality of the 1950

race, Jaguar's prospects looked promising.

The cars had been subjected to works preparation although they were entered privately in case of abject failure, Jaguar always being conscious of their public image. Work carried out included the fitting of special Lockheed clutches, larger Newton-type shock absorbers, careful attention to electrical equipment and water pumps, new halfshafts and 3.27:1 final drives (standard ratio with the ENV axle was 3.64:1). In deference to the poor quality fuel (80 octane) Bill Heynes had specified near standard tuning with 8:1 compression and standard manifold and carburettors, thus making them as near production level as any car ever to have raced at Le Mans

post-war. The catalogued options of aero screens, mirror cowl and lightweight bucket seats were fitted together with a 24-gallon (109 litres) tank, while spares and tools were carried in a box next to the driver. Additional spotlights were fitted to each car either side of the grille and the rear spats removed, but unfortunately, nothing significant was done about the brakes, despite all the previous warnings, which was to cost them dearly. This was certainly on Johnson's mind and he had raised the subject with co-driver Hadley who favoured harder linings on the grounds of wear, while Johnson wanted softer ones. In the event, Hadley prevailed and they used Ferodo VG95 linings, while the other two cars used Mintex 14 equipment.

The total weight ready to go with the driver on board was approximately 30cwt (1,524kg). L. H. 'Nick' Haines was also concerned about the brakes and suggested a front brake adjustment modification, although history does not record whether this was actually carried out. Haines was an Australian who had served in the RAF during the war and had started the Belgian Jaguar distributors with Madame Joska Bourgeois. In 1949 he had finished seventh at Le Mans in the Aston Martin DB1 shared with A. W. Jones, while his partner Peter Clark had driven HRGs at the Sarthe in 1938/39 and 1949. To ensure familiarity, both Hadley and Clark had been loaned XK120s before Le Mans, and tellingly Peter Clark had

Peter Whitehead rounds Arnage in 660042, the XK120 sporting the ubiquitous Lucas spotlights to supplement the rather feeble headlights that are wearing what appear to be cloth protectors. Another standard 'mod' is the small leather bonnet strap just visible above the grille. (Ludvigsen Library)

come to the conclusion that the brakes were not adequate even for fast road driving, never mind racing. Indeed, Clark was to recall that 'I was endlessly assisting the mechanics with changing brake shoes and brake drums, as various permutations and combinations were tried in a search for a compromise between stopping power and duration of wear.' Meanwhile Bert Hadley, to his great surprise, was the quickest of the XKs in practice, a fitting comment on his modesty and wheelmanship.

The competition at Le Mans in 1950 was still a mixture of converted grand prix cars (Talbot Lago), many production sports cars, three Ferraris, some pre-war machinery (Delahaye and Bentley), lots of little French DB Panhard, Renault, Simca and Simca-Gordini variants and even two diesel entries. Since the previous year (the first post-war event which was won by Chinetti's Ferrari with a little help from Lord Selsdon) the track had been resurfaced and improved, so speeds were up as expected. It was 8.383 miles (13.49km) to a lap and featured a very long straight with a kink, of almost 3.5 miles (5.6km) in length, which meant sustained high speeds for hour after hour.

Come the race the Sommer/Serafini Ferrari 195S led for the first two hours with the Louis and Jean-Louis Rosier Talbot in second. The Jaguars were running sixth (Whitehead), seventh (Hadley) and 12th (Haines), but already those brakes were playing up and Whitehead's first stop took seven minutes while all four brakes were adjusted. By midnight Hadley had taken over from Johnson for his second stint and they had risen to fourth place but the other two cars were much further back in 11th and 15th positions. By now the Ferraris had either retired or faded which left the Talbot Lagos in command, which was hardly surprising considering they were detuned 4.5-litre racing cars fitted with offset bodies, cycle wings and lights. Nevertheless, the XKs were going well in forward mode, if not in the stopping department; Peter Clark having to be careful not to exceed his rpm limit which still gave him over 130mph (209kph).

As the race continued the leading Talbot was delayed by a broken rocker and by 7am the Johnson/Hadley Jaguar was in second place, the harder brake linings proving their worth. However,

with just three hours to go with the car lying in third having been delayed by a burst tyre, the centre plate of the clutch broke and all drive was lost. In 1990, Hadley was to recall that prior to the race Johnson had conducted a series of violent standing starts with different ignition settings, and these had undoubtedly weakened the clutch centre. Other than for this failure a second place would almost certainly have been possible in what was a genuine, only slightly modified road car. Johnson's fastest lap of nearly 97mph (156kph) compared favourably with Rosier's new lap record in the Talbot of 102.830mph (165.45kph). The other two cars soldiered on with their brake problems, the Haines/Clark car reaching eighth at 9am on Sunday but dropping back to finish 12th after an oil-on-clutch problem and a further reduction in their pace when told not to use the clutch at all. Whitehead and Marshall were 15th and both cars were still in good fettle otherwise.

The final result was a victory for the Talbot Lago of father and son Louis Rosier/Jean-Louis Rosier who covered 2,153.121 miles (3,464.37km) at 89.713mph (144.348kph). Finishing fourth in their Nash-Healey were two future Jaguar stars, Duncan Hamilton and Tony Rolt. There were 16 British cars entered of which 14 finished.

1950 results

12th Nick Haines/Peter Clark Jaguar XK120 (660041) 1,946.901 miles (3,232.563km), 81.120mph (130.522kph).
15th Peter Whitehead/Johnny Marshall Jaguar XK120 (660042) 1,886.305 miles (3,035.065km).

So, despite the almost inevitable braking problems and the probably unnecessary retirement of Johnson's car, the exercise had been a success. Bill Heynes and 'Lofty' England returned to Coventry convinced that a purpose-built machine using their standard mechanicals in a lightweight, streamlined body would do the trick. While all this drama was going on William Lyons had gone to watch the Isle of Man Senior TT motorcycle race scheduled that weekend, thus ensuring an apparently low key stance toward the race, a subterfuge he did not need to indulge in again!

Chapter 2

1951 – Surprise, surprise!

Following Le Mans the three cars returned to the Jaguar factory and in August 1950 were prepared for the forthcoming production car race at Silverstone where the Italian maestro Tazio Nuvolari was to drive an XK120. After a few laps his failing health ended any such intentions and indeed his racing career. The race was won by Peter Walker from Tony Rolt in Nick Haines's car. Then in September, Jaguar's competition year which was already benefiting from Ian Appleyard's Alpine Rally triumph, was crowned by Stirling Moss winning the Dundrod TT in Tommy Wisdom's XK120 660057 in a virtuoso display from Peter Whitehead in the old 1949 car, 670002.

The final outing of note for the year saw Leslie Johnson and Stirling Moss average 107.46mph (172.90kph) at Montlhéry on 24 October over 24 hours in Johnson's car, but despite this it was obvious that for serious racing the XK was too heavy and too production based. At the Earl's Court Motor Show that month, where the Mk VII Jaguar was making its debut, Lyons gave Heynes the go-ahead for the new XK120C. This had a mainly tubular frame with drilled channel-section base members and a stressed scuttle to increase rigidity to the centre section and stop vertical distortion. The body was designed by ex-Bristol Aircraft man Malcolm Sayer, and the whole

Left to right are XKC001, XKC002 and XKC003, all brand-new and sparkling outside Browns Lane in 1951. Note the 'v'-shaped bonnet louvres and that No. 23 has not yet been fitted with the grille-mounted spotlight visible on the other two cars. How sad that these three subtly different original C-types were ultimately scrapped. In the background, Mk VII body shells await the production line. (Ludvigsen Library)

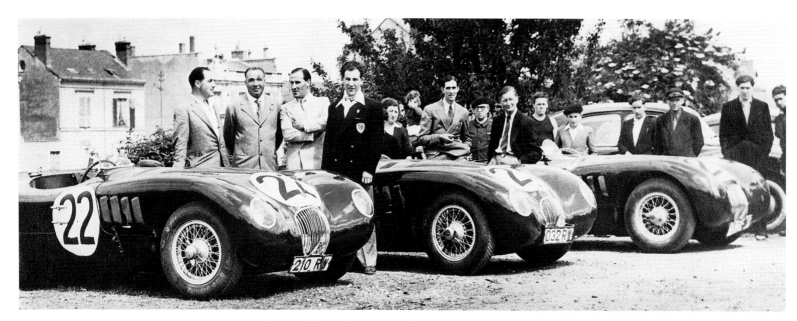

Cars and drivers at Le Mans with local French residents before the 'off'. Left to right are Jack Fairman, Clemente Biondetti, Leslie Johnson and Stirling Moss behind No. 22, and Peters Walker and Whitehead are behind No. 23. Biondetti's battle-scarred face stands out as does the very sartorially correct attire of Mr Moss with BRDC-badged blazer, prominent shirt collar and crevat. (Ludvigsen Library)

structure was substantially lighter than the XK120. Front suspension was similar to its predecessor, but improved with torsion bar and wishbone independent operation and anti-roll bar while the rear used a rigid axle with torsion bars. Wire wheels, which were still not fitted to the production cars were used, saving weight and providing some extra brake cooling. The new

Lockheed drum brakes were self adjusting.

Construction took place in the old Swallow Road factory, nobody breathed a word of what was going on, and the secret survived right up to the eve of Le Mans 1951. Today this would not be possible, but it does suggest that the British motoring press was probably being discreet, given that the car had to be tested at Silverstone and

A pre-race garage scene with the C-types and an XK120 in attendance. The sign hanging above No. 23 warns that the garage is closed on holidays (Saint's days?) and Sundays after 11am. (LAT Photographic)

Lindley (better known today as MIRA), in May and June that year. Before this however, the standard XKs remained the centre of attention and Leslie Johnson was back at Montlhéry going even faster in a further modified car to record 131.20mph (211.10kph) over one hour from a standing start. Meanwhile Biondetti had used one of his XK-cum-Ferrari based specials to win the Firenze-Fiesole hill-climb, and then it was Mille Miglia time again.

This proved to be a disaster with both the Johnson and Moss XKs crashing out on oil at the same corner within 20 miles (32km) of the start. Johnson's car was immobile, but after some throttle linkage repairs, Moss was able to struggle on with his mangled car only to get stuck in reverse gear later on. Their co-drivers Lea and Rainbow respectively were Jaguar factory mechanics who were to become well-known members of the Le Mans works team. In the meantime, Biondetti's special had also retired when chassis flexing had caused the fan to slice through the bottom water hose, thus 'cooking' the engine. So ended another Mille Miglia fiasco for Jaguar. There were to be more.

Back in England things were looking better with the *Daily Express* Silverstone meeting moved to

'Lofty' England sits in the winning car (XKC003) during a typically wet practice day. Contrast the pristine, unmarked finish of the car with its post-race, paint-chipped and begrimed condition. (Rodolfo Mailander/Ludvigsen Library)

May and here, Stirling Moss drove the first steel-bodied XK120, registered JWK 675, to win from Charlie Dodson (pre-war Austin racer and also 1928 and 1929 Senior TT motorcycle winner) and Duncan Hamilton both also in XKs. Elsewhere, Johnny Claes won at Spa in the old HKV 500 chassis No. 670002 and 1930's grand prix and latter day Talbot Lago driver Louis Chiron drove an

Stirling has apparently already dented the nose of XKC002 as he storms away after a typically meteoric Le Mans start in company with the three Cunningham C2Rs and the Hay/Clarke pre-war Bentley (14). (LAT Photographic)

Not perhaps the best photograph, but this is a rare shot of four-times Mille Miglia winner (1938, 1947/48/49) Clemente Biondetti in XKC001. He died in February 1955 after a long battle with cancer. (LAT Photographic)

Peter Walker accelerates away from Mulsanne Corner in the winning car accompanied by the two tiny Renault 4CVs of Lecat/Senffleben (54) and Clause/Clause (55). While the C-type would have been reaching 145mph (233kph) or more on Mulsanne, the tiny Renaults would probably have struggled to reach 75mph (120kph). (LAT Photographic)

XK120 in the Ulster Handicap at Dundrod in June. He was unplaced while the race was won by a certain Mike Hawthorn in his ancient TT Riley. Tommy Wisdom returned to Oporto on 17 June along with fellow Jaguarists Hamilton and George Wicken for the Portuguese Grand Prix. They all retired.

Ever cautious and always aware of the pitfalls, William Lyons had taken the precaution earlier in 1951 of having three special lightweight XK120 bodies constructed in case the new car was too late for Le Mans. These were designated LT1, LT2 and LT3 and while retaining the standard car's profile were quite different in detail. The bodies were made of magnesium alloy, there was no external boot lid with the rear of the body being one piece. Similarly the front wings and bonnet were integral while the doors were shallower, ending at the sill line. Total weight saving was approximately 3cwt (153kg). In the event they were never needed and all survived, LT2 and LT3 being bought by Charles Hornburg, Jaguar's Western United States distributor and mounted on production chassis. They went on to enjoy a very active racing life in America while LT1 was bought by Bob Berry who put it's lightweight body on his own car, MWK 120, and campaigned very successfully in British national racing in 1954. Bob Berry's involvement with Jaguar began at Le Mans 1951 when he helped John Lea rebuild the engine of XKC001 after it had swallowed a plug electrode during practice. His mother was French and the young Robert's fluency in the language, and his general abilities, became a real asset as the pressure built.

As a result, he gave up his studies at Cambridge and joined Jaguar, staying with them until 1980.

Apparently the press was still blissfully unaware of what was about to be revealed as *Autosport* suggested on the day before the race that Jaguar would probably use their well-tried XK120! In typical Jaguar fashion of the period the three XK120Cs, or C-type as they became known, were driven to Le Mans by team manager 'Lofty' England, Jack Emerson and Phil Weaver along with Bill Heynes in his Mk VII. Mechanics John Lea and Joe Sutton followed up in a Bedford van while the boss flew out later with Joe Wright in the Dunlop plane. The team was based at the Hotel de Paris with its private garages at Le Mans.

Le Mans 1951

The official Jaguar entries were:

No. 20 Peter Walker/Peter Whitehead Jaguar C-type XKC003. Engine E1003-8. 204bhp at 5,750rpm.
No. 22 Stirling Moss/Jack Fairman Jaguar C-type XKC002. Engine E1002-8. 205bhp at 5,750rpm.
No. 23 Leslie Johnson/Clemente Biondetti Jaguar C-type XKC001. Engine E1004-8. 202bhp at 5,500rpm.

No. 21 Bob Lawrie/Ivan Waller Jaguar XK120 (660449). Reg AEN 546.

All the C-types were running on 8.5:1 compression ratios in deference to the 80-octane fuel and were still using the small, 1.75-in SU carburettors. Bob Lawrie's XK120 was a very standard steel-bodied roadster.

Moss in XKC002 exiting White House and about to lap the Cunningham C2R of Fitch/Walters. In the background unprotected spectators stand in front of the cottage and sit on its roof. Track passes? Who needs them! (Rodolfo Mailander/Ludvigsen Library)

Another view of Stirling, showing the lovely, elegant and rounded lines of the C-type that so epitomised Jaguar's aesthetic values. The ever-present Le Mans sand banks can be seen in the background, just waiting to trap the unwary. (Ludvigsen Library)

Linen helmets were still acceptable in 1951 as Ivan Waller demonstrates en route to 11th place in his XK120 (660449). The very standard steel-bodied roadster is still wearing its typically period club badges, one of which looks suspiciously like an Aston Martin one. Tsk, tsk! (Paul Skilleter)

The first Le Mans win for Jaguar. Peter Whitehead (driving) and Peter Walker on their celebratory lap in XKC003 pass the pits, assembled onlookers, photographers, pit crew and the inevitable gendarme. (Rodolfo Mailander/Ludvigsen Library)

The fruits of Jaguar's labours were very quickly apparent as Peter Walker broke the lap record on Wednesday evening in the dark by over three seconds recording 4min 50sec according to the team's timing (officially one of the Cunningham entries was credited with the fastest practice time of 5min 3sec). Malcolm Sayer's mathematically designed body shape with its smaller frontal area than the XK120 needed less power to push it through the air and speeds exceeding 145mph (233kph) were achieved. None of the other drivers came close which may have been partly due to Walker's bravery as the French Marchal headlamps were inadequate. After words from Mr England, Marchal produced some greatly improved units for the race. There were problems too for car No. 23 as already noted when Biondetti suffered a plug electrode breaking off and falling into the engine which necessitated a rebuild by John Lea. Additionally, during one of the wet practice sessions, Moss collided lightly with the back of

Mort Morris-Goodall's Aston Martin DB2 which had stopped to avoid a crashing Porsche. Fortunately damage was only superficial. By the end of practice it was becoming apparent that the new Jaguars were very formidable.

The main opposition in 1951 was still the old grand prix Talbot Lagos adapted with offset bodies, cycle wings and lights, and they were worthy rivals. There were six in all and two of them were driven by Argentinian aces Froilan Gonzalez (with Onofre Marimon), and soon-to-win the first of his five World Driver Championships Juan Manuel Fangio sharing with Louis Rosier. Others were driven by Talbot regulars including the ill-fated Pierre 'Levegh' and would pose a real threat if necessary. In this bumper year for entries there were no less than nine Ferraris, five Aston Martins, two Allards and three Cunninghams amongst the more serious contenders with a total of 60 starters. Regardless of practice times the cars were lined up in echelon according to engine size, so race numbers give a good clue as to where they started.

At the traditional run and jump-in start Chaboud, Talbot, was first away, but by the end of lap one Gonzalez thundered by in the big Talbot four seconds ahead of Moss who was followed by Tom Cole's Allard and Biondetti in No. 23 Jaguar. The other Jaguar of Peter Walker was sixth ahead of Briggs Cunningham in one of his own Cunningham C2Rs. Already the big engined Ferrari 340 Americas were proving surprisingly slow, possibly due to clutch troubles and the race looked like a straight fight between the Jaguars and the quicker Talbots. In reality however it was no match as Moss passed Gonzalez on lap four and drove off into the distance and Jaguar were soon holding first, third and sixth, Moss acting as the hare while the other two drove at a predetermined pace. After one hour Moss led from Gonzalez with Biondetti and Whitehead third and fourth and by four hours it was 1, 2 and 3 for the Coventry firm with the Talbots back in fourth and fifth. Moss, whose first Le Mans this was, had smashed the lap record repeatedly and left it at 4min 46.8sec, a speed of 105.232mph (169.318kph) – a reflection not only of Stirling's pace but also Jaguar's aerodynamics courtesy of Mr Sayer. Further back was Peter Walker, who in those days was as fast as

Moss, stayed in touch without straining the car, which was to prove fortuitous.

Suddenly, at about 8.30am Biondetti, who had continued driving after the first stops, noticed his oil pressure disappearing and he managed to nurse the car back to the pits. An inspection by John Lea showed oil aplenty, but no pressure and so the car was retired at 50 laps completed, thus denying Johnson a drive. At six hours with heavy rain now falling Fairman was leading in No. 22 from Whitehead, the Talbots were third and fourth with the best of the Ferraris now fifth driven by pre-war Bentley TT expert Eddie Hall. Soon however, more grief was to descend upon Jaguar as Moss, now back in the leading car had a connecting rod break at Arnage on lap 92 (or lap 94, depending on who you believe) due to a sudden loss of oil pressure. This catastrophic failure was caused by the fracture of a copper oil pipe in the sump due to vibration and the resultant dry bearings. Thereafter Jaguar always used steel pipes.

Now there was just one C-type, and Walker and Whitehead were left way out in the lead which at half distance (4am) was seven laps over the

Peter Whitehead tries not to run over various unobservant French persons as he parks up XKC003 after the race. Just look at the huge paint chips and filthy condition of the car compared with its pre-race appearance. In the background can be seen the eighth-placed Ferrari 340 America of 1949 winner Luigi Chinetti and the old Bentley of Hay/Clarke that finished 22nd. (Paul Skilleter)

Peter Walker (left) looks like a naughty schoolboy while Peter Whitehead has apparently just suffered a terrible disappointment rather than winning the most famous motor race in the world. Apart from Walker's barely noticeable grin there is not a single smiling face on view. It looks like a wake rather than a victory photograph. Very strange. (Ludvigsen Library)

Gonzalez/Marimon Talbot and the Walters/Fitch Cunningham. The Jaguar had speed in hand, but it had to be driven very smoothly to avoid as much vibration as possible. So while Jaguar worried and waited, the private XK120 of Lawrie/Waller circulated steadily with only brake adjustments (no surprise here) and exhaust repairs interrupting its progress in midfield. Instead it was the opposition who were cracking up with Rosier's Talbot retiring with a split oil tank and Gonzalez falling out with head gasket failure soon after half distance. The Walters/Fitch Cunningham was now second, albeit eight laps adrift by two thirds distance while the

Hall/Navone Ferrari had slowed to a crawl with terminal clutch troubles. Moving nicely through the field were the Aston Martin DB2s, the highest of which was third (Macklin/Thompson). The best of the remaining Talbots meanwhile had advanced to fifth by 8am and to second by midday Sunday (Meyrat/Mairesse) with the Rolt/Hamilton Nash-engined Healey coupé the remaining top six runner.

By now the Cunningham was also one of the walking wounded with valve trouble, but managed to struggle on to the end very slowly, losing many places and finally finishing 18th. Happily the remaining works Jaguar survived, and despite its greatly reduced pace, Walker and Whitehead won at a record average speed and distance by nine laps from the Talbot of Meyrat/Mairesse with the similar car of 'Levegh'/Marchand fourth. Aston Martins were third, fifth, seventh, 10th and 13th, so all five Feltham cars finished! They were never to be so reliable again. Rolt/Hamilton were sixth in the Nash-Healey and the Lawrie/Waller XK120 finished a meritorious 11th.

1951 results

1st Peter Walker/Peter Whitehead Jaguar XK120C XKC003 2,243.886 miles (3,610.412km), 93.495mph (150.433kph).
2nd Pierre Meyrat/Guy Mairesse Talbot Lago 4.5 2,166.108 miles (3,485.268km), 90.253mph (145.217kph).
3rd Lance Macklin/Eric Thompson Aston Martin DB2 2,160.445 miles (3,476.156km), 90.018mph (144.839kph).
11th Bob Lawrie/Ivan Waller Jaguar XK120 1,980.436 miles (3,186.522km), 82.517mph (132.770kph).

By any standards Le Mans 1951 was a tremendous achievement for Jaguar and their new car and but for the fractured copper oil pipes they would probably have finished 1, 2, 3. There is no doubt that they had the best car, but the result also reinforced Jaguar's inherent racing philosophy of designing to win at Le Mans as laid down by William Lyons. This was the sports car race above all else that carried the highest prestige, most kudos and greatest commercial rewards.

Chapter 3

1952 – Development and over reaction

Predictably and deservedly Jaguar were much fêted for their Le Mans triumph, the winning car even appearing at the Festival of Britain in London, while one of the other team cars appeared at the 1951 British Grand Prix at Silverstone with the winning number '20'. This was, of course, in stark contrast to the chaotic BRM V16 saga in grand prix racing.

Following Le Mans, Jaguar's next major race was the Tourist Trophy at Dundrod in Northern Ireland in September, where they ran the three Le Mans cars, XKC001 for Leslie Johnson, XKC002 for Stirling Moss and XKC003 for Peter Walker. This quickly turned into a walkover for Jaguar, as Moss won his second TT from Peter Walker, but Leslie Johnson began to fall back, his performance suffering due to his ongoing poor health. This prompted 'Lofty' England to replace him with reserve driver Tony Rolt, who set fastest lap and climbed back to third overall, fourth on handicap.

The three C-types with XKC002 nearest the camera, showing their new noses and elongated tails. Standing behind No. 19 is Jaguar mechanic Joe Sutton, while the RAF roundel can be seen adorning the flank of the Moss/Walker car, XKC011. (Rodolfo Mailander/Ludvigsen Library)

A rear view of XKC002 showing the extraordinary length of the tail. No wonder 'Lofty' England complained of weaving and 'lift' at speed on Mulsanne when you note the way the wing is cut away from the rear wheel, leaving a huge space for air to build up under the tail. (Rodolfo Mailander/Ludvigsen Library)

Johnson did not drive officially for Jaguar again, while Rolt, who was known to England from pre-war ERA racing, became a full team member.

As a final flourish Jaguar then entered Moss in the late September Goodwood meeting, where he won two short races to no-one's great surprise. One irony of the instant success of Jaguar was that had there been a World Sports Car Championship (it actually began in 1953), then the Coventry firm having won two out of the four classic sports car races (Mille Miglia, Le Mans, Targa Florio and the Tourist Trophy), would have been champions. They were never to win the original version, but did achieve the modern equivalent 36 years later.

All this caused much excitement and pent up demand for the C-type (as it was now referred to) and only space limitations had prevented the production intentions. This further complicated the question of allocation; who was to be lucky and who was not. Duncan Hamilton (who became a

works driver in 1952) and Tommy Wisdom received the initial two cars, Wisdom being the first to race a 'customer' car at Monaco in 1952. (Yours for just £2,327!) Into the new year Jaguar announced its Le Mans drivers which featured two new faces. These were Duncan Hamilton, already well known for his ability behind the wheel of various machinery, and Ian Stewart, a young, talented Scotsman who was a known XK120 driver and a member of Ecurie Ecosse. They joined the established team of Moss, Walker, Whitehead and Tony Rolt.

Obviously Jaguar needed more racing development and public exposure, so a limited competition programme was undertaken for this purpose. Thus it was that Moss raced at the 1952 Easter Goodwood with XKC003, and no less a person than the future MP and noted raconteur Alan Clark, then reporting for *Road & Track*, spotted the fitment of the embryonic disc brakes.

Moss came fourth in the handicap sports car race, being easily the quickest car in the event. This was the first time disc brakes were used in racing and they were still not absolutely reliable, Moss's pace reflecting this at Goodwood. Nevertheless after this, XKC003 was prepared for the forthcoming Mille Miglia complete with the new brakes, on 4 May 1952, and driven to Brescia by Norman Dewis who had recently arrived from Lea Francis. He was to share the car with Moss in the race which began when Stirling started from the road, rather than the famous ramp which was very slippery due to heavy rain.

They were motoring well, having passed several front runners including Piero Taruffi (Ferrari) and Rudolf Caracciola in one of the new coupé 300SL Mercedes, but after the C-type threw a tread, Moss was dismayed to find that Karl Kling in another Mercedes had made up four minutes on him from the start. Caracciola, of course, had retaken his position as a result of this delay. Moss repassed Kling, although still behind on elapsed time, but shortly after Ravenna a cracked exhaust manifold caused Dewis to nearly pass out from leaking fumes. Further down the road, having caught up with Caracciola again, Moss passed only to crash off the road at the following corner. Amazingly the car survived knocking over several posts and lurched back on to the road, and after gathering themselves together, Moss and Dewis continued to Rome. By now the C-type was becoming rather battered, with worn out rear shock absorbers and a leaking fuel tank. Eventually, and still pressing on, Moss lost the front end going down the north side of the Raticosa, and the resultant steering damage ended their race. Contemporary reports suggest that had Moss simply driven to finish, then he would have made fourth place, but that would not have been Stirling Moss.

Post-race notes indicated that Moss had been passed by Kling in the Mercedes when he was flat out at over 150mph (241kph). However, the 1952 300SL only produced 171bhp (although it did have a very low drag coefficient of 0.25) while the C-type in its early form would surely have struggled to reach such a high velocity, at least on a level road. The gearing of the Jaguar here was 3.31:1 which meant pulling 6,000rpm in top gear to reach

150mph (241kph) so theoretically it was possible. Notwithstanding this the real problem was not Moss's ability or Jaguar's performance, but the apparently overstated potential of the Mercedes, highlighted by the subsequent telegram sent to William Lyons by Moss, who demanded: 'Must have more speed for Le Mans'. Despite 'Lofty' England's misgivings Lyons responded with consequences that could hardly have been worse.

For the meantime however, there was the May Silverstone meeting to consider. XKC003 was still *hors de combat*, so drivers Rolt, Moss and Walker used XKC001, XKC002 and a new car, XKC011, respectively. In practice Rolt crashed and briefly used Walker's car until his own was repaired. It reappeared from the factory with Panhard rod rear suspension, as distinct from the standard car's offset 'A' bracket location. Moss won the race easily from the old enemy Aston Martin, while Walker stopped with no brakes, which would only work if the pedal was pumped vigorously before each corner, presumably pad 'knock-off' which typified early disc brakes. He restarted to finish seventh, but Rolt retired with a rear hub failure. So, despite Jaguar winning the sports car race and the saloon car event (Moss again, this time in a Mk VII), all

The nose of XKC001, which was driven by Rolt/Hamilton, clearly showing the damaged paint above the number that denotes the fitting of the standard radiator and header tank robbed off Duncan Hamilton's own production C-type (XKC004) that was was en route to Portugal. A similar 'mod' was performed on the Moss/Walker car (XKC011) using parts from Tommy Wisdom's XKC003 that was returning from the Monaco sports car race. The third car (XKC002) had no such donor and was stuck with the new set-up. (Rodolfo Mailander/Ludvigsen Library)

XKC002 during scrutineering, with Gordon Gardner who drove the Jaguar Bedford spares transporter. The milling crowds, archetypal small boys and intimate atmosphere typify Continental races of the 1950s, in stark contrast to the ultra hostile, rigorously controlled and ruthless regime of modern motor racing that denies all direct public access. (Collection Bernard Viart/Paul Skilleter)

was not well with England complaining about lack of preparation and general carelessness. A line from his post-race report reads: 'I must say that, in my opinion, to attempt to race in this manner is a complete waste of time and will only result in an unsatisfactory performance which we cannot really afford if we wish to maintain our prestige'. 'Lofty' England was also concerned that the disc brakes were being raced too soon because of Moss, and that they needed more development.

Also on the schedule was the Monaco Grand Prix, which in 1952, was for sports cars with Moss driving XKC003 and Tommy Wisdom in his and

Brighton Jaguar distributor Bill Cannell's newly delivered XKC005. (Duncan Hamilton had raced his C-type XKC004 in the British Empire Trophy on the Isle of Man but retired with rear axle failure.) On pole Moss led away, was caught and passed by Manzon's very quick Gordini and then both became entangled in a multi-car accident caused by oil dropped from Reg Parnell's blown up Aston at St Devote. Manzon was out, but Moss got going again with minor frontal damage after helping to clear the road. He was subsequently blackflagged being deemed to have received outside assistance. Tommy Wisdom meanwhile drove steadily to sixth place, the race being won by Eugenio Castellotti in a Ferrari. Jaguar's foreign adventures were not bringing much joy in 1952, but much worse was to come.

In contrast to the 1951 race the 1952 Le Mans had much stiffer opposition for Jaguar's three works C-types, not least the Mercedes-Benz 300SLs that had so rattled Moss on the Mille Miglia. Additionally, strong entries from Aston Martin, Cunningham, Ferrari and the still potent Talbot Lagos could not be underestimated, but inevitably the legendary Mercedes invincibility was most feared.

Le Mans 1952

The Jaguar entries were:

No. 17 Stirling Moss/Peter Walker Jaguar C-type
    XKC011. Engine E1005-8.
No. 18 Tony Rolt/Duncan Hamilton Jaguar C-type
    XKC001. Engine E1001-8.
No. 19 Peter Whitehead/Ian Stewart Jaguar C-type
    XKC002. Engine E1002-8.

(This information, as to who drove which actual car has only recently resurfaced after decades in obscurity and has been supplied by Terry Larson and Penny Graham who owns XKC011.)

Power was still around 200bhp. As a result of the flap over Mercedes's pace in Italy, the C-types appeared with very elegant elongated noses and tails hastily designed by Malcolm Sayer for aerodynamic gain. This had necessitated mounting the header tank on the bulkhead and no opportunity for proper testing thereafter with predictably dire consequences. The night before practice 'Lofty' England tried the cars at speed on the Mulsanne Straight and noted a pronounced but controllable weaving at speed due to lift attributable to the new body shape. Practice itself soon revealed a much worse problem as each car overheated and then had to be abandoned trackside until the session ended, there being no tunnel under the circuit in 1952. However, XKC003 was on hand returning from Monaco and Duncan Hamilton's XKC004 was en route to

Portugal, so these were robbed of their standard radiator and integral header tanks for two of the works cars, but the third was stuck with the new system and obviously doomed. Just to help matters along Stirling was demanding disc brakes and although three sets were flown to Dinard and collected by Bob Berry, they were understandably not fitted in the pre-race chaos.

While all this Coventry angst was in full flow Mercedes-Benz displayed a roof-mounted lever-actuated air brake 'wing' which sat horizontally at speed and could be tilted to the vertical plane for extra retardation. Although it seemed to work well during practice it was not used in the race, but achieved a psychological gain over an already rattled opposition. Ironically, had they persisted with this the full aerodynamic implications might have become apparent in due course, but they were concerned only with stopping, as 1955 was to prove. Pre-war grand prix champion Hermann Lang in the No. 21 Mercedes-Benz set a lap of 4min 40sec, some six seconds quicker than Moss's 1951 mark with Alberto Ascari just a tenth slower in the works Ferrari 250 Sport. Also very rapid but

The famous Le Mans type start. Moss, as ever, has reached his car first (second from left), with the tall figure of Tony Rolt just behind. Third Jaguar driver, Ian Stewart, has just reached the nose of his car. Looking further down the echelon it is noticeable how far behind some of the other drivers are. High above flies a balloon in the shape of a giant sparking plug. (Rodolfo Mailander/Ludvigsen Library)

not expected to last was the 2.3 Gordini of Robert Manzon/Jean Behra.

So to the race and 4pm on Saturday, 14 June 1952. With so many cars of larger capacity ahead of them in the echelon, the Jaguars were well down the 57-car field but the customary 'lightning' Moss Le Mans start saw Stirling up to fourth by the Dunlop bridge behind the two Cunninghams of Phil Walters and John Fitch and Leslie Johnson's Nash-Healey. Completion of lap one saw Walters still in front from Moss, followed by Simon and Ascari (Ferraris), Rolt and Stewart (Jaguars) and Levegh's barchetta style Talbot seventh. Very soon the Ascari Ferrari pitted with clutch slip but the Manzon Gordini now appeared in fourth having overtaken the Rolt and Stewart Jaguars. Before the first hour was up Ian Stewart had pitted briefly with No. 19

Stirling Moss leads the Phil Walters Cunningham C4R in XKC011 (now owned by Penny Graham) as he heads toward the Dunlop bridge early in the race. This was the only C-type not to retire with head gasket failure. (Rodolfo Mailander/ Ludvigsen Library)

Jaguar and then departed at reduced speed to be followed shortly after by Tony Rolt in No. 18. The Stewart car (which was still using the new header tank system) soon retired with head gasket failure but the Rolt/Hamilton car struggled on slowly, having stopped again to take on some Radweld unnoticed, eking out the prescribed minimum 28 laps before they were officially allowed to replenish fluids. Water was added but as Hamilton noted in his autobiography, *Touch Wood*, 'Unfortunately the damage had been done, and as the water was put in steam came out of the exhaust pipe; sadly we pushed the car away.' Works mechanic Frank Rainbow, who was working with Jack Emerson, recalled: 'I remember pouring in about five gallons of water and Jack remarking that I should stop, as it was running out of the exhaust pipe and into his

shoes. We had an engine full of water!'

The Moss car had already retired but not for the overheating/head gasket failure reason. Instead, a small piece of the timing chain tensioner had snapped off and become lodged under the relief valve in the oil suction pipe, leading to oil starvation and terminal engine failure. Whether this car would have survived the race anyway is a moot point given the demise of the Rolt/Hamilton machine despite having the proven standard radiator/header tank set-up. What is not in doubt is that had Jaguar persevered with their existing car then they probably would have won the race anyway as Mercedes-Benz were running at a very conservative pace and were outpaced by the leading Levegh Talbot. Tragically, as history recalls, this car suffered crankshaft failure after Pierre Levegh had driven it singe-handedly for 23 hours, nursing it along with an engine vibration that he had noticed long before. Rather than stop and warn his co-driver Pierre Marchand, who might not have been so mechanically sympathetic, and thus

alerting Mercedes, he chose to drive on 'oh so carefully', but alas the engine broke anyway.

The other front runners had faded away and Mercedes-Benz enjoyed a 1, 2 triumph with Hermann Lang/Fritz Riess in the winning car. Afterwards the Germans waited in vain for their national anthem to be played, for as Duncan Hamilton observed, 'When I passed in front of the spectators who stood below a plaque erected on the stands in memory of Robert Benoist, founder of the race, who was executed by the Germans in 1944, I could understand why.' A worthy third place fell to the Johnson/Wisdom Nash-Healey followed by the Cunningham/Spear Cunningham, the much delayed Simon/Vincent Ferrari and the Valenzano/Ippocampo Lancia Aurelia. *Après* their Sarthe debacle Bill Heynes sat down and carefully summarised the allocation of responsibilities and duties, appointments and modus operandi of the Jaguar engineering and design staff, to avoid any repeat of such an occurrence. This in turn generated a response from

XKC002 at rest just before Mulsanne Corner at the end of the Mulsanne Straight. In the background, cars approach at maximum speed before braking for the 30mph right-hander. Once again it is worth noting that spectators including the inevitable small boy, and perhaps but not necessarily some race officials, are on the scene. (Paul Skilleter)

Tony Rolt in the Esses lapping a trio of Renault 4CVs before the inevitable head gasket failure. This was one of the most disappointing and unnecessary Jaguar Le Mans failures ever, as the leading Talbot and ultimately winning Mercedes were not as fast as the standard C-type in Le Mans trim. So easy to say with the benefit of hindsight. (LAT Photographic)

Phil Weaver who was to operate the Special Project Department, pointing out further inconsistencies and the lack of certain essential facilities and equipment, only some of which he received.

Thereafter, Jaguar's season improved with Stirling Moss winning the sports car supporting race at Reims for the French Grand Prix in Wisdom's XKC005 fitted with the still-experimental Dunlop disc brakes for the occasion. A further dose of good news was the setting of three world records at Montlhéry by an XK120 FHC (chassis No. 669002) driven by Leslie Johnson, Jack Fairman, Bert Hadley and Stirling Moss. They pounded around the dramatic French track for a week, averaging over 100mph and proving that Jaguars were reliable after all. Sadly,

this was not reflected at Goodwood for the Nine-Hour race with one car crashing (Ian Stewart), another losing a wheel (Duncan Hamilton) and the fastest one (Moss/Walker) suffering a rear axle bracket failure, although the car was repaired and finished fifth. In America, the C-type had arrived and Phil Hill was winning in Charles Hornburg's XKC007 with George Weaver and John Fitch also winning with Max Hoffman's XKC009.

The reality of the year had been greatly increased competition activity without adequate facilities and a much stronger opposition. This was being addressed, but 1952 was something of a curate's egg for Jaguar and as is so often the way in motor racing, the second year was much tougher than the first.

Chapter 4

1953 – England expects

In America Jaguar was enjoying a sales bonanza and had become the biggest dollar earner of imported cars in the country during 1952.

Despite this the Coventry marque failed to enter any works cars in the Sebring 12-hour race on 8 March 1953, even though this was the inaugural round of the new FIA World Championship for Sports Cars. The Sebring event was particularly gruelling but at least an American privately entered C-type came third (XKC010), driven by Sherwood Johnston/Robert Wilder.

Back home, Mort Morris-Goodall, Jaguar's new competitions manager was budgeting for 14 events during the year, not counting six championship rounds. With the co-operation of the British private owners (Hamilton, Wisdom, Stewart, Holt, Johnson, Scott-Douglas, Swift and Whitehead), it was hoped to cover all the more appropriate events. Le Mans of course remained the primary objective, the more so after the 1952 debacle.

In April, Jaguar returned to Jabbeke and ran a Mk VII, XK120 roadster and a C-type, the latter

Joe Sutton with ever-present 'fag' in mouth and XKC053 at the sand test. For some strange and arcane reason the idea was that when revved up the car's exhaust should not disturb the sand on the ground! As usual the onlookers include a man in uniform and of course two small boys. (Collection Bernard Viart/Paul Skilleter)

recording 148.435mph (238.832kph) over one kilometre. There were no great surprises here and it was the last time that the 1952 long-nose Le Mans bonnet was used, there being no discernible difference in terminal velocity over the standard body shape. Thereafter the Mille Miglia and the May Silverstone meeting beckoned, and neither brought any joy. The famous Italian road race was another disaster with the only proper works car of Moss/Morris-Goodall (XKC011) retiring early with rear axle problems near Ravenna. The other two competitive C-types of Rolt/Hayden (in Wisdom's XKC005) and Leslie Johnson in his XKC008 (uniquely fitted with overdrive) also retired. Three other C-types were running but all dropped out, tragically in one case with the Descollanges car (XKC016) crashing and killing co-driver Pierre Ugnon. This was the last time that Jaguar officially entered the Italian road race, leaving future attempts to brave amateurs.

One week later Stirling Moss won the touring

car race at the *Daily Express* Trophy meeting at Silverstone in a Mk VII, but overturned the new works C-type (XKC037) in practice for the sports car event. In the race brake fade intervened and a slightly detuned Stirling finally finished seventh, having been second quickest during practice. Elsewhere a fatal accident involving Jean Heurtaux's XKC035 at a French hill-climb caused some speculation as to possible mechanical failure, but ultimately this was disproved. On a happier note Peter Whitehead and Tom Cole won the Hyères 12-hour road race near Toulon in Whitehead's C-type just a week before Le Mans but few could have forseen the extent of the forthcoming triumph.

Le Mans 1953 was arguably Jaguar's most convincing win of the decade against the strongest opposition despite various problems, of which more anon. Ranged against them were full factory entries from Alfa Romeo, Ferrari, Lancia, Gordini, Aston Martin and Talbot with Cunningham joining in, the

This lovely Rudy Mailander photograph shows the full Jaguar line-up with XKC052 in the foregound and Jaguar mechanic Frank Rainbow directly behind. Further along in shirtsleeves and tie is William Lyons behind No. 17 (XKC053). (Rodolfo Mailander/Ludvigsen Library)

latter's 5.5-litre C5R, a real threat and a potential winner. Of these the three works Ferraris and Alfa Romeos were the most formidable. Ferrari's pairings were current World Champion Alberto Ascari sharing the 4.5-litre 375MM coupé with his friend Luigi Villoresi and two 4.1-litre 340MM spyders for 1950 World Champion 'Nino' Farina/ Mike Hawthorn and the Marzotto brothers Paulo and Giannino. Alfa Romeo fielded 1951 World Champion Juan Manuel Fangio with his countryman and protégé Onofre Marimon, 1952 Le Mans winner Fritz Riess/Karl Kling and long-time Alfa racer and test driver Consalvo Sanesi with Piero Carini. This time nothing was left to chance at Browns Lane and Bill Heynes had requested the building of five engines towards the end of 1952 in preparation for the race. Interestingly, the specification called for the use of three 2-in SU carburettors with Webers on order to be tried as a comparison. In early 1953, John Heath of HWM turned up at Harry Weslake's Rye works with a set of Webers and manifold to fit a Jaguar cylinder head. Weslake tried the set-up and recorded 218.5bhp at 5,250rpm with big gains in mid-range power and torque as well as a modest increase at peak rpm. Subsequently the Webers were first used in competition on a Jaguar engine when HWM 1 was raced at Shelsey Walsh driven by George Abecassis in early June, prior to Le Mans.

Three new cars were made (XKC051, '052 and '053) and although they looked familiar, underneath they were subtly different. Apart from the stronger engines they had lighter gauge bodies and some chassis tubes, aircraft style 'bag' fuel tanks, redesigned rear suspension with Panhard rods and a second pair of trailing links, a lightweight battery and of course the Dunlop disc brakes. Dry weight was now 2,013lb (913kg) compared to the production car's 2,102lb (953kg). A small diversion was caused by the release of photographs of an experimental prototype that was due to be tested at Jabbeke, Le Mans and Reims but in fact never raced. *Autosport* dubbed it '*a disco volante*' after a similar Alfa Romeo.

Apart from the three cars already mentioned, Jaguar took a spare chassis (XKC012) and the Belgian Ecurie Francorchamp team was allocated XKC047, this originally being destined for rally use

by Ian Appleyard but then discarded. Unlike the works entries this was essentially a production specification car with drum brakes and SUs. It gave 209bhp at 5,750rpm and was repainted from Appleyard's familiar white to bright yellow denoting Belgium's national racing colours.

This head-on shot of XKC052 depicts the bluff front of the C-type, the grille-mounted spotlight and the air intake for the new Weber carburettor set-up. (Rodolfo Mailander/ Ludvigsen Library)

Le Mans 1953

The Jaguar entries were:

No. 17 Stirling Moss/Peter Walker XKC053.
    Engine E1055-8-9. Trade plate 164 WK.
No. 18 Tony Rolt/Duncan Hamilton XKC051.
    Engine E1053-9. Trade plate 774 RW.

The 40DCO Weber carburettors and cold airbox revealed on one of the works C-types, looking rather more impressive than the familiar twin SU arrangement of the production cars. (Rodolfo Mailander/Ludvigsen Library)

During practice one of the Pegasos crashed at the Dunlop Curve and here Duncan Hamilton has stopped XKC051 to have a look. Car No. 5 is the Duntov/Merrick Allard J2R (JRX 3043) and the nose of one of the Nash-Healeys is just visible on the left. Duntov was of course Zora Arkus Duntov of Chevrolet Corvette fame. Note the tyre marks and ambulance in attendance. (Rodolfo Mailander/Ludvigsen Library)

Moss (XKC053) and Rolt (XKC051) chase Villoresi's Ferrari 375MM (0318AM) through the Esses early in the race. (Rodolfo Mailander/ Ludvigsen Library)

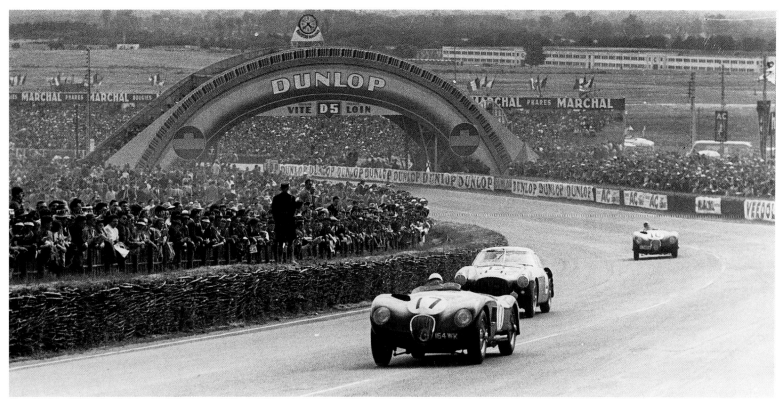

No. 19 Peter Whitehead/Ian Stewart XKC052.
   Engine E 1054-8-9. Trade plate 194 WK.
No. 18 XKC012. Engine E1052-8 (spare car).
No. 20 Roger Laurent/Charles de Tornaco
   XKC047. Engine E1047-9.

Practice times were not truly indicative of race pace but for the record, Hamilton was the quickest Jaguar with a 4min 37sec lap, well inside the lap record while the Belgian car driven by de Tornaco recorded 5min 03sec. Norman Dewis used the spare car, XKC012, and set a 5min 05sec lap. This car was also bearing race number 18 and against the regulations was on the circuit at the same time as the official number 18, XKC051. Dewis did eight laps and the organisers disqualified the Rolt/Hamilton car, although it must be said here that accounts vary as to the exact circumstances. Fortunately, after William Lyons payed a fine the car was reinstated. The team personnel were spread between the Hotel de Paris and Hotel des Ifs with the cars garaged at the warehouse of a Paris Jaguar enthusiast M. Carre in the Rue de

Sarthe. However, some drivers and family preferred the existing arrangements from previous years (see sidebar).

Sydney Allard enjoyed a brief moment of glory leading for one lap in one of his own brutal creations before quickly retiring to leave the 4.5-litre Ferrari coupé of Villoresi duelling with the Moss and Rolt Jaguars. Peter Whitehead meanwhile was driving to preset orders at a

A good idea of the size of the crowd can be gathered in this Mailander picture with Moss now leading Villoresi's Ferrari and Rolt following on. The clock above the Dunlop bridge tells us it is 4.40pm, on Saturday, 13 June 1953. (Rodolfo Mailander/Ludvigsen Library)

The Belgian-entered XKC047 rounds Arnage, on its way to an eventual ninth place, driven by Roger Laurent and Charles de Tornaco. (Archives Serge Pozzoli)

A pit stop on Sunday for XKC053 with Stirling running round the front of the car, mechanic Joe Sutton on the left, 'Lofty' England leaning forward over the pit counter and Bill Heynes seated and pointing just beyond. The car is absolutely filthy and the ribbing for strengthening the new lightweight body panels can clearly be seen on the tail. A rather nice touch is the GB plate just above the spare wheel panel. At far right is Jock Thompson, another of the Jaguar pit crew. (Rodolfo Mailander/Ludvigsen Library)

'Hey, don't stretch my pully Duncan.' 'Lofty' and Hamilton give Rolt a helping hand as Len Hayden leans across the top of XKC051 to help Gordon Gardner who seems to be struggling with the right-hand bonnet strap. In the background, wearing a suit and dark glasses between Jacques Swaters and the man in a baseball cap, is Belgian Jaguar importer Joska Bourgeois who, left her fortune to Geoffrey Robinson, the man who was briefly Jaguar's managing director in the 1970s and who later became a Labour MP. (Ludvigsen Library)

reported 4,900rpm and sparing the machinery in case of possible troubles besetting the other Jaguars. It is worth noting that the big Ferrari was running a detuned 1951/52 grand prix engine and had well in excess of 300bhp, but despite this and Ascari's formidable speed it was only able to match the Jaguars rather than outpace them. Behind them the Alfa Romeos and the Chinetti/Cole 4.1 spyder Ferrari were well in touch, although Fangio retired one of the Alfas early on with a broken gearbox. The Astons were not faring well either with Denis Poore in trouble and Parnell crashing his DB3S, and Talbot were also in the wars. One other major threat disappeared when Mike Hawthorn's works Ferrari was disqualified for taking on brake fluid too early. Jaguar did not escape however with Moss in the pits with fuel starvation and misfiring that looked serious but was caused by dirty fuel, not exactly unknown at Le Mans in those days. This cost the Moss/Walker car 4min 11sec for a precautionary plug change and then 6min 49sec when the blocked fuel filter was discovered and replaced, dropping them to 21st place. After this the car was on song again and began the long haul back up the field.

At 8pm, with four hours gone, Rolt/Hamilton were just 1.3 seconds ahead of the Villoresi/Ascari Ferrari on 51 laps, with two works Alfa Romeos of Kling/Riess and Sanesi/Carini next up followed by the Trintignant/Schell Gordini, all on 50 laps.

Home and dry! Hamilton acknowledges the flag after one of his and Jaguar's finest performances. (Rodolfo Mailander/Ludvigsen Library)

Moss (with Peter Walker) finishes second in XKC053, perhaps a little frustrated after the car's earlier delays. Stirling was never to win Le Mans although he was second again in 1956 for Aston Martin. (Rodolfo Mailander/Ludvigsen Library)

Duncan Hamilton

Speaking to Angela Hamilton at her delightful Somerset home in December 2000, she recalled that Duncan, herself and the Rolts, Tony and Lois, always stayed at a private house outside Le Mans which belonged to la famille Lamotte. They drove to Le Mans every year from 1950 to 1958. When Duncan and Tony won in 1953 they were ecstatic and provided a wonderful celebratory meal and much champagne.

Angela met Duncan in Mombasa, he being in the Fleet Air Arm, she serving in the WRNS. They married in June 1946 and Duncan spent 18 months working for well-known motor dealers Henlys before setting up on his own in Byfleet where he stayed for many years. During the late 1950s the operation was moved to Bagshot, and today the business continues under his son Adrian, near Hook in Hampshire.

Duncan Hamilton was, Angela remembers, relatively laid back before a race, unlike Peter Whitehead who was very twitchy. Of the other drivers she thought that Tony Rolt was very smooth and probably better than Duncan, and amusingly, Stirling Moss used to call Duncan 'porky boy'! Having arrived at Le Mans on race day in 1953, Duncan discovered he had left his lucky Swiss red scarf (a present from Angela) behind and she had to return to the Lamotte household to retrieve it. Getting back in time through the very heavy traffic was quite a feat. It was at this race that somebody (possibly old friend and commentator James Tilling) gave Duncan an orange which was left in the cockpit of the car and thereafter became one of his mascots. This unique object, now mummified, still survives with son Adrian!

Angela Hamilton describes those days as carefree, and being young, she did not worry too much about the dangers of racing, this being a lot safer than the war, only recently ended. Amongst her more vivid experiences was a lap around the old Nürburgring with Duncan in his C-type, wedged into the tiny and very narrow passenger seat.

Duncan Hamilton died in 1994.

Rounding out the top six was the large Cunningham C5R of Walters/Fitch. With night setting in the battle became ever more fierce and, only a brief stop by the Ferrari when leading, dropped it to fourth place with the Alfas sneaking in front of their Maranello rivals. The Gordinis were beginning to fade and the supercharged Lancias had also disappointed. The Ferrari was back in front when Jaguar refuelled, but by midnight Rolt/Hamilton had regained the lead 1min 56sec ahead of Villoresi/Ascari with the Kling/Riess Alfa third, all on 101 laps. The other Alfa, the Walters/Fitch Cunningham and the Whitehead/Stewart Jaguar were next up with 99 laps and the Moss/Walker car was now ninth.

During the early hours the Jaguars continued their punishing pace and by 2am were leading by a lap from the Ferrari, with Moss up to sixth. At the halfway mark (4am) the remaining two Alfas had retired and the Cunningham was up to third with the Whitehead/Stewart Jaguar fourth and the Moss/Walker car fifth. Rolt/Hamilton had gained two laps on the big Ferrari and in his book *Touch Wood*, Hamilton observed that 'I was never in danger of overshooting at Mulsanne whereas poor Ascari was obliged to brake early just to make sure.' The Dunlop disc brakes were proving decisive. Further back the Belgian-entered C-type was enjoying a reliable if somewhat steady run in 12th place. As the hours progressed it became obvious that the Ferrari was beginning to suffer clutch slip and after stopping at approximately 8.30am it dropped to fifth and then to eighth retiring in the 19th hour, a sad end for such a gallant effort. Sadder still was the death of Tom Cole who had crashed at the notorious White House section earlier in the morning, being thrown out of his open Ferrari into a ditch.

So Rolt/Hamilton continued on their way to victory and had in fact led the race for virtually the entire distance, while Moss/Walker climbed to second by 10am on Sunday. The Whitehead/Walker car was fourth having been delayed by collapsing bodywork and the Cunningham was running strongly in third. At 2pm the existing race distance/speed record had been passed and by 4pm on Sunday Tony Rolt and Duncan Hamilton had covered 2,540.200 miles (4,087.18km) at an average speed of 105.841mph (170.298kph), a crushing victory, with the other two team cars second and fourth and the Belgian-entered Jaguar ninth. The significant increase in race speed over 1952 had been generated not only by fierce competition and quicker cars but also by the uncharacteristically kind weather that had remained dry throughout. Despite the very best efforts of the cream of the Continental teams and their world champion drivers Jaguar had outperformed and outlasted them. Although Ascari had set a new lap record of 4min 27.4sec the Jaguars had matched his pace and ultimately the Italian car had broken. One of the works Ferraris survived to finish fifth driven by the Marzottos but it was over 80 miles behind at the finish. The *Automobile Club de l'Ouest* published a list of timed speeds over a measured kilometre on the Mulsanne Straight that indicate just how well matched the major competitors were. However, these figures should be treated with some caution as they were not necessarily recorded at the fastest point and over the years variations have been quoted. For the record they were:

Cunningham C5R 154.81mph (249.09kph)
Alfa Romeo DV 152.80mph (245.86kph)
Jaguar C-type 151.97mph (244.52kph)
Ferrari 4.1 spyder 151.06mph (243.06kph)
Ferrari 4.5 375 coupé 150.34mph (241.90kph)
Jaguar C-type (production spec, ninth placed)
    143.39mph (230.71kph).

The winning Jaguar according to Jaguar's own records spent 15min 16sec in the pits during the race as compared with the delayed Moss/Walker car which was stopped for 28min 13sec. 'Lofty' England also reckoned that the time lost with the broken louvres on XKC052 had cost them third place.

1953 results

1st Tony Rolt/Duncan Hamilton Jaguar C-type XKC051
    304 laps 2,540.200 miles (4,087.182km),
    105.841mph (170.298kph).
2nd Stirling Moss/Peter Walker Jaguar C-type XKC053
    300 laps 2,511.074 miles (4,040.318km),
    104.628mph (168.346kph).
3rd Phil Walters/John Fitch Cunningham C5R 299 laps
    2,498.112 miles (4,019.462km), 104.088mph
    (167.477kph).
4th Peter Whitehead/Ian Stewart Jaguar C-type
    XKC052 297 laps 2,485.896 miles (3,999.806km),
    103.579mph (166.658kph).
9th Roger Laurent/Charles de Tornaco Jaguar C-type
    XKC047 275 laps 2300.815 miles (3702.011km)
    95.867mph (154.250kph).

Après Le Mans, Duncan Hamilton travelled to Oporto with his own XKC004 but suffered serious injuries in a huge shunt caused by the incompetent driving of a privately entered Ferrari. Happily he fully recovered. The works meanwhile went to the

Isle of Man with XKC011 and Moss but were unable to beat Parnell's Aston Martin DB3S. Reims was a better bet however and Stirling Moss/Peter Whitehead (described in the programme as Moos and Whithead) outlasted the Ferrari and Gordini opposition to win the 12-hour race with the Le Mans 'spare' car, XKC012. In September, Jaguar should have won the Goodwood Nine Hours but a combination of oil surge and wet sump engines combined with

Hamilton driving with Rolt and Jaguar pit crew Len Hayden and Gordon Gardner making it a four-seater C-type. The aeroscreen has been split in half by a bird that Hamilton struck at maximum velocity on the Mulsanne Straight. It also broke Duncan's nose! (Rodolfo Mailander/Ludvigsen Library)

A very happy scene indeed. Stirling Moss, Peter Walker and an unknown Frenchman help Angela and Duncan Hamilton and Tony and Lois Rolt celebrate their finest hour. Hamilton's stringback driving gloves were de rigueur for the period as was the Herbert Johnson helmet, although the American-style rubber one-piece tank goggles did not become commonplace until the end of the decade. Directly behind Angela Hamilton is Jaguar mechanic Ted Brookes, while Len Hayden can be glimpsed behind Rolt's right ear. (Rodolfo Mailander/ Ludvigsen Library)

Ian Stewart climbing out of the fourth-placed XKC052 with Peter Whitehead alongside for the post-race photocall. The collapsed and broken right-hand bonnet louvres can be clearly seen, while the trade plate is almost obscured by the combination of filth and crushed insects after 24 hours of racing. (Collection Bernard Viart/Paul Skilleter)

En route home the Jaguar team, including the Belgian-entered XKC047, stopped at this café on the A40, a somewhat more exotic class of customer than the usual pre-war old bangers and Fordson lorries that characterised England of the period. (Adrian Hamilton)

Goodwood's mainly right-hand bends caused bearing failure. This together with some inter-team rivalry between Duncan Hamilton and Peter Walker resulted in two retirements and the surviving Whitehead/Stewart car managing third.

Management were very unhappy! The TT at Dundrod saw Moss come third (fourth on handicap) despite gearbox failure and having to give the Aston Martins a one-lap start (the TT was still run using the unfair and outmoded handicap system). Had they won then Jaguar would have beaten Ferrari to become the first manufacturer to win the World Championship for Sports Cars. Instead they lost by just three points.

The rest of the year played out with William Lyons declining an invitation to run in the Carrera PanAmericana. A car was prepared however (XKC038) with a heavier gauge body but was not ultimately used. It was later sold to Duncan Hamilton who raced it in 1954 when he was not driving the works cars. Notwithstanding, 1953 had been a stellar year for Jaguar in racing and rallying, and for England in general; there had been the coronation of Queen Elizabeth II and Mount Everest had been conquered, so nearly everybody had something to be happy about. The C-type however needed replacement and Jaguar was not resting on its laurels as 1954 would reveal.

Chapter 5

1954 – From C to D

On 20 October 1953, Jaguar returned to Jabbeke, the second time that year, partly as a result of Pegaso exceeding 150mph (241kph) on the Belgian arterial road. Coventry was determined to prove it made the world's fastest production cars and this was done conclusively.

Norman Dewis averaged 172.412mph (277.410kph) over a mean mile in a specially prepared XK120 (MDU 524, chassis No. 660896), but perhaps of more significance was the appearance of what Malcolm Sayer described as an XK120C Mk II. It was the ultimate development of the C-type and carried the chassis number XKC054 (according to Andrew Whyte, although more recently Philip Porter quotes XKC201, a nomenclature probably used for expediency in

The missing link, almost. This is the hybrid machine that was known as the 'light alloy' car, also XKC054 and elsewhere as XKC201. It was taken to Jabbeke in October 1953 and tested at Le Mans, Reims and Silverstone, but never raced. (Paul Skilleter)

Tony Rolt at Le Mans in April 1954 with the first D-type (XKC401), where he unofficially broke the lap record by five seconds. This is Arnage and the car's incorrect registration number (it should have been OVC 501) is clearly visible. As with the 'light alloy' car, it was never raced, but thankfully still survives, leading a busy life with the Jaguar Daimler Heritage Trust. (Collection Bernard Viart/Paul Skilleter)

Bob Berry sits in the still unpainted XKC401 which displays the short almost dumpy nose and the vestigial screen. (Ludvigsen Library)

dealing with customs) but featured a very different almost D-type body style. It had its first run at Silverstone in May 1953 driven by Norman Dewis and was seen again during testing at Silverstone, Le Mans and Reims in the first half of 1954.

At Jabbeke the car averaged 178.383mph (287.018kph) for the flying mile, so it had exceeded 180mph (290kph), the first Jaguar to do so. Bereft of any driver's headrest or fin it looked like a portly D-type, albeit with wire wheels and a Perspex bubble instead of a screen. Interestingly, a photograph of the car at high speed in Belgium shows no sign of the aerodynamic lift and nose up attitude that afflicted the D-type and most other front-engined sports racing cars of the era pre-spoilers and other such aerodynamic aids.

At this time the decision to make the D-type had already been made, and meanwhile testing continued with the 'light alloy car' as it was christened. Norman Dewis and Tony Rolt drove it at Silverstone in November fitted with SU carburettors and an all-syncromesh gearbox. By December Claude Baily had issued a project specification and the construction of six prototype Le Mans cars was set in motion. At this stage, the new car was being referred to as a Series 4 XK120C.

Testing the 'light alloy car' resumed at Silverstone in January 1954 with Stirling Moss, who complained of too much understeer and poor pedal layout and the need to reposition the steering wheel. By February a proper specification for the new car had been set out that included dry sump lubrication and an alternative 'wide angle' cylinder head design. Unlike its famous predecessor the new car was a full monocoque built using some of the knowledge obtained making Stirling bomber aircraft wings during the Second World War. Suddenly, the C-type was obsolete. Then, between 5 and 11 April private tyre testing was undertaken at Reims, again with the light alloy car and also with XKC011 which was fitted with a new design of alloy wheel that would soon become familiar on the D-type. This was a necessity in the light of previous experience of broken spokes on wire wheels caused by the huge weight of the cast-iron block Jaguar engine and gearbox which weighed about 6cwt (300kg) and the increasing grip offered by continuing tyre development. Even allowing for this, it is to be wondered how or why Jaguar's main rivals continued with wire wheels throughout the 1950s, and in the case of Ferrari sports racing cars, right up to the end of 1964!

The first proper test for the D-type, as it was now called, was at RAF Gaydon, a venue organised by one Elmer Richard Protheroe, later to be a successful Jaguar racer, and his CO at the base. Dewis, Rolt and Hamilton tried the car and in his autobiography Duncan states that 'Lofty had marked out a course so that we could sample the car's handling characteristics and, true to form, I was the first person to spin off.' Shortly thereafter an opportunity arose to go to Le Mans, it being in use for the *Rallye de Sablé Solesmes* on 8/9 May 1954. With the agreement of the *Automobile Club de l'Ouest* Tony Rolt was able to use the new unpainted prototype, XKC401, in which he lapped over five seconds inside Ascari's 1953 record to record 4min 22.2sec. A small problem arose upon returning to 'Fortress' England when HM Customs noted the bare alloy car had the number OKV 501 painted on it rather than the correct registration OVC 501! In an uncharacteristically magnanimous mood the officers allowed the car to return to Coventry where the number was quickly amended. Subsequently this car was used only for testing and was never actually raced, but at least it was not broken up like the three original C-types and is still in use with the Jaguar Daimler Heritage Trust today.

The first published details appeared in *The Motor* on Wednesday, 12 May 1954 in an article headed 'JAGUAR for Le Mans' which showed the still unpainted car with a central spotlight in the air intake. In his capacity as head of public relations for Jaguar, Ernest Rankin had already briefed the press on 5 May with some details of the new car and the team drivers for Le Mans. Originally it had been intended to run two cars at the BRDC *Daily Express* International Trophy the following Saturday (15 May) but although two were indeed entered, this was wishful thinking. William Lyons wrote a polite and slightly contrite letter to the secretary of the BRDC, Desmond Scannell, apologising for their withdrawal. He pointed out

that they had to take full advantage of the 18 remaining days before their departure for Le Mans. In reality Jaguar were struggling to meet their schedule, but Lyons assured Scannell that the cars were progressing very satisfactorily, and all the

XKC402 displaying its original form with neatly mounted nearside spotlamp and 17-inch diameter wheels. Just visible above the racing number roundel is the trademark Jaguar logo of red lettering on a white background. (Rodolfo Mailander/Ludvigsen Library)

Early D-type engine that still used the production type camshaft covers with a screw-in oil cap mounting and welded-on scavenge pipes. (Rodolfo Mailander/Ludvigsen Library)

Cockpit of the Moss/Walker car (XKC403) showing the curved dashboard unique to the original 1954 cars. The sharp, vertical ends to the screen were in contrast to the nicely rounded item on the Rolt/Hamilton car. Look carefully and you can just see a spare ignition key fixed to the dashboard under the rev counter. (Rodolfo Mailander/ Ludvigsen Library)

tests were quite up to expectations. He also wrote to Basil Cardew, the motoring correspondent of the *Daily Express*, in similar mode. It is hard to imagine the head of any major manufacturer writing such a missive today to a mere journalist, no matter how distinguished.

Le Mans 1954 was now upon them. 'D' day had arrived!

Expectations were high, perhaps unfairly so, as Jaguar arrived at Le Mans with its most concerted effort yet to continue where the C-type had left off. The sheer magnitude of their task is best illustrated by simply pointing out that they were going to try to win a high-speed 24-hour race with a brand new and unraced car that combined technical innovation with a relative lack of testing.

Unlike 1953 the opposition was rather less numerous, with Lancia withdrawing despite having won the Mille Miglia and Mercedes-Benz not yet

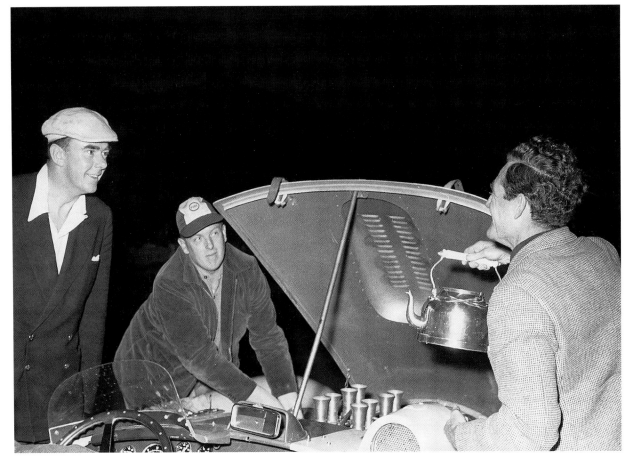

It wasn't all work and no play. Famous American sportsman and entrant Briggs Cunningham is presumably offering 'Lofty' a cup of tea over the bonnet of one of his C4Rs during night practice. (Rodolfo Mailander/ Ludvigsen Library)

ready with their new sports racing car. It should be noted that of course both these manufacturers were busy getting their new F1 cars ready while Alfa Romeo had retired from racing. So once again Ferrari were the chief threat with three 5-litre V12 375 'Plus' models to be driven by Froilan Gonzalez/Maurice Trintignant, Umberto Maglioli/Paolo Marzotto and Louis Rosier/Robert Manzon. The only other likely challengers were Aston Martin who had entered four DB3Ss (one supercharged) and a V12 Lagonda, and the omnipresent Cunninghams, two C4Rs and one Cunningham-styled Ferrari 375MM with a 4.5-litre engine and water-cooled brakes!

Le Mans 1954

The complete Jaguar entry was:

No. 12 Stirling Moss/Peter Walker Jaguar D-type XKC403. Engine E2003-9. Reg OKV 2.
No. 14 Duncan Hamilton/Tony Rolt Jaguar D-type XKC402. Engine E2004-9. Reg OKV 1.
No. 15 Peter Whitehead/Ken Wharton Jaguar D-type XKC404. Engine E2005-9. Reg OKV 3.
No. 16 Roger Laurent/Jacques Swaters Jaguar C-type XKC047. Engine E1047-9.

Spare engines E2006-9 and E2007-9 were not used.

All four Jaguars are visible in this Rudy Mailander view taken just after the start with Ken Wharton (15) in XKC404 briefly leading Moss (12) in XKC403 and Tony Rolt (14) in XKC402 alongside Roger Laurent in the Belgian C-type XKC047/012. No. 18 is Rubirosa's Ferrari 375MM (0380AM) and the two Talbot Lagos are No. 9 Louis Rosier (110 005) and No. 10 Pierre Bouillon aka Pierre Levegh (110 056). (Rodolfo Mailander/ Ludvigsen Library)

Despite its hurried construction from the remains of XKC047 and the donor XKC012, the Belgian-entered C-type went well enough to finish fourth. Here, Roger Laurent leads Carroll Shelby in his privately owned (hence the American racing colours) but works-prepared Aston Martin DB3S (3) through the Esses early on Saturday. Following is a Gordini and one of the ill fated coupé Aston Martin DB3Ss. (Ludvigsen Library)

Power for the D-types was quoted at 246/7bhp but there is some evidence that the engine in XKC402 gave 255.5bhp on test. Note that the chassis numbers were still in the XKC series and the cars were registered OKV 1, '2 and '3 respectively. There had been one driver change as Ian Stewart had retired due to family and business ties and his replacement was sometime ERA, BRM and hill-climb maestro Ken Wharton. Once again Ecurie Francorchamps was running its C-type (XKC047) now works prepared to 1953 specification with Webers and disc brakes, to be driven by Jacques Swaters and Roger Laurent. Sadly, Laurent's 1953 co-driver Charles de Tornaco had died in a Ferrari testing accident at Modena late that year. However

the C-type very nearly did not make it as works mechanic Frank Rainbow spun it off the road after overtaking a small Renault en route near Montebourg. The car lost its nearside front suspension and sustained other serious damage and was not repairable in time. Fortunately Jaguar had XKC012 *sans* engine back at the factory and this was loaded up and taken across to Le Mans where Ted Brookes and Les Bottrill transferred the engine and the more important mechanical components from the crashed car. There was no time to repaint it in Belgian yellow but the dark green car was given a yellow bonnet stripe as a gesture and the organisers accepted the new car as still being XKC047.

Inevitably there were other problems including some concern over lighting regulations, the rules stating that all lamps and bulbs had to be approved by the French *Service des Mines*. When 'Lofty' England wrote to Raymond Acat at Le Mans about this he was told that as long as the lights were yellow then the choice of equipment was free. Another cause for concern was tyre wear and this was solved by Dunlop's new Stabilia tyre which gave greatly improved performance. In passing it is worth noting that as late as 28 May Bill Heynes had issued a memo to those concerned detailing some 45 adjustments and modifications for Le Mans. No wonder they had cancelled their Silverstone entries.

Practice had shown that the new very sleek and really quite small Jaguars were well matched in terms of speed with the large, brutal Ferraris which had 1,500cc and 100bhp more than the Coventry cars. The Maglioli Ferrari and Walker's Jaguar both lapped in approximately 4min 18sec, nearly 10 seconds inside the 1953 record so once again speeds were rising dramatically. With cars lining up

In the opening stages Moss in XKC403 had quite a battle with the 4.9 Ferraris, and here he is leading Marzotto's car (0394AM) through the Esses on Saturday afternoon. (Rodolfo Mailander/Ludvigsen Library)

This photograph illustrates perfectly the rounded edges and extreme rake of the screen plus the 17-inch wheels of XKC401 (OKV 1) as Rolt speeds through the French countryside. Unusually there is no visible front-end lift. (Paul Skilleter)

in echelon at Le Mans according to their engine capacity, largest first, the Jaguars were starting in 12th, 13th and 14th in the line up. The Ferraris and the Cunningham led away with Gonzalez, Marzotto and Manzon leading on lap one followed by Moss, Rolt and Wharton, the last named having sustained some minor nearside front wing damage on the opening lap. For a while Moss shadowed the Ferraris and then began to close in, passing first Manzon and then Marzotto to lie second to Gonzalez. These four were now on their own and when it started raining Rolt rose to fourth displacing Manzon. Moss led briefly but the Jaguar and Ferraris were very evenly matched.

Fate now intervened when shortly after Moss's initial 32-lap stint, co-driver Peter Walker came in with misfiring and the fuel filter was changed. It transpired that the fuel filters as fitted were faulty and each car in turn suffered substantial delays including 8min 47sec for the Rolt/Hamilton car. These vicissitudes dropped the Moss/Walker car to 27th place at 8pm, Walker having lost 33 minutes out on the circuit at one point, Rolt/Hamilton

falling to seventh and the remaining D-type to eighth briefly although they were not so badly affected. Early casualties had included the V12 Lagonda that Eric Thompson had crashed at the Esses and the leading Talbot of Levegh which had retired with front suspension damage. Parnell in the supercharged Aston had benefited from Jaguar's misfortune and had risen to fifth while the other two works Astons with special coupé bodies were now seventh and eighth. For now the Ferraris held sway but the Whitehead/Wharton Jaguar was moving up nicely as was Hamilton. Come the midnight hour and Moss had climbed back to 11th but was then stricken with brake problems culminating in brake failure approaching the end of the Mulsanne Straight. Fortunately Moss was able to stop the car eventually by using the gearbox and handbrake but went some considerable distance up the escape road in doing so. He got the car back to the pits and the D-type did one more lap with Walker before retiring.

Now Ken Wharton was up to second and the Maglioli/Marzotto Ferrari was out with back axle problems. Tony Rolt had recovered to fourth and the old Belgian-entered C-type was up to ninth and going well. The next casualty was the Whitehead/ Wharton car which developed a gearbox malady and could only struggle round in top gear, placing a huge strain on the engine, resulting in its retirement in the 12th hour. The weather meanwhile was deteriorating in typical Le Mans fashion and this was to Jaguar's advantage. While Gonzalez was able to maintain a good pace in the brutish Ferrari in the wet conditions Trintignant could not and was losing ground rapidly to the fast advancing Rolt/Hamilton Jaguar. Ferrari then lost Rosier/Manzon to gearbox failure, so it was one prancing horse versus one Coventry cat. The steady Cunningham of Spear/Johnston was now third. Both the coupé Astons were out after dramatic crashes near White House and after the race the Feltham team were left with nothing but a pile of wrecked and broken motor cars.

As the rain increased the chase continued, see-sawing back and forth depending on who was driving the lead Ferrari. A very real cause for concern was the amount of oil and water being consumed by the remaining Jaguar, over three gallons of Shell and six gallons of water in total by race end. Fortunately it did not seem to affect the engine's performance, helped no doubt by the very wet conditions. By 10am on Sunday Rolt was on the same lap as the leading Ferrari but then had a contretemps with a Talbot and ended up hitting the bank at Arnage necessitating a stop that lost a further two and a half minutes. The gap was out to one lap and 33 seconds and Hamilton discovered that the car's handling had changed as a result of the frontal damage.

When Trintignant took over the Ferrari at approximately midday the rain had abated and Hamilton's rate of gain lessened. He stopped at 1.37pm and Rolt took over with the weather seemingly still improving, but then the rain returned. Trintignant came in for the last time, fuel and oil were added and Gonzalez prepared to depart. Drama! The Ferrari would not start and against the regulations four or more mechanics were working on the car at once to get it started – only two were allowed. Hamilton, observing this suggested to William Lyons that Jaguar might

protest the flagrant breach, but as Hamilton stated in *Touch Wood* Lyons replied that, 'If we win this race Duncan, it will be the British way – outright, not as a result of protest'. Such moral integrity was conspicuously lacking elsewhere however, as history relates. This delay allowed Rolt to make up a lap but then he came into the pits waving his goggles and demanding a visor due to the dreadful conditions. He was quickly waved out again.

The Ferrari meanwhile had finally got going after some seven minutes, but any hopes that it was sickening were soon dispelled by Gonzalez's pace. Poor Tony Rolt was still struggling with the torrential downpour and had to come in and it was decided that rather than waste time exchanging his goggles for a visor it was quicker to simply change drivers. Also there was some concern regarding the very ambiguous Le Mans rules concerning what could or could not be done if Rolt had remained in the car. In any case Rolt came in, stopped the car and got out, only to see Hamilton, suitably attired with visor, jump in and depart.

Rolt looks none-too-happy as he squeeezes out of OKV 1 while the plombeur *and mechanics get to work.* (Rodolfo Mailander/Ludvigsen Library)

Duncan Hamilton exits White House during a brief period of sunshine on Sunday. The nose-up attitude of the D-type is quite pronounced as Hamilton presses on trying desperately to catch the leading Ferrari. (Rodolfo Mailander/Ludvigsen Library)

Rolt was understandably annoyed and afterwards Rankin, Jaguar's PR chief, wrote to several journals explaining the decision to allow Hamilton to finish the race. Hamilton was at his best in the worst conditions and he really tried, his efforts memorably captured by the Random Films crew who were filming the race for Jaguar. Gonzalez, who was then arguably one of the fastest drivers in the world, could not be caught and he won by just 1min 45sec, or 1min 30sec depending on whom you believe.

Perhaps the most frustrating aspect of the final result was that the Jaguar lost over 11 minutes with the fuel filter delays and minor accident damage. The former was avoidable had the cars been ready earlier and better tested, but the Arnage shunt was not their fault and this alone cost them the race. Additionally, despite its huge engine and power advantage the Ferrari was only quicker on acceleration out of the slower corners and considerably slower on Mulsanne compared with the Jaguar over the timed kilometre (160mph/257kph to 173mph/278kph). It must also be noted that without Gonzalez they probably could not have done it as he was much quicker than his co-driver, and he also set the fastest race lap and a new record of 4min 16.8sec. Race speed average and mileage were slower than 1953, but only due to the atrocious weather conditions.

Pre-race predictions of a winning average exceeding 110mph (177kph) would surely have been realised had it remained dry. Nevertheless Jaguar had achieved great things given that the D-type was still brand new and only sheer misfortune and piffling problems had stopped them from winning again. On the debit side they had once more gone to Le Mans with an unknown quantity just as in 1952. They were lucky to get away with it. Almost as meritorious was the fourth place achieved by the quickly built up Belgian-entered C-type although they were 206 miles adrift at the end.

Now wearing a visor in deference to the very wet conditions Duncan Hamilton crosses the line to finish second after one of his greatest drives. (Rodolfo Mailander/Ludvigsen Library)

Jacques Swaters takes the chequered flag for fourth place with the Belgian C-type (047/012) that he shared with Roger Laurent. (Rodolfo Mailander/Ludvigsen Library)

Duncan Hamilton toasts partner Tony Rolt after their heroic drive in OKV 1. Major A. P. R. Rolt had enjoyed some success pre-war winning various races in ERA R5B including the 1939 British Empire Trophy at Donington. During the Second World War he had been incarcerated in the infamous Colditz Castle. He drove Rob Walker's ERA-Delage and Connaught amongst others before retiring in 1956 to concentrate on his business interests. (Adrian Hamilton)

1954 results

1st Froilan Gonzalez/Maurice Trintignant Ferrari 375 'Plus' (0396AM) 302 laps, 2,523.476 miles (4,060.272km), 105.145mph (169.178kph).

2nd Tony Rolt/Duncan Hamilton Jaguar D-type XKC402 301 laps, 2,520.935 miles (4,056.184km), 105.038mph (169.006kph).

3rd Bill Spear/Sherwood Johnston Cunningham C4R (R5217) 283 laps, 2,367.377 miles (3,809.110km), 98.640mph (158.712kph).

4th Roger Laurent /Jacques Swaters Jaguar C-type XKC012/047 277 laps, 2,314.677 miles (3,724.315km), 96.444mph (155.178kph).

The apparent anomoly of the Ferrari being credited with one lap more when it was only 2.5 miles ahead is explained by the fact that every other car's position is based on actual completed laps at the moment the winning car crosses the line.

After the race Peter Walker had said: 'We will have our revenge on July 3rd!' He was talking about the Reims 12-hour race and for the third time in a row Jaguar did indeed win, albeit against lesser opposition and only one works Ferrari, a smaller, 3-litre four-cylinder model. Ken Wharton/Peter Whitehead won in XKC404 from Tony Rolt/Duncan Hamilton in XKC402 after the latter were drastically slowed by a leaking differential, the legacy of an earlier collision with Behra's Gordini. The third car, driven by Moss/Walker, retired with propshaft failure and the Belgian C-type driven again by Laurent/Swaters, was third.

The last major outing for the D-types in 1954 was at Dundrod for the TT and once again the race was run on a handicap basis. To try to take advantage of this Jaguar turned up with three cars, one with the usual 3.4 engine (XKC402) but the other two with short stroke (76.5mm) 2.5-litre XK engines (XKC403 and a new car, XKD406). Moss/Walker in the new car had piston failure having run in third on handicap, but this was not unexpected as they had suffered a similar problem in practice. Destroked XK engines never worked well as Jaguar were to rediscover in 1958. The Whitehead/Wharton car however finished fifth on handicap but the standard engined car of Rolt/Hamilton retired after a poor run at 33 laps. Already doubts were surfacing about the crude rear suspension of the D-type that slowed them considerably on bumpy road courses like Dundrod, a fact commented upon by *Autosport* technical editor John Bolster. Later on, in October, XKC402 was returning from the Paris Salon when driver Joe Sutton swerved to avoid the original mad cow (French style) and crumpled both ends. For those who believe that buying an ex-works car confers some hidden advantage, Jaguar Competition Department's handwritten notes to Joe Sutton as recorded in Andrew Whyte's *Jaguar Sports Racing & Works Competition Cars from 1954* tellingly states that he was to bring OKV 1 'back to standard in every respect … car being sold to Duncan Hamilton on return from France.'

Now, 1955 beckoned, and it was going to be a memorable year for all the wrong reasons.

Chapter 6

1955 – Long nose casts a long shadow

At the end of 1954, Bill Heynes had written to Alfred Moss concerning the matter of whether or not Stirling would be driving for Jaguar again in 1955. Moss junior had already been to Italy to try a Ferrari but turned down Maranello's proposals, and had also spoken to Mercedes-Benz. The latter's Esso/Castrol contracts clashed with Stirling's but the Germans were willing to accommodate him by running his car on Shell. For the time being the decision rested with Stirling who had yet to visit Mercedes, but Heynes shrewdly observed that if Moss signed with the Germans for grand prix racing he would probably have to drive their new sports cars as well.

Ultimately of course Stirling departed, his career in need of some high profile results that neither his privately entered Maserati in F1 or his sports car races with Jaguar had more recently provided. Jaguar's racing policy too was an apparent source of discontent, insofar as they were almost solely focused on Le Mans first and everything else thereafter. In fact there were considerable changes in the driver line-up that saw Ken Wharton, Peter Walker and Peter Whitehead dropped. This drew adverse comments from Wharton and Walker which caused William Lyons to issue a press statement explaining the decisions. Wharton was not being considered again anyway as he had also become Daimler's competitions manager without consulting Jaguar, while Walker was unwilling to take part in the obligatory driver tests, feeling that Jaguar should know his abilities well enough by now. Notwithstanding this he had signed for Aston

Martin, so the dismissal was largely irrelevant, pride and face-saving apart. As with Wharton, Peter Whitehead was simply dropped, having already been informed that his services would probably not be required in 1955.

The big news was that Mike Hawthorn had been signed up, this being made somewhat easier by Mike's decision to race for Tony Vandervell's Vanwall team in F1. (He had driven for Ferrari in 1953 and '54.) Ironically this would not last beyond

Looking suitably proper in blazer and slacks, Duncan Hamilton seems less than happy while co-driver Tony Rolt, in his beloved dark glasses, fiddles in the cockpit of their car XKD506. Between them is the tall, bespectacled figure of Cunningham driver Bill Spear. The height and curvature of the wrap around screen must have made Le Mans type starts very tricky for tall, large men like Rolt and Hawthorn. (Collection Bernard Viart/Paul Skilleter)

Briggs Cunningham's first Jaguar entry at Le Mans was with XKD507, seen here during scrutineering. Although it was to the latest long-nose configuration it did not have the new 35/40 cylinder head engine and long rear exiting tail pipes. Instead it used the standard side exhaust. In fact, the works cars also used a standard centre section but with the side exhaust outlet blanked off. (Collection Bernard Viart/Paul Skilleter)

This is XKD503, the works-prepared Belgian Ecurie Francorchamps entry looked after by Les Botterill who is leaning on the screen, and Ted Brookes is at the rear holding the tailfin. Unlike the other Jaguars it used 17-inch wheels. (Collection Bernard Viart/Paul Skilleter)

the Belgian Grand Prix at Spa, and Mike parted company with the Acton concern ostensibly to join Lancia who promptly withdrew from racing! Having never quite burnt his bridges in Italy Hawthorn pitched up again at Ferrari for F1 while retaining his Jaguar sports car drive. Such musical chairs would never be allowed today. On 31 January 1955 Jaguar announced the signing and on 14 February they issued a press release naming their other drivers for the season. Apart from Rolt and Hamilton they were all newcomers: Jimmy Stewart (elder brother of Jackie and an Ecurie Ecosse regular), Desmond Titterington, and Don Beauman. 'Lofty' England also kept Ivor Bueb in play by suggesting he would use him should an occasion arise. Beauman had got the nod over Bueb at Hawthorn's request as Mike recalled in his book *Challenge Me the Race:* 'I had argued strongly in favour of Don Beauman, who was a friend of mine and in a sense a protégé, as my garage prepared his cars and I advised him on his racing.

Night practice was a regular feature of Le Mans and this is Mike Hawthorn accelerating away from the pits in XKD505. Note that the identifying white nose has not yet been painted on the car, but the tailfin does have a vertical white edge unlike the other works D-types. (Rodolfo Mailander/Ludvigsen Library)

Here are the D-types lined up with the winning car in the foreground. Whoever painted the nose of No. 6 presumably used a horse's tail. Bob Penney is standing by No. 6 with colleague Joe Sutton behind No. 7, the Rolt/Hamilton car (XKD506). No. 8 is XKD508 for Beauman/Dewis and No. 10 the Belgian car XKD503 for Claes/Swaters. (Rodolfo Mailander/Ludvigsen Library)

Beauman therefore got the job and Bueb was furious.' Later at Le Mans this was to prove slightly awkward but was quickly resolved. England had also made informal approaches to Ascari and Villoresi, both now ex-Maranello.

Jaguar's racing activities, Le Mans aside, were to include the May Silverstone sports car race, Reims 12 hours, Aintree sports car race (British GP meeting), Nürburgring 1,000km and the Tourist Trophy at Dundrod. Privately Duncan Hamilton was quick to use OKV 1, travelling to Agadir and Dakar in Africa in late February with mixed results. Of more note was the announcement earlier in the month by famous American entrant, racer and sportsman Briggs Cunningham, that he would be racing Jaguars in 1955. Included in the plan was a Le Mans entry and for the next eight years the familiar white with two blue stripes colour scheme was to grace many Jaguar and Jaguar-powered machines. Shortly afterwards, Phil Walters set a new American speed record at

This is the front nearside suspension of XKD506, the chassis number of which can just be discerned stamped on the top of the shock absorber mounting. The Dunlop six-pad caliper clearly shows the graduated wear indicator that was only used on the works cars. (Rodolfo Mailander/Ludvigsen Library)

The cockpit of XKD505, which is instantly recognisable by the four-spoke steering wheel, a particular fad of Mike Hawthorn. Jaguar had hoped to get away with using an interior rear-view mirror that is just visible above the handbrake, but the organisers insisted on a proper external mirror. The strange looking cylindrical unit and plumbing is a CAV fuel filter designed to alleviate any further problems with dirty fuel, a recurring problem at Le Mans during the period. (Rodolfo Mailander/Ludvigsen Library)

Daytona in XKD406, returning an average speed of 164.138mph (264.098kph) over a measured mile, 12mph (19kph) faster than the next quickest car, a 4.5-litre Ferrari. Then came Sebring and the same car, now entered by Cunningham and driven by Mike Hawthorn and Phil Walters, won despite an erroneous protest by the second-placed Ferrari owned by Allen Guiberson. Silverstone in May had Hawthorn driving XKC404, now fitted with a wide-angle head – was this the first racing appearance of the 35/40 cylinder head? He led easily until a top hose burst, slowing to finish fourth with team-mates Rolt third and Hamilton fifth.

The first public appearance of the new Mercedes-Benz 300SLR came in the Mille Miglia and Moss partnered by Denis Jenkinson won at a record average speed with team-mate Fangio second. In their next race, the Eifelrennen at the Nürburgring, they looked every bit as formidable as their grand prix counterparts with straight-eight 3-litre engines. Fangio and Moss duly finished 1, 2 but Titterington and Stewart both suffered brake failure in practice and crashed their Ecurie Ecosse 'customer' D-types. It transpired later that this was the dreaded brake pad 'knock-off', a problem that plagued early Dunlop disc brakes and may even have been the cause of Moss's near miss and retirement at Le Mans in 1954. Titterington was most unhappy about the brakes and the handling as well, and was effectively *hors de combat* until post Le Mans. Stewart decided to retire on the spot apparently due to injuring his arm badly for a second time, but it was really the extreme anguish of his mother about racing that caused him to stop. Although Titterington made it to Le Mans it was only to lend moral support so Jaguar now had to fill two seats for the 24-hour race. May was an unhappy month too for Italy when Alberto Ascari crashed during private testing at Monza in a Ferrari and was killed instantly, only a week after surviving his now famous dive into Monte Carlo's harbour. But even darker clouds were just over the horizon.

Le Mans and once again Jaguar was going to use a new car, albeit a development of the existing D-type, the target being better performance and specifically a higher top speed. Work had started in December 1954, instigated by Claude Baily under

Project Specification ZX501/50. As in 1952, they were facing Mercedes-Benz, this time with a much better car than before and with the world's two greatest drivers, Fangio and Moss. Meanwhile a new 'production' D-type (XKD503) was built for Ecurie Francorchamps and prepared for Le Mans with works modifications. The 1955 version now had a steel frame that bolted to the front and rear bulkheads and along the floor of the tub, replacing the original and damage-prone magnesium alloy structure that had been integral with the tub. Six cars were prepared for the 1955 race including XKD503, but the other five were all fitted with the new 'long nose' body configuration, 7½in (190mm) longer, with twin front brake cooling intakes and rear exiting exhausts replacing the familiar, earlier side-mounted version. A bigger dynamo and 100-watt bulbs meant the additional front-mounted spotlight was now deleted. Designed as ever by Malcolm Sayer this was one of the most beautiful and sleek of all the sports racing cars of the period. The six were XKD504 (spare), XKD505, XKD506 and XKD508 from Jaguar and XKD507 for Briggs Cunningham. The works cars all had the latest bigger valves and wide angle 35/40 cylinder head that offered approximately 270bhp, while the American car had a regular specification unit but was works tweaked as per the Belgian entry. It also retained the standard D-type side exhaust system. There was one other Jaguar powered car, Peter Whitehead's Cooper-Jaguar shared with his half brother Graham (see sidebar).

Le Mans 1955

The full Jaguar line-up was as follows:

No. 6 Mike Hawthorn/Ivor Bueb XKD505. Engine
    E3002-9 (changed for E3006-9 after practice).
    Trade plate 774 RW.
No. 7 Duncan Hamilton/Tony Rolt XKD506.
    Engine E3003-9. Trade plate 732 RW.
No. 8 Don Beauman/Norman Dewis XKD508.
    Engine E3005-9. Trade plate 194 WK.
No. 9 Bill Spear/Phil Walters XKD507. Engine
    E3004-9 (Briggs Cunningham).
No. 10 Johnny Claes/Jacques Swaters XKD503.
    Engine E2011-9 (Ecurie Francorchamps).

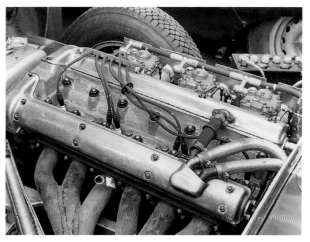

A works 3.4-litre 35/40 cylinder head engine. Only one such wide-angle head 3.4 unit still races today, in Ben Eastick's long-nose version that uses an ex-Hawthorn motor. (Rodolfo Mailander/Ludvigsen Library)

No. 11 Peter Whitehead/GrahamWhitehead
    Cooper-Jaguar T38 Mk II (CJ/1/55). Engine
    E2013-9 (Peter Whitehead).

It is seen here that long-time Jaguar tester Norman Dewis was replacing the still unfit Desmond Titterington. Legendary motoring journalist, race and rally driver Tommy Wisdom wrote in *Sporting Life* on 10 June: 'At long last a British motor racing team has given a chance to a man from the bench.' Sadly not enough of a chance as it turned out.

The opposition was very daunting and led by the three Mercedes-Benz 300SLRs to be driven by

The engine (E2013-9) in Peter Whitehead's Cooper-Jaguar (CJ/1/55). This is a standard D-type unit, and pity the poor mechanics who had to remove it and its ancillaries from under that tubular frame. (Rodolfo Mailander/Ludvigsen Library)

Fangio/Moss, Karl Kling/André Simon and John Fitch/Pierre Levegh. Levegh, whose real name was Bouillon, had led Le Mans for 23 hours in 1952 nursing his sick Talbot Lago until finally it broke, handing an undeserved victory to Mercedes-Benz. As a reward and in respect of his considerable Le Mans experience the sometimes emotional and sentimental Mercedes-Benz team manager Alfred

The Whitehead brothers

Peter and Graham Whitehead had the same mother who had wed two brothers, the first of which died and she then married the other. Hence they were half brothers. Tragically Peter was killed while travelling as a passenger with Graham in a 3.4 Mk 1 Jaguar during the 1958 Tour de France.

Neubauer offered him a drive. Originally Neubauer had wanted Belgian racing journalist Paul Frère but he had already agreed to drive for Aston Martin. Such is the quite arbitrary nature of fate. The Mercedes-Benz lacked disc brakes, but instead had a cockpit operated air brake panel that rose up on the rear deck and, of course, desmodronic valve operation. It also had fuel injection. Power was normally 302bhp at 7,500rpm but the 7,000rpm limit proposed for Le Mans in the interests of reliability reduced output to 276bhp. Generally the engines were considered unbreakable no matter what, but Jaguar pundits reckoned either the drum brakes or clutch would be their weak spot. In reality the air brake worked brilliantly as it did not destabilise the car so much under heavy braking and also conveyed some downforce, a little understood factor then. During testing at Hockenheim John Fitch had first noted this stabilising effect on fast bends. The 300SLR also enjoyed the advantage of a five-speed gearbox unlike its Coventry rival.

Also prominent but perhaps overshadowed this time were the three works Ferrari 121LMs, 4.4-litre six-cylinder devices to be handled by Eugenio Castellotti/Paulo Marzotto, Umberto Maglioli/Phil Hill and Maurice Trintignant/Harry Schell. Castellotti was very much the rising star at the time and future American F1 World Champion Phil Hill was competing in his first Le Mans. This was a very fast and powerful car as Moss had discovered on the Mille Miglia, and certainly the most powerful in the race, being quoted as 360bhp at 6,000rpm. Like the Mercedes it too had a five-speed gearbox. The others in the field were not serious challengers except by default, the works Maserati 300S and Aston Martin DB3S entries being the best of the rest. Cunningham brought along a new, beautifully engineered and very handsome looking C6R with a 3-litre Meyer Drake engine, but it was not competitive.

Tragically, even before this fateful event, a personal tragedy befell William Lyons when his son John was killed in a road accident while driving one of the works Mk VIIs near Valognes when he collided with a US military bus. This cast a shadow over everybody but the work went on. In his book *Touch Wood* Duncan Hamilton recalled how both Mrs Heynes and Mrs Lyons had dreamed that 'Tony and I had been killed at Le Mans.' This had understandably been linked to the accident and gave Hamilton quite a lot to think about. Practice was not without incident either as Hawthorn suffered a blown engine in the spare car XKD504, according to Tommy Wisdom, and Moss was hit up the rear by a little French DB as he was leaving the pits and then struck the counter. Maserati ace Jean Behra was injured and unable to race as a result. Practice as ever was a case of not giving too much away and Castellotti made fastest time in the big Ferrari with 4min 14.1sec, an improvement on the 1954 times, but there was much more to come.

Random Films were covering Le Mans again for Jaguar and they show race day bright and sunny with a Cunningham mechanic wearing an umbrella hat as he tends XKD507 before the start. Hawthorn twiddles his famous blue and white polka dot bow-tie and Hamilton winks at the camera as he and Rolt leave their caravan after a driver briefing with 'Lofty' England. Also shown is the RAF roundel adorning the Rolt/Hamilton car that epitomised the mood of Germany versus England and Neubauer versus England as Raymond Baxter's jingoistic film commentary makes plain. With the benefit of hindsight the extreme narrowness of the road and totally exposed pits plus the proximity of the spectators make for uncomfortable viewing as the film dwells on the scene and the happy, milling crowd. For now however it is a warm day with a wonderful entry and everybody is anticipating a tremendous race.

The patter of driver's feet and the sudden roar of exhausts at 4pm on 11 June denoted the beginning of the most notorious motor race in history. Castellotti led away from Maglioli, Beauman and Hawthorn. Being smaller engined the Mercs were back in the ruck with Fangio more delayed than normal having supposedly got the gearlever up his trouser leg during the Le Mans run and jump in start! Also delayed at the start was Tony Rolt. Exiting Tertre Rouge on lap one Beauman pulled over to let Hawthorn go by and by the end of the lap the two Ferraris led from Hawthorn, Beauman and Phil Walters in the

Tony Rolt in XKD506 at the beginning of the Mulsanne Straight followed by one of the Mercedes-Benz 300SLRs. Unprotected trees and public spectators trackside were normal fare at Continental races in the 1950s. (Rodolfo Mailander/Ludvigsen Library)

Phil Walters in the Cunningham D-type (XKD507) and Salvadori's Aston Martin DB3S enjoyed a tussle early in the race, although the much faster Jaguar was surely being driven conservatively. Here they leave the Esses en route to Tertre Rouge. The huge and densely packed crowd is impressive. (Rodolfo Mailander/Ludvigsen Library)

Cunningham Jaguar. The works Aston Martin of Roy Salvadori was well up but the first Mercedes were back in 12th and 13th places (Levegh and Kling) with Fangio and Rolt slicing their way through the field. Gradually Hawthorn reeled in first Maglioli and then Castellotti while Fangio advanced rapidly on to their tails. Using his superior brakes Hawthorn slipped by Castellotti at Mulsanne Corner on lap 16 with Fangio in close attendance. Two laps later and Fangio was past the Ferrari as well and the battle was well and truly on. (See sidebar.)

Lap times had tumbled in this opening stint with Castellotti, Hawthorn and Fangio taking turns to decimate the old mark. In his book *Challenge Me the Race* Hawthorn had reported that his car had suffered a huge detonation in practice on Mulsanne, like an explosion, after which it seemed to return to normal. The same thing had happened to Bueb apparently. Therefore, according to Mike, a new engine had been fitted for the race: 'It had only been run in briefly on the test-bed and I was told to take it easy during the first few hours of the race. What a forlorn hope! Few engines have known such a hectic running-in period as this one was to have.' Hawthorn's car had an engine change the night before the race after a persistent and incurable misfire developed. While doing this it was discovered that a tooth had broken off one of the gears, so the gearbox was changed as well. Apart from a few kilometres on local roads before the race the car started with a fresh engine and gearbox.

So, with a brand new motor Hawthorn and Fangio were now lapping in under 4min 10sec and Mike reported reaching 5,800/5,900rpm in top on Mulsanne. The D-type was running 16-inch diameter wheels (the Belgian-entered XKD503 was running 17-inch wheels and both this and the Cunningham car had a final drive ratio of 2.79:1) and apparently 2.67:1 gearing. This gave 180–185mph (290–298kph) on the Mulsanne Straight. Unlike Mike's car, which had had its windscreen height trimmed for easier visibility, the Dewis/Beauman car retained the original profile and Norman got another 200rpm on Mulsanne reaching nearly 190mph (306kph). Mike also stated in his book: 'When we went round a slow corner like Mulsanne, the Jaguar could hold the Mercedes on acceleration in first or second gears. When Fangio got into the third speed of his five-speed gearbox he could draw ahead, but once I got into top on my four-speed box I could gain on him.' The Ferrari by contrast had obviously inferior brakes and handling but: 'on acceleration Castellotti just left us both standing, laying incredible long black tracks of molten rubber on the road as he roared away.' Fangio was now leading by a small margin with the Ferrari fading away and here was Mike again: 'I suppose at this stage I was momentarily mesmerised by the legend of Mercedes superiority. Here was this squat silver projectile, handled by the world's best driver, with its fuel injection and desmodronic valve gear, its complicated suspension and its out-of-this-world air brake. It seemed natural that it should eventually take the lead. Then I came to my senses and thought: "Damn it, why should a German car beat a British car?" As there was no-one in sight but me to stop it, I got down to it and caught up with him again.'

Mike Hawthorn

Hawthorn and Fangio were not, on paper at least, well matched. The Englishman was not a prolific race winner despite his meteoric rise to fame, and had won only two Grands Prix at this time (1953 French and 1954 Spanish). Remarkably, despite becoming the first ever English World Champion, he was to win only one more championship Grand Prix, at Reims in 1958. Yet he had successfully beaten Fangio to win the 1953 French GP and was to match him at Dundrod in 1955, despite the D-type's marked inferiority to Fangio's Mercedes on the bumpy Ards roads. He was embroiled again with Fangio at Reims in 1957 and shortly afterwards during Fangio's legendary 1957 German Grand Prix, Hawthorn had hung on to finish only 3.6 seconds behind in the Argentinian's greatest ever race. Despite his cavalier attitude to life and what turned out to be kidney disease, Mike Hawthorn, when his health and constitution allowed, was one of the very best. Certainly nobody could drive a D-type like Mike and he was much admired and supported to the end of his career by 'Lofty' England. In stark contrast Fangio was on his way to a third World Championship and had already won 15 Grands Prix up to this time.

Hawthorn's well-known anti-German sentiments were never far away.

However, the D-type certainly had the higher maximum speed and was the quickest overall with Hawthorn leaving the lap record at 4min 6.6sec on lap 28, no less than 10.2 seconds inside the previous mark! The leaders had lapped everybody up to sixth place and the battle continued with relentless ferocity with Hawthorn now a few seconds ahead of Fangio. On lap 35 he caught up with Levegh's Mercedes to lap him. Having got by he also passed Macklin's Austin-Healey 100S and then lifted off and braked ready to stop at the pits for the first driver change and refuelling. This was at approximately 6.27pm. What happened next has been the subject of endless supposition, close scrutiny and much moral outrage, but the basic facts are undeniable. (See sidebar.)

The huge accident completely changed the entire pattern of the race, not surprisingly. Hawthorn had overshot and exited the car via the Cunningham pit and had to be persuaded by 'Lofty' England to get back in and do another lap before returning to hand over to Ivor Bueb. According to Chris Nixon in *Mon Ami Mate*, Hawthorn was distraught and telling everybody around him that it was all his fault, while Lofty and

Graham Whitehead in brother Peter's Cooper-Jaguar leads Levegh's Mercedes-Benz 300SLR into the Esses. Unlike Fangio's car at the exact same spot in the earlier picture he is not using the air brake. (Rodolfo Mailander/Ludvigsen Library)

The photograph taken by Geoff Goddard when he returned to the pits after the Levegh tragedy. I have included this picture because the crash cannot be ignored, but for reasons of taste and respect it is not one of the graphic and horrific images that can be found elsewhere. (Geoff Goddard/Grand Prix Library)

others sought to reassure him otherwise. Meanwhile poor Ivor Bueb was left with the task of racing the D-type for the first time in the worst possible circumstances. While all this horror was taking place the other two cars driven by Beauman and Rolt were circulating in eighth and ninth with the Cunningham Jaguar in seventh. As the race progressed the American car began to lose way caused by debris from its disintegrating airbox getting into the valvegear, ultimately causing retirement at around 10pm. Even earlier the Cooper-Jaguar had suffered bearing failure, but the Belgian D-type was motoring steadily in ninth place at 8pm.

For now Mercedes were still racing and Moss in the Fangio car was walking away from the field, Bueb holding second but a lap down and unable to match Hawthorn's earlier pace. This was always going to be a problem for Jaguar, regardless of any other factors, as Moss was even quicker than Fangio in a sports car. Had Titterington been available the relative mismatch would not have been so great. Behind these two the Ferrari of Maglioli/Hill was now third followed by the

Hamilton and Dewis Jaguars and then the first of the Maseratis. Early leader Castellotti's Ferrari now driven by Marzotto, had faded to seventh, its engine failing due to the caning it had received in the opening stint. The other Mercedes of Kling/Simon was temporarily back in 10th position but would soon regain lost ground. Four hours on at midnight and the leading Mercedes was now two laps clear of the Jaguar with the other Mercedes up to third with the Beauman/Dewis and Rolt/Hamilton D-types fourth and fifth. Shortly afterwards, Beauman went off at Arnage and was stuck in the sand, but after heroic efforts to extricate himself had almost succeeded, was pushed back in again by Chapman's Lotus. So ended a fine drive by him and Norman Dewis. All the Ferraris had now retired to the benefit of Maserati and Aston Martin, but there was dramatic news shortly after 1.30am. Mercedes-Benz, after consultation with their board in Stuttgart, withdrew from the race, an honourable and worthy gesture which was much appreciated, especially by the French public. Not however by Jaguar, who were racing on like everybody else, at the organiser's

The abandoned Beauman/Dewis XKD508 at Arnage as the Lund/Waeffler prototype MG Ex182 (the forerunner of the production MGA) passes by. (LAT Photographic)

Len Hayden looks back up the track on the grim, wet Sunday, and well he might after the events on Saturday. The plombeur is resealing the radiator cap on XKD505 as refuelling is completed prior to Ivor Bueb taking over. The very minimal, strip-like rear view mirror (sic) was as flat as Jaguar could make it to lessen any aerodynamic drag, but how much could be seen in it, especially at speed? Bob Penney with flat cap and glasses is at far right. (Collection Bernard Viart/Paul Skilleter)

The Le Mans accident

At 6.27pm on lap 35 Hawthorn was due to make his first stop. On the approach to the pits he had pulled in front of Macklin's Austin-Healey 100S before braking, Macklin had pulled out to the left from behind the D-type and into the path of the Levegh Mercedes that was travelling much faster than the Healey. The hapless Levegh according to Fangio had just enough time to stick his hand up to warn the fast-closing Argentinian before he struck the nearside rear of the Healey and was launched into the air. Impact speed was over 130mph (209kph). The car was now airborne and hit a concrete section of the trackside bank which was part of the tunnel that connected the pits and the spectator enclosures on the other side of the track. It stopped within a very short distance and burst open, the fuel exploded, and the engine and much of the front of the Mercedes scythed its way through the dense crowd. Levegh was thrown out and killed instantly as were more than 80 spectators, while the wrecked Healey spun up the road hitting the Jaguar pits and then bouncing back into the road opposite with Macklin jumping out unharmed. The Random Films clip clearly shows that Macklin is in shock as are others including Kling who stopped in a daze at the Jaguar pit to be waved on by a calm 'Lofty' England.

In his book *Touch Wood* Duncan Hamilton states: 'A gendarme lay dead at my feet, hit by something, I know not what. A photographer and another man were also on the ground. The scene on the other side of the road was indescribable; the dead and the dying were everywhere; the cries of pain, anguish and despair screamed catastrophe.'

In 1999, famous racing photographer Geoff Goddard recalled how, as a young man, he had been photographing at the Esses when Colin Chapman had motored by very slowly in his Lotus IX pointing back up the hill to the pits and urging Geoff to return. When he got there he took some pictures of the burning wreckage from the pits side and then crossed over the track. There he observed the French laying out bodies close to some stalls which continued serving food. It was to leave a lasting impression and one of profound disgust that anybody could consider eating in such a situation. Inevitably the aftermath of such an event led to the cancellation of many races including the French Grand Prix and Reims 12-hour race, the German, Swiss and Spanish Grands Prix and much else besides. Switzerland banned circuit motor racing permanently, a situation still existing today.

There was much criticism and demonisation of those involved. Veteran race organiser and French motorsport icon Charles Faroux was maligned for not stopping the race. In defence he pointed out that had such action been taken the immediate evacuation of the huge crowds would have hampered the medical services and rescue operations badly. It was better to allow the race to continue and clear up the chaos gradually. Mike Hawthorn became the target for blame, and he was perhaps the catalyst in the affair. Certainly the French press were sure that it was the Englishman's fault. Levegh too came in for some adverse comments as Chris Nixon noted in his biography of Hawthorn and Collins *Mon Ami Mate* in 1991, by some British commentators. It was suggested that he was too old at 50 and not up to racing such a potent car, but in fact he was running sixth at the time of the crash and leading his team-mate Kling. In more recent times there has been speculation as to whether Macklin had swerved out too far across the road, but given the relative narrowness of the track this seems unfair. Was he concentrating too much on the Mercedes coming up behind him and not paying enough attention to what was going on in front? Others have pointed out that Hawthorn had braked very hard in front of the Healey which did not have anything like the stopping power of the Jaguar and Macklin had had no choice but to swerve out to avoid hitting the D-type in the rear. Shortly afterwards at a hearing at Le Mans, Lance Macklin asserted that Hawthorn had made an error, an accusation refuted by Jaguar's Ernest Rankin.

Hawthorn stated in *Challenge Me the Race*, written in collaboration with Gordon Wilkins two years afterwards, that: 'When I passed Macklin, I was travelling about 25mph (40kph) faster than he was and I decided I had ample time to get ahead before braking for the pits. Certainly I had disc brakes which could pull me up very quickly, but so had he. But when a faster car passes you it is almost automatic to glance in your mirror to see if there is another one coming. Now, during the briefest possible glance in the driving mirror, Macklin's car would have travelled 80 to 100 feet. And if he happened to miss my signal (Hawthorn raising his arm to indicate he was pulling into the pits) and found me braking unexpectedly, he would travel another 50 feet before the brain could get a message to the foot to put the brakes on. What we do know is that Macklin, taken by surprise, for some reason, pulled over to the left and from that moment Levegh's plight was desperate.' Macklin always denied that there had been a hand signal. It is only fair to include Hawthorn's comments even though they were written long after the event. In any case they are confirmed by his statement to Jaguar at the time and in a cine film taken by one of the spectators, who was himself injured and hospitalised for three months, which helped exonerate Hawthorn from direct blame for the accident. It distinctly shows Macklin's Healey swerving out from behind Hawthorn's Jaguar and over the centre line of the road. Years later professional opinion from eye-witness and respected racing journalist Paul Frère also concluded that Hawthorn could not be held to blame but the consequences rumbled on for years. It is really only safe to say that the fundamental cause was the narrowness of the road and the inadequate spectator protection. Despite this disaster the pits remained open to the roads until the early 1970s and even then there was only a narrow barrier of Armco between the competing cars and stationary vehicles.

One final and unknown factor has lingered down through the decades. Europe, even ten years on from the Second World War, was full of displaced and sometimes stateless persons. The official death toll was put at 80 plus, but as Angela Hamilton told the author in 2000, it was probably much higher as some bodies were never identified.

behest to maintain some semblance of order and to prevent a mass exodus. This of course made Jaguar appear to be rather heartless, when quite the opposite was true and caused the much maligned Hawthorn even more press opprobrium post-race.

Meanwhile the Rolt/Hamilton Jaguar was in trouble. An oil seal had failed and it had lost first and second gears, and although still driveable, the very high Le Mans gearing would have destroyed the engine so it was withdrawn after 15 hours.

Ivor Bueb drove a faultless race under appalling circumstances even though he could not be expected to match Hawthorn's extraordinary pace. Bueb went on to win Le Mans again in 1957 for Ecurie Ecosse and probably would have done so in 1956 but for the fuel injection problems on the Jaguar that year. (Rodolfo Mailander/ Ludvigsen Library)

Johnny Claes, Belgian band leader and racing driver accelerates away from Tertre Rouge on Sunday morning in XKD503 on his way to third place with co-driver Jacques Swaters. Already a sick man in 1954 he nevertheless had a reasonable 1955 season but finally succumbed to tuberculosis in February 1956. (Rodolfo Mailander/Ludvigsen Library)

The end is thankfully near as Hawthorn passes the pits followed by Claes in the Belgian D-type. Just how narrow the racing line is can be judged by Rudy Mailander's picture and the uphill gradient that is not normally apparent in most photographs. In the background the telescopic effect of distance and perspective exaggerates the road's curves leading up from White House. (Rodolfo Mailander/Ludvigsen Library)

It was now just a case of driving to the finish, Sunday having become wet and miserable. The second-placed Maserati 300S of Musso/Valenzano finally dropped out after 20 hours leaving the Collins/Frère Aston Martin DB3S second and the Belgian D-type in third. So a very subdued Hawthorn drove the final miles to a pyrrhic victory, overshadowed by the ghastly events of Saturday and the soon-to-be-highly unpleasant consequences. (See sidebar.)

As for the Jaguar versus Mercedes-Benz question, there is no denying that Mercedes had a driver advantage in their lead car, if not in the others. Certainly the leading Jaguar was as quick but it lacked a competitive second driver, and would surely have continued to lose ground every time Bueb took over. On the other hand could Mercedes have been broken by a continuing flat-out pace? Rumours of clutch problems circulated, but Mercedes looked bulletproof and no confirmation of any such trouble has ever surfaced, whereas one Jaguar suffered gearbox failure

anyway and the other was crashed. The race and distance records were broken again but not by a significant margin due to the wet Sunday weather, and so Jaguar won their third Le Mans.

1955 results

1st Mike Hawthorn/Ivor Bueb Jaguar D-type XKD505 307 laps 2,569.601 miles (4,134.488km), 107.067mph (172.271kph).

2nd Peter Collins/Paul Frère Aston Martin DB3S (DB3S/6) 302 laps, 2,530.852 miles (4,072.141km), 105.452mph (169.672kph).

3rd Johnny Claes/Jacques Swaters Jaguar D-type XKD503 296 laps, 2,477.358 miles (3,986.069km), 103.161mph (165.986kph).

As already noted the aftermath of Le Mans caused many cancellations including Jaguar's happy hunting ground at Reims, and their appearance in the sports car race at the Aintree British Grand Prix meeting was disappointing. An unwell and off-form Hawthorn could only manage fifth place behind four works Aston Martins. The last ever Tourist Trophy at Dundrod however saw Jaguar back on form, but inexplicably Coventry entered only one car against three Mercedes-Benz 300SLRs. Also entered was Bob Berry/Ninian Sanderson in Jack Broadhead's ex-works 1954 D-type OKV 2 (XKC403). In the race, Hawthorn, partnered by an equally impressive Desmond Titterington, had the better of a duel with Fangio, setting an all-time lap record of 4min 42sec, but in wet conditions Moss, driving with John Fitch in another 300SLR, was unstoppable. Finally the Jaguar's crankshaft broke and with Bob Berry having crashed out of third very early on, the race was a Mercedes-Benz 1, 2, 3 benefit. Prior to the race the Le Mans-winning XKD505 had been overhauled for the TT and tested with a De Dion rear axle but this had been withdrawn with driveshaft coupling problems.

This was the last outing for the works in 1955

Trauma counselling

In more recent times the counselling of persons involved in any disasters, large or small, has become commonplace. Even those attending the scene, police and rescue personnel included, are offered help. Regardless of blame it is to be wondered what demons poor Hawthorn suffered for the rest of his short life, as such an horrific event would create a devastating mental trauma. Macklin too had suffered a very frightening and shocking experience, but in those days you were just expected to grin and bear it. Perhaps on reflection this is the only practical way to cope with such terrible tragedies.

and was followed by a press release from Ernest Rankin on 12 December 1955 announcing Jaguar's continued participation in selected sports car races for 1956. Unlike Mercedes-Benz, which had unexpectedly withdrawn from competition, apparently because they had won nearly everything in Grand Prix and sports car racing, Jaguar would carry on.

No happy smiling faces in 1955. Polensky and von Frankenberg share the photocall with a grim-faced Mike Hawthorn and Bill Heynes. Ivor Bueb with cigarette stands on the other side of the D-type with 'Lofty' England directly behind him. Porsche team manager Huschke von Hanstein wearing trenchcoat and scarf is on the far left in front of a gendarme. (Rodolfo Mailander/Ludvigsen Library)

Chapter 7

1956 – Jaguar win, but retire

Apart from the loss of several races post Le Mans, another casualty was the withdrawal of Mercedes-Benz from competition, the Stuttgart firm having won just about everything during 1954/55. This in turn meant a lot of toing and froing on the driver front, with Fangio going to Ferrari and Moss to Maserati for F1. Jaguar had intended to run both Stirling and Hawthorn but negotiations foundered on who was or was not going to be No. 1. So Mike stayed put while Stirling went to Aston Martin for sports car racing, although on occasion he also drove for Maserati (and won at the Nürburgring). All very confusing.

Jaguar's testing was undertaken at Lindley (known as MIRA today), Goodwood and Silverstone for the new season and many new drivers were tested including motorbike aces Geoff Duke (trying cars again) and John Surtees. Additionally a new batch of long nose D-types was produced for 1956 which featured some lightening of non-stressed panelling and detail redesigning of bracketry that saved 50–60lb (22–27kg) per car. Engine development continued and 275bhp at 5,750rpm was quoted while the suspension was subtly modified with a thicker front anti-roll bar and a rear anti-roll bar was added to increase roll stiffness.

Sebring was one of Jaguar's chosen races and they had four long-nose cars running, entered jointly with and running in Briggs Cunningham livery. Three were existing 1955 cars and the fourth was the new XKD601, running with Lucas fuel injection in its first public appearance and driven by Hawthorn/Titterington. This car led the race at the four hour mark until brake trouble (always a problem at Sebring) caused it to slow and finally retire with seized brakes. A similar fate befell the Hamilton/Bueb car (XKD508) and Spear/Johnston (XKD504) suffered valve failure after seven hours without second gear. At Silverstone for the *Daily Express* Trophy meeting Jaguar had entered Hawthorn (XKD603), Titterington (XKD604 with De Dion rear axle) and Fairman (XKD504). The race was a disaster with Titterington the victim of some heavy-handed driving by Salvadori in a works Aston and Mike retiring with seized steering after

A closer view in colour shows the three works D-types with Len Hayden walking out of picture to the left and 'Lofty' England in blazer in the background talking to an official. (Collection Bernard Viart/Paul Skilleter)

breaking the lap record (1min 47sec). Fairman also retired with a broken drive shaft. This was the only race appearance of the De Dion rear end on a D-type and unfortunately XKD604 was written off. At the Nürburgring 1,000km Hawthorn/Titterington (XKD601) had led briefly then run in third or fourth place before a collision with a slower car and then half-shaft failure had stopped them just before the end. The other car of Frère/Hamilton (XKD603) was crashed in practice by Frère and replaced by the older XKD504 but retired on lap six with a broken gearbox.

With Le Mans delayed due to the much needed circuit alterations, Reims was next up and was a triumph for Jaguar with Duncan Hamilton/Ivor Bueb (XKD605) with fuel injection winning from Frère/Hawthorn (XKD601) and Fairman/Titterington (XKD603). Unfortunately, Hamilton had disobeyed pit signals to slow down, instead going quicker and quicker, a result according to Hamilton in *Touch Wood,* of lifting off earlier for the right-hander past the pits. Basically, Hamilton's fuel injection car was quicker and he was determined to win, especially as he had lost the race in 1954. Whatever the reason, 'Lofty' England took a dim view of the situation, and despite his otherwise good relations with 'Lofty' and winning to boot, Duncan was sacked on the spot! In time the situation would be amicably resolved, but by then Jaguar had retired so Hamilton missed the last ever race for the works D-types. This unfortunate incident aside, Jaguar had another

good day at Reims, perfect in fact, finishing 1, 2 and 3 with the Ecosse D-type XKD501 fourth.

The rescheduled Sarthe classic on 28/29 July 1956 looked a foregone conclusion as far as Jaguar was concerned. They had the three fastest cars in the race by a large margin and their opposition was, compared with previous years, not very impressive. Certainly there were works Astons and Ferraris, but the former were still not powerful enough and the latter had reduced their cars from 4.4 litres in 1955 down to 2.5 litres and four cylinders in 1956. This was due to Le Mans being run on a new set of regulations that allowed prototypes only up to 2.5 litres, anything bigger had to be a series production car (the D-type and Aston's DB3S qualified, the latter on the basis that provision had been made for 50 cars, although in fact only 31 were ever built). Additionally the race was not part of that year's championship. Aston Martin also entered a new car, the DBR1 but running here with a 2.5-litre unit as per the rules.

Another feature of the new regulations was an obligatory full-width screen with wiper that had not been necessary at any of the other venues. Cars were supposed to be proper two-seaters with adequate passenger accommodation and leg room. The passenger hatch was not allowed so Malcolm Sayer devised a flexible Vybak tonneau for the D-types that ran from the top of the screen to the back of the second seat to lessen aerodynamic drag. Also affected were the lighting and the seat cushions which had to be a minimum of 19.7 inches (500mm) wide! Pure red tape and bureaucratic nonsense. Additionally, the doors had to be deeper and wider, and there was a limit on fuel tank capacity of 130 litres (28.6gal) with a maximum of 120 litres (26.4gal) only allowed upon refuelling after a minimum of 34 laps. This meant achieving no less than 25.7l/100km (11mpg) and was the first time (but not the last) that fuel consumption was linked to speed. It also spoiled the race as events would unfold. Consequently the car had lost some of its sleekness and the increased frontal area caused by the minimum height full-width screen took 20mph (32kph) off the top speed. Alterations to the circuit addressed the lack of road width and spectator protection and the start/finish line area was changed considerably with spectators moved

The three works cars (opposite), Ecurie Ecosse's XKD501 and the Belgian entry XKD573 showing their new high windscreens. No. 1 is driven by Len Hayden, No. 2 by Joe Sutton, No. 3 by 'Lofty' England. No. 4 is driven by 'Wilkie' Wilkinson and No. 5 by Ted Brookes. No. 2 is the original entry XKD606 before it was crashed and replaced by XKD603. (Collection Bernard Viart/Paul Skilleter)

This overhead view of the Ecurie Ecosse XKD501 reveals 'Wilkie' Wilkinson's penchant for painting cockpit interiors matt black, including the steering wheel spokes as here. (Collection Bernard Viart/Paul Skilleter)

Even by 1956 Jack Fairman was a veteran, having driven for all and sundry over the years. He had been part of Jaguar's first C-type assault in 1951, driving with Stirling Moss, a partnership that was renewed at Aston Martin in 1959. Here he is all togged up in nice new overalls and pristine stringback gloves and rarin' to go. He was sharing XKD602 with Ken Wharton. Note the early pattern Mk 8 motorcycle goggles. (LAT Photographic)

back. Even so, the pits were still exposed, a feature that presumably survived due to the traditional run and jump-in Le Mans type start. (It finally ended after 1969, safety harnesses making the exercise redundant and unsafe. That year, Jacky Ickx strolled to his car thus making the point.)

Jaguar's drivers for this race had been adversely affected by Hamilton's dismissal (Duncan secured a seat at Ferrari, much to his amusement, but continued to race Jaguars elsewhere privately.) He was replaced by Ken Wharton, back from his exile, while Tony Rolt had effectively retired. Jack Fairman had found his way back into Jaguars for the season and Desmond Titterington was driving in his last Le Mans. He was, Hawthorn excepted, the fastest driver in the team, but en route to premature retirement at the end of the year due to family and business pressures. Once again the Belgians were entered, with a new 'customer' car, XKD573 and Ecurie Ecosse was having its first Le Mans with XKD501, prepared by 'Wilkie' Wilkinson. All the D-types bar the Scottish car, were works prepared. An unusual entry was Robert Walshaw's very standard XK140FHC s/e.

Le Mans 1956

The complete list of Jaguar entries was:

No. 1 Mike Hawthorn/Ivor Bueb XKD605. Engine E4007-9 (changed to E4003-9 for race). Trade plate 393 RW.
No. 2 Paul Frère/Desmond Titterington XKD606. Engine E4006-9. (Crashed in practice and withdrawn.) Replaced by spare car XKD603. Engine E4005-9. Trade plate 774 RW.
No. 3 Jack Fairman/Ken Wharton XKD602. Engine E4004-9. Trade plate 351 RW.
No. 4 Ron Flockhart/Ninian Sanderson XKD501. Engine E2036-9. Reg MWS 301. (Ecurie Ecosse)
No. 5 Jacques Swaters/Freddy Rouselle XKD573. Engine E2079-9. Trade plate 164 WK. (Equipe Nationale Belge)
No. 6 Robert Walshaw/Peter Bolton XK140 FHC S804231. Engine G4060/9S. Reg PWT 846. (Robert Walshaw)

During practice Titterington had suffered an off-

circuit excursion in XKD606 and this was replaced for the race with XKD603. Practice had confirmed Jaguar's superiority with Hawthorn predictably quickest, his 4min 17sec lap, over 10 seconds adrift of the 1955 record, despite a slightly faster and marginally shorter circuit (8.364 miles/13.458km as against 8.383 miles/ 13.488km), after the necessary alterations. Gearing seems to have been 2.69:1 giving 32.3mph (51.97kph) per 1,000rpm in top. Power was quoted at 263.5bhp for the injection engine on the No. 1 car and typically 272bhp for the Weber set-up, although the injection unit retained its mid-range torque advantage and better throttle response.

The works Aston Martins had Moss/Collins and Walker/Salvadori in DB3Ss with Reg Parnell and Tony Brooks in the new DBR1/250. Ferrari had entered three 625LMs that were effectively early Testa Rossa type cars fitted with the old four-cylinder F1 engine for Trintignant/Gendebien, Simon/P. Hill and de Portago/Hamilton. These were the only other competitive cars in the larger class and it is easy to see that the works Jaguars

The leading cars have departed leaving the Belgian D-type lagging behind at the start of the 1956 Le Mans. No. 7 is a Mercedes-Benz 300SL followed by the two works Ferraris (Nos 10 and 11) and the prototype Aston Martin DBR1. This picture reveals how the spectators have been moved back following the 1955 tragedy, but by modern safety standards it still looks, and is, totally inadequate. A collision here could have produced another catastrophe, especially given the totally unprotected pits. (Collection Bernard Viart/Paul Skilleter)

This is the first lap at Mulsanne with Fairman in XKD602 leading Frère in XKD603, before the accident on lap two at the Esses. (Collection Bernard Viart/Paul Skilleter)

Paul Frère (2) lost it at the Esses on lap two causing Jack Fairman (3) to spin in avoidance. Unfortunately Fairman was hit by de Portago's Ferrari (11) and in a trice both Jaguars were out plus the Ferrari that was coincidentally to be driven by Duncan Hamilton, recently sacked by 'Lofty' England for disobeying team orders at Reims. (Photo Junior/Paul Skilleter)

The battered XKD602 afterwards with Bob Penney looking very fed up in the background. This car and XKD603 were rebuilt into a new XKD603. (Ludvigsen Library)

had a capacity and power advantage in their favour.

It was already raining when the race started and this caught out both Frère and Fairman at the Esses on lap two when they were in fifth and sixth positions. The newly resurfaced track was incredibly slippery. Hawthorn was already in the lead followed by Moss and by lap three was the only works Jaguar left. Frère had spun and Fairman had also lost it avoiding his team-mate, but having managed to avoid the bank he was then hit in the rear by de Portago's Ferrari. All three cars were eliminated and XKD602 and '603 were subsequently cannibalised to make a new XKD603. Writing in his book *Starting Grid to Chequered Flag*, Paul Frère was suitably contrite about his culpability, having already crashed XKD603 at the Nürburgring. 'When I got back to the pits, after half an hour's walk, Hawthorn's car was standing there. All hope for a win by our team had vanished. I could find no words to explain my despair to he, who had taken upon himself the responsibility of picking a foreign driver for the Jaguar team. But "Lofty" knows about racing, knows its risks and the fact that human beings are not infallible. Before I even opened my mouth he seemed to understand my confusion and made not the slightest reproach.'

Fairman's car had petrol injection and it is to be wondered whether he would have suffered the same fate as Hawthorn, whose car began misfiring on lap three. The engine had been changed in practice after weak settings had burnt out a piston and now it would struggle for nearly seven hours with a persistent misfire. Finally the problem was traced to a hairline crack in a fuel line and thereafter it ran perfectly. Sadly however, full use could not be made of the performance due to the punitive fuel restrictions and it might have finished higher but for this. In all, the problem cost Jaguar 22 laps. Hawthorn related in *Challenge Me the Race*, 'As I handed over to Ivor I said: "Well, at least we've made a little money. We should share £500 for the fastest lap!" Then somebody said: "But there's no prize for the fastest lap this year." And there wasn't.'

Fortunately Ecurie Ecosse stepped into the breach and Ron Flockhart began a game of cat and mouse with Moss's works Aston, the superior speed of the D-type offsetting the driver skills of

Some things are just not meant to be and for Jaguar Le Mans 1956 was one of them, at least from the factory's standpoint. Hawthorn and 'Lofty' England stare down disconsolately at the reluctant Jaguar as Bob Penney desperately tries to find the cause of the misfiring. (Collection Bernard Viart/Paul Skilleter)

Ron Flockhart in the Ecosse Jaguar (4) had quite a duel with Moss in the works Aston Martin DB3S (8) and here they are in the Esses with Walker's Aston Martin (9). The Jaguar's superior speed was enough to cancel out the brilliance of the Aston's two grand prix aces, Moss and Collins. Walker later crashed badly, suffering head injuries from which he never fully recovered. His later life was spent in decline and he finally died impoverished in 1984. (Collection Bernard Viart/Paul Skilleter)

Freddy Rouselle cranks over the Belgian-entered XKD573 into Mulsanne Corner followed by the rare and unusual looking Salmson 2300S of Nercessian/Monneret. (Ludvigsen Library)

Ron Flockhart pits in XKD501 as 'Wilkie' waits to refuel and Stan Sproat attends to something on the nearside. Note the litter in the air intake and the plombeur with the pincers waiting to unseal the radiator cap in case of water replenishment. (LAT Photographic)

the incomparable Stirling. Behind them raced Walker (Aston Martin) and Simon (Ferrari), Manzon (Gordini) and Gendebien (Ferrari). By 8pm the Aston was leading just from the Ecosse D-type, while the Belgian Jaguar was seventh and the XK140 was circulating steadily in 23rd position. At midnight, Flockhart/Sanderson just led from the Aston with the works Ferrari of Trintignant/ Gendebien third, the Belgian Jaguar sixth, the XK140 17th and Hawthorn/Bueb now 20th. By 4am the Aston was leading again and both it and the Scottish Jaguar had covered 146 wet laps, four

up on the third-placed Trintignant/Gendebien Ferrari. The Belgian D-type had dropped one place to seventh and Hawthorn/Bueb were now 11th, three ahead of the impressive XK140.

During the early hours the Ecurie Ecosse D-type had regained the lead and there it stayed to the end despite the best efforts of Aston's GP stars. At around 7.30am Peter Walker crashed the second works Aston, just past the Dunlop Bridge and suffered head injuries from which he never fully recovered. By 10am the Jaguar had a two-lap lead, the Aston suffering from a gearbox malady that had taken the edge off its performance. Ferrari ran third and the Belgian Jaguar fourth while Hawthorn/Bueb were up to seventh and the XK was now 11th. Thus the race run in intermittently very wet conditions petered out with Ecurie Ecosse winning at their first attempt, to the undisguised joy of Scotsmen everywhere, by just

over a lap. (See sidebar.) The only notable changes were that Hawthorn/Bueb rose to sixth and sadly the Walshaw/Bolton XK140 was disqualified with only four hours to go for allegedly taking on fuel after 33 instead of 34 laps some hours earlier. (Many years later Peter Bolton claimed the organisers had got the wrong race number and it should have been the winning car

Almost unbelievable. The first Le Mans entered and the first victory for Ecurie Ecosse as Flockhart crosses the line in triumph, but only just as XKD501's engine is suffering from an almost burnt-out No. 5 piston. (Jaguar)

Ecurie Ecosse luck

Just how lucky Ecurie Ecosse were to win at Le Mans in 1956 is highlighted by Ecurie Ecosse chief mechanic Stan Sproat who told me during the writing of this book that XKD501's No. 5 piston was almost burnt out together with the combustion chamber. Stan had already lowered the compression ratio to counteract the poor fuel quality, but it was still too high and the engine only just lasted until the end of the race.

Messrs Collins and Moss (nearest camera) and Ninian Sanderson chat up les jeunes filles while behind them Stan Sproat (looking straight at camera), 'Wilkie' Wilkinson and David Murray of Ecurie Ecosse enjoy the moment. It is 4.25pm on Sunday, 29 July 1956. (Collection Bernard Viart/Paul Skilleter)

that was penalised, but this is impossible to substantiate.)

1956 results

1st Ron Flockhart/Ninian Sanderson Jaguar D-type XKD501 300 laps, 2,507.183 miles (4,034.057km), 104.465mph (168.084kph).
2nd Stirling Moss/Peter Collins Aston Martin DB3S (DB3S/9) 299 laps, 2,497.057 miles

(4,017.764km), 104.044mph (167.406kph).
3rd Olivier Gendebien/Maurice Trintignant Ferrari 625LM (0644) 293 laps, 2,446.713 miles (3,936.761km), 101.946mph (164.031kph).
4th Jacques Swaters/Freddy Rouselle Jaguar D-type XKD573 284 laps, 2,371.564 miles (3,815.846km), 98.815mph (158.993kph).
5th Wolfgang von Trips/Richard von Frankenberg Porsche 550RS (0104) 282 laps, 2,356.389 miles (3,791.430km), 98.182mph (157.975kph).
6th Mike Hawthorn/Ivor Bueb Jaguar D-type XKD605 280 laps, 2,336.280 miles (3,759.075km), 97.345mph (156.628kph).

Mike Hawthorn set fastest lap at 4min 20sec, a new record on what was considered to be a sufficiently different layout. This and his officially recorded fastest timed speed on the Mulsanne Straight of 156.77mph (252.24kph) shows just how much the new regulations had slowed the cars, although it was, as ever, probably a shade pessimistic. Nevertheless speeds were well down and this with the wet conditions meant that no distance records were broken. Sadly, during September, Jack Emerson, XK engine development guru, who had contributed greatly to the Jaguar's Le Mans successes, died age 65.

Après Le Mans Jaguar simply stopped racing officially but did not announce this until 13 October in a press release headed 'Jaguar to suspend racing'. They cited various reasons for this, production priorities being foremost, and suggested that they might return in 1958 or later, depending upon circumstances. The reality was that William Lyons was more concerned with making a profit and his Le Mans victories, plus others, had boosted sales worldwide but now it was time to take advantage of this rather than continuing to expend vast sums on competition. He had never been interested in winning the Sports Car Championship and the D-type's development had only ever been seriously aimed at Le Mans. Experiments with De Dion rear axles and even a stillborn five-speed gearbox that would have enabled the D-type to win even on the bumpy and less smooth venues, were only spasmodic. For Le Mans however the D-type was an almost perfect weapon and there was one last hurrah in it.

'Wilkie' Wilkinson

Walter Ernest Wilkinson who became famous as 'Wilkie' Wilkinson was born on 7 August 1903 in Friern Barnet, North London. His father Chris hailed from Yorkshire and his mother from the Old Kent Road in London. His racing career began as riding mechanic to Giulio Ramponi in 1930, moving to Brooklands with the Bellevue Garage and MG racing team and also acting as mechanic for band leader Billy Cotton with his ERA.

After the war he resumed his racing activities with Reg Parnell and he did some driving, mainly in ERAs. By the early 1950s he was working for accountant David Murray, the founder of Ecurie Ecosse and partner with 'Wilkie' in Merchiston Motors, and had begun his long association with Jaguars. By 1956 Ecurie Ecosse had been racing Jaguars for five years, including the 1953 ex-works C-types, so 'Wilkie' knew all about the Coventry cars. Their singleton entry at Le Mans 1956 was with their first D-type purchased new in May 1955 that had already enjoyed a busy and robust competition life. 'Wilkie' left Ecurie Ecosse in 1961 and joined BRM at Bourne where he stayed until his retirement in 1972.

Chapter 8

1957 – Whitewash

Although Jaguar had ended its official participation in racing there were of course many D-types in the field and the car was still competitive, so 1957 was going to be another busy year. However there was a problem with surplus 'production' D-types which would probably not be sold, so a shrewd marketing strategy was undertaken and on 21 January 1957 a press release introduced the XKSS, in effect a partially sanitised road-going version of the D-type. It was to be for export only initially and a price of $6,900 in America was quoted.

Sixteen cars were completed with two D-types being converted later, but on 12 February Jaguar's service department and the northern end of the factory at Browns Lane were gutted by fire. Thus

The original contract on Duncan Hamilton & Co. letterhead signed over a 6d stamp by Masten Gregory and witnessed by Frank Kennington, Duncan Hamilton's pit manager, for his drive at Le Mans 1957 with Hamilton. (Adrian Hamilton)

The list of personnel and duties for the Hamilton equipe also detailing the trade suppliers and accommodation of those involved. (Adrian Hamilton)

and perhaps fortuitiously XKSS production ceased almost as quickly as it had begun, for there was only a limited number of chassis available, the D-type production line and parts sanction having long since been disbanded. Jaguar recovered quickly from the fire and in any case had to concentrate on their new cars, the 3.4 Mk 1 saloon and later the XK150, the first production Jaguar sports car with disc brakes.

Production aside racing went on and Ecurie Ecosse had bought three of the works long-nose D-types in October 1956. Graham Gauld wrote in his story of the Scottish team, *Ecurie Ecosse,* that Jaguar offered the cars for a deposit of £1,000 per car on the basis that they remained Jaguar's property, or an option to buy them outright for £3,000 each! They were XKD504, the 1955 Le Mans 'spare' and Jaguar's fuel injection testing car, XKD603 and XKD606. This was agreed on the basis that Ecurie Ecosse would undertake a full season of World Sports Car Championship rounds, something Jaguar had never done, and that they would not alter the specification without Jaguar's agreement. Additionally Jaguar retained the right to nominate two drivers for any car entered at Sebring and Le Mans. This caused some dismay when Jaguar loaned Hawthorn and Bueb to

Cunningham at Sebring, but in any case, Ecosse were not there. In the first round at Buenos Aires Ron Flockhart well and truly stuffed poor XKD606, knocking over a concrete lamp post in practice and substantially wrecking the front of the car. It did not appear again until Le Mans, of which more later. The other car, XKD603, driven by Ninian Sanderson and sometime Maserati grand prix racer Roberto Mieres finished a worthy 4th.

Sebring 1957 was the next round after Buenos Aires and this was a works entry by proxy with Hawthorn and Bueb driving XKD605 with a new, larger 3.8 engine. This development had originated from Alfred Momo at Cunningham and had been adopted and approved by Jaguar. (The early 3.8 engines had their blocks stamped 3.75.) It was painted in Cunningham colours and despite a brake pipe failure, finished third behind the works Maseratis, with its sister car fifth. This was the last time that Hawthorn drove a D-type in a race. Cunningham had become a successful Jaguar entrant and the car stayed on in America. In England a new Jaguar-engined car had appeared that dominated British national racing, and later American sports car racing with Cunningham, for nearly three years – the Lister.

Back on the championship trail, Ecurie Ecosse

Len Hayden in Hamilton's XKD601. Note that the public are now kept at bay by a wooden fence. The later, 1956 series long-nose D-types can be differentiated from their 1955 counterparts by the recessed bonnet straps, just visible here. (I wonder if the XK140DHC (OCA 451) on the extreme right, still exists?) (Collection Bernard Viart/Paul Skilleter)

The Belgian Equipe Nationale Belge XKD573 was driven by Paul Frère and Freddy Rouselle. No access problems here for the masses as Ted Brookes (hands on hips) surveys the scene. Note how tall the windscreen is and the puny windscreen wiper. (Collection Bernard Viart/Paul Skilleter)

Ron Flockhart nearing maximum speed past the Hotel des Hunaudieres Restaurant on the Mulsanne Straight in XKD606 displaying the characteristic front-end lift. The car is travelling at 180mph (290kph) and the camera's focal plane shutter distortion accounts for the rearward leaning building. (Paul Skilleter)

Compare the French Los Amigos-entered XKD513 short-nose production car driven here by 'Mary' (Jean Brousselet) and Hamilton's ex-works long-nose XKD601. A piece of the sidescreen on Duncan's car has broken off. (Edward Eves/Ludvigsen Library)

had escaped into private hands, this being XKD601 bought by Duncan Hamilton which he was saving for Le Mans. It was to be in many ways, Jaguar's finest hour at the French classic in 1957 even though they were no longer actually racing themselves. However it should not be forgotten that Jaguar race-prepared all the engines for the five entries and three of the cars completely, engines included. This was factory support in the truest sense and much better service than could be had at Maranello for instance.

Happily, Le Mans 1957 had reverted to its traditional June date and prototypes of unlimited capacity were back in favour. Gone too were the petty fuel restrictions that limited tank size and the minimum distance between refuelling had been reduced to 30 laps, rather than 34. Cars however, still had to have full-width screens and two identical seats and also a working hood! This last item was presumably a sop to the original concept of running road-equipped touring cars and illustrates perfectly the unrealistic mindset of bureaucracy. The omens for a good race were strong. Aston Martin, Ferrari and Maserati all entered their latest cars, Aston fresh from its Nürburgring victory with the potent DBR1/300. There were three works Astons, two of the 3-litre DBR1 cars and a new 3.7-litre version based on the old 1954 Lagonda V12 known as the DBR2. These were driven by Tony Brooks/Noel Cunningham-Reid, Les Leston/Salvadori and Peter and Graham Whitehead. Ferrari were sporting four works cars, two 4.1-litre 335Ss, one 3.7-litre 315S and a 3-litre Testa Rossa. Drivers included Mike Hawthorn, Peter Collins, Phil Hill and Olivier Gendebien. Maserati looked the most formidable on paper with Fangio and Moss on the driving roster, but their Le Mans form was pretty dismal. Potentially they had the fastest car, the awesome 450S that had won at Sebring, and they fielded two of the beasts. Behra and Simon had the conventional open car but Moss and Harry Schell were in a Zagato coupé abomination that was uncomfortable to drive and nearly impossible to see out of. Fangio was nominated as reserve driver and wisely gave the race a miss. They also had a 300S for Bonnier/Scarlatti but this was not a serious contender.

entered the Mille Miglia with Ron Flockhart driving the 1956 Le Mans-winning XKD501. Car and driver did very well until the D started to come unstitched around the rear and the fuel tank broke loose, leading to retirement. This was the last ever Mille Miglia, its inevitable demise hastened by the fatal accident that befell 'Fon' de Portago and Gurner ('Ed') Nelson's works Ferrari that crashed, killing themselves and nine spectators – four adults and five children. After this, Ecurie Ecosse went to the Nürburgring with three cars, finishing eighth, 11th and 16th. Meanwhile another long-nose car

Le Mans 1957

There were five Jaguars in total: two from Ecurie Ecosse and three others:

No. 3 Ron Flockhart/Ivor Bueb XKD606. Engine E5005-9. Trade plate 341 SG. (Ecurie Ecosse)
No. 4 Duncan Hamilton/Masten Gregory XKD601. Engine E5006-9. Reg 2 CPG. (Duncan Hamilton)
No. 15 Ninian Sanderson/John Lawrence XKD603. Engine E4007-9. Trade plate 376 SG. (Ecurie Ecosse)
No. 16 Paul Frère/Freddy Rouselle XKD573. Engine E2079-9 (the same quoted number as 1956 but a new unit). Reg NKV 479. (Equipe Nationale Belge)
No. 17 Jean Lucas/'Mary' (Jean Brousselet) XKD513. Engine E2022-9. Reg 6478 AT 69 Los Amigos. (Henri Peignaux)

The No. 3 and No. 4 cars had 3.8-litre engines built by Bill Wilkinson who had assumed Jack Emerson's role, Hamilton's had the familiar 45DC03 Weber set-up but the Ecosse car had Lucas fuel injection. They developed 288.2bhp at 5,500rpm and 297.5bhp at 5,750rpm respectively. The injection engine was on loan and remained Jaguar's property. XKD606 meanwhile had been rebuilt from its Argentinian shunt with a new front frame, nearside front suspension and bonnet assembly. Gearing on this car was 2.69:1. The other cars including the Ecosse second string used 3.4 units on Webers. As a comparison the ENB D-type's new engine (not a wide angle head unit) was giving 257.2bhp at 6,000rpm. It had also acquired a new gearbox. Practice proved nothing much except how fast the Italian brigade were with Fangio the quickest in the Maserati 450S with 3min 58.1sec, the first sub four-minute lap at Le Mans. By contrast the Jaguars were relatively sedate with Hamilton quickest on 4min 8sec, but this was never a guide to their race form or outright speed, as history indicates. The Ecosse fuel injection car was in fact misfiring prior to practice, as 'Wilkie' Wilkinson recalled, caused apparently by a hairline crack (sounds familiar?), a blocked fuel filter and faulty fuel pump. Another problem was finding the

right settings for the varied atmospheric conditions at Le Mans, the Lucas fuel injection not then fully developed. A near miss on the Mulsanne Straight during public hours with a Citroën while testing the car flat out at nearly 180mph (290kph) gave 'Wilkie' quite a scare. Chief mechanic Stan Sproat, who had been working with the Lucas technician, cured the problem. It lapped in 4min 10.8sec while the smaller-engined sister car managed 4min 14.6sec.

There were 54 starters for the 1957 Le Mans 24-hour race, but only 20 classified finishers. Much of the mortality amongst the bigger engined cars occurred early on and robbed the race of any real drama. Moss was first to his car as usual in the Le Mans start, but by the time he had got himself

Ninian Sanderson sweeps through Arnage in XKD603. This rear view illustrates perfectly how big the tailfin was on the long-nose cars. (Edward Eves/Ludvigsen Library)

Ivor the Driver Bueb at Arnage in the winning car (XKD606). He was never a real 'ace', but was certainly very capable in sports cars and always went well at Le Mans where his two victories represented the peak of his career. (Edward Eves/ Ludvigsen Library)

Pit stop for the Belgian D-type XKD573. Ted Brookes leans over the passenger side of the cockpit. (LAT Photographic)

wedged into the Maserati's cramped cockpit, Peter Collins was away and gone in the Ferrari 335S. At the end of lap one he came by in the lead from Brooks in the DBR1 Aston and Moss's coupé 'Maser' followed by Gendebien in the Testa Rossa Ferrari, Hawthorn Ferrari 335S and Flockhart in the first of the Jaguars. Incredibly, Collins was out by lap three with piston failure, but Hawthorn quickly took over at the front and by 5pm the order was Hawthorn followed by Behra and Moss (Maseratis), Gendebien (Ferrari) and then Flockhart (Jaguar) and Brooks (Aston Martin). Hawthorn stayed in front until he stopped just short of 6pm, when during a protracted pit stop caused by being unable to shut the spare wheel panel, both Maseratis overtook him. Ecurie Ecosse

had also had a spot of bother when John Lawrence brought in XKD603 with a very rough sounding engine, but a change of plugs cured the problem.

Now disaster visited Maserati as first the Moss car started to develop terminal rear axle problems and then after stopping for fuel and a driver change, the other 'Maser' now driven by Simon crashed. Schell managed a few laps in the Moss car but he was out by lap 38, and that was the end of the Trident's challenge. Musso having taken over from Hawthorn was getting a move on however but he too was destined to retire before too long. All this left the Aston Martin of Brooks briefly in the lead until his stop where upon the Ecosse Jaguar now driven by Bueb took over. Just as in 1956 it was a Scottish Jaguar versus a works Aston Martin,

Ninian Sanderson leaves the Esses on his way to Tertre Rouge in the second-placed Ecurie Ecosse XKD603. (LAT Photographic)

Jock Lawrence in the Ecurie Ecosse XKD603 chased by Masten Gregory in Hamilton's XKD601 as they brake for Tertre Rouge. No Armco then, just a long line of high straw bales and of course the ability to take pictures almost on top of the cars as this one was, right on the track's edge. (Collection Bernard Viart/Paul Skilleter)

The piece of steel that was used to patch up the floor of XKD601 after the burnt exhaust escapade. (Geoff Goddard/ Grand Prix Library)

Jock Lawrence leaps out of XKD603 as Ninian Sanderson on the pit counter with David Murray waits to take over. 'Wilkie' is refuelling. John 'Jock' Lawrence stopped racing in 1959 and emigrated to Australia before returning to England in later life. He died in 2000. (Collection Bernard Viart/Paul Skilleter)

with 'Johnny Foreigner' lurking in the wings. Still well up but gradually losing ground to the bigger engined cars was the Testa Rossa Ferrari, Gendebien being rather more effective than co-driver Trintignant. The other 3.8 D-type of Gregory, who was driving steadily to orders, had the benefit of what was very nearly a Jaguar 'works' pit team with 'Lofty' England and Malcolm Sayer

on hand and Len Hayden, Jaguar's chief mechanic assisting Robin Freeman. Frank Kennington was Hamilton's team manager and also present were former HWM racer Tony Gaze and Michael Head (father of Williams F1 designer Patrick Head).

Hamilton suffered an alarming incident during his opening stint in XKD601 that he related in *Touch Wood*: 'I lapped steadily for over two hours and then, while doing about 180mph (290kph) on the Mulsanne Straight, my lights went out. I had just taken my line for the curve (there was a distinct right-hand kink on Mulsanne) and how I got round that corner I do not know. I kept my foot down and let my memory do the rest. My speed was so great that braking was out of the question, and to have lifted my foot off the throttle would have been disastrous: the torque reversal at such speed would have sent me off the road.' Fortunately he followed another car back to the pits where the lights were fixed, only for them to fail again when Masten was back in the car. A third set of bulbs was fitted and these lasted until dawn, but as Hamilton further relates, 'But our troubles were only beginning. Masten came in to say there

was a glow in the cockpit and he reckoned there must be a fire somewhere. Neither Len Hayden nor Robin Freeman could find anything wrong so I went off to do a trial lap. There certainly was a glow in the cockpit, near the passenger's seat, but when driving at racing speeds in the dark you cannot examine the passenger's seat. I waited until I was round Mulsanne Corner (a bottom gear corner) and then, before opening up, took a good look to my left. The floor of the car was a mass of flames and I guessed rightly that the exhaust pipe had fractured and the escaping flames had burnt through the floor.' Returning to the pits someone pointed out that the left shoulder of his sweater was badly singed. The exhaust was not repairable but the floor was and it was patched up with a heavy duty steel plate that kept the flames at bay. Slipping ignition timing had led to the overheated exhaust and the car lost a huge amount of time, its total stoppage time for the race being 126min 36sec. This dropped it to 20th and thereafter the car spent the rest of the race regaining lost ground. (See sidebar.)

Prior to this the Flockhart/Bueb car was leading

Ron Flockhart rounds Arnage early in the race in XKD606.

and there it stayed right to the end. Behind them came the Brooks/Cunningham-Reid Aston and the Gendebien/Trintignant Ferrari followed by Hamilton's Jaguar before its dramas, the second Ecosse car of Sanderson/Lawrence and the other works Ferrari of Lewis-Evans/Severi. (Who remembers now that sometime Connaught and then Vanwall driver Stuart Lewis-Evans drove for

Can we really do this again? David Murray (nearest camera), Jock Lawrence and 'Wilkie' Wilkinson suffer those final anxious moments. Further along an impassive 'Lofty' England just waits for the inevitable. (Paul Skilleter)

Masten Gregory

Angela Hamilton described the slight, bespectacled Masten Gregory as laconic and recalled his reply when asked how the car was going during one of its pit stops. He replied: 'It's all right when it's not on fire!' A chain smoker and rumoured user of illegal substances, he died prematurely in 1985, aged 53.

Flockhart and Sanderson arrive and Ecurie Ecosse have reached their pinnacle. With changing regulations for 1958 Ecurie Ecosse were never to win a championship sports car race again, although they did manage two victories at Silverstone and Spa in 1958 with their Lister-Jaguar driven by Masten Gregory. (LAT Photographic)

Ferrari?) At midnight the Scottish Jaguar and the Aston were alone on 112 laps, three clear of the second Ecosse car with the now failing Testa Rossa Ferrari fourth, Rouselle fifth in the ENB D-type and the French Jaguar of Lucas/Brousselet eighth. Sometime after 1am the second DBR1 Aston of Leston/Salvadori retired with engine maladies caused by loss of gears and at 4am, halfway, Jaguars were running first, second, third and fourth, the Belgian car now in second place after the smaller-engined Ecosse Jaguar had been delayed by blown headlight bulbs, and then a lap

scoring error caused further consternation. Gone was the second-placed Aston Martin after Tony Brooks had slid off at Tertre Rouge when grappling with the Aston's sticking gearbox, and with him the last effective threat to total Jaguar domination. The Gendebien Ferrari was also out long before while the surviving works Ferrari of Lewis-Evans/Severi was delayed and several miles back.

Just before 7am, the Belgian Jaguar driven by Rouselle, stopped near Mulsanne Corner but he eventually got it back to the pits after discovering that the points in the distributor had closed up, which lost them nearly an hour. This dropped them back behind the surviving Ferrari and probably cost them second place. Three hours later and Flockhart/Bueb were sailing serenely on seven laps clear of their team-mate with the French and Belgian Jaguars third and fourth, Frère having caught and passed the surviving Ferrari which was suffering from sand ingested earlier in the race and had very little braking. Frère remarks in *Starting*

Grid to Chequered Flag that XKD573 was reaching 165mph (265kph) on Mulsanne, which was almost identical to the French car but 6mph (10kph) slower than the 3.4-litre Ecosse car. This reflects the superior aerodynamics of the long-nose version and its more powerful wide-angle head engine. By contrast, Masten Gregory had been timed at 178.8mph (287.7kph) in XKD601 and this car had climbed back to ninth position at 7am.

There was nothing left to do now but drive steadily to the finish for Ecurie Ecosse who for the second year running were leading Le Mans. In fact, the only excitement was provided by the progress up the field of the Hamilton/Gregory car, but it was so far back that not until the 23rd hour did it appear in sixth place after the works Porsche of Storez/Crawford retired. In *Touch Wood*, Hamilton wrote of his pursuit of the Lewis-Evans/Severi Ferrari to make it a Jaguar 1, 2, 3, 4, 5: 'We tried desperately to overtake the Ferrari and would have done so had the race lasted a little longer. Due to a misunderstanding I believed that the Ferrari and I were on the same lap and, making a great effort, I

caught and passed it right on the line only to discover it was a lap ahead. Some very stupid over-excited Scotsmen ran on to the road and had it not been for the fact that my disc brakes were still in perfect working order many of them would have been killed.'

Despite spending half the race driving at a very conservative pace due to lack of any real competition bar the lone Aston Martin, Ron Flockhart/Ivor Bueb won at a record average speed that was not exceeded until 1961. It could so easily have been much faster, and was a magnificent achievement by Ecurie Ecosse, winning for the second year in a row. Comparisons with 1956 make for interesting if rather puzzling reading. Hawthorn's works fuel injection long-nose D-type had lapped in 4min 17sec during practice and 4min 20sec in the race (presumably when it was not raining) as fastest car. Yet in 1957 the two 'customer' short-nose cars of ENB and Los Amigos had lapped in 4min 10sec (Rouselle) and 4min 14sec (Lucas) without the benefit of a wide-angle head engine and the superior aerodynamics of the

Jean Brousselet ('Mary') drives the French Los Amigos/Henri Peignaux XKD513 with co-driver Jean Lucas on the tail as they are congratulated after finishing third. No. 26 is the old Maserati A6GCS (2079) of Guyot/Parsy that came in 12th. (Paul Skilleter)

Ron Flockhart seems reflective, but Ivor is more interested in the fizzy stuff. None of that champagne spraying nonsense in 1957 thank you. 'Wilkie' Wilkinson stands on the nearside of XKD606 and looks quite happy about it all. Flockhart was to die when his Second World War Mustang fighter plane broke up in mid-air turbulence near Melbourne, Australia in April 1962 during preparations for a London–Sydney air record attempt. (Collection Bernard Viart/Paul Skilleter)

long-nose car, according to Malcolm Sayer's pit notes. The second-string Ecosse car was even quicker, lapping in 4min 11sec (Sanderson) and the two 3.8s achieved 4min 6sec (Bueb) and 4min 8sec (Gregory) respectively. Maximum speeds were up too, highlighting the inconsistency of the Le Mans timing, but those lap times really are a puzzle. Could the lack of pace the previous year have been caused by those fuel restrictions that led to the Jaguars being overgeared or were the obviously higher windscreens used in 1956 responsible?

1957 results

1st Ron Flockhart/Ivor Bueb Jaguar D-type XKD606
   327 laps, 2,732.230 miles (4,396.158km),
   113.845mph (183.177kph).
2nd Ninian Sanderson/John Lawrence Jaguar D-type
   XKD603 319 laps, 2,665.388 miles (4,288.609km),
   111.058mph (178.692kph).
3rd Jean Lucas/Jean Brousselet Jaguar D-type XKD513
   317 laps, 2,644.025 miles (4,254.236km),
   110.167mph (177.259kph).
4th Paul Frère/Freddy Rouselle Jaguar D-type XKD573
   310 laps, 2,590.638 miles (4,168.337km),
   107.943mph (173.680kph).
5th Stuart Lewis-Evans/Martino Severi Ferrari 315S
   (0684) 300 laps, 2,505.126 miles (4,030.478km),
   104.380mph (167.947kph).
6th Duncan Hamilton/Masten Gregory Jaguar D-type
   XKD601 299 laps, 2,496.072 miles (4,016.180km),
   104.003mph (167.341kph).

This was an unprecedented victory and quite unbelievable given the strength of the opposition, although in hindsight the Italian habit of producing ever more new cars with ever more power, was not conducive to reliability. Aston Martin continued their Le Mans woes, but the DBR1 was not fast enough to beat a 3.8 Jaguar here anyway. It is worth considering too what would have happened had Hamilton/Gregory not been so delayed. Assuming reliability was maintained this would have been a winning or second-placed car. Regardless of any such conjecture Jaguar had utterly dominated Le Mans with privately entered, albeit works assisted, cars and had achieved their greatest ever win. It was a high tide mark for

Jaguar at Le Mans (and Ecurie Ecosse) that has never been bettered.

After the crowning glory and subsequent adulation Ecurie Ecosse travelled to Monza for the Race of Two Worlds (Monzanapolis) where Indy roadster cars challenged the supposed best of Europe on the combined road and banked Monza track. This resulted in Jack Fairman scoring a worthy fourth place in XKD603 despite tyre problems. In August, Ecurie Ecosse raced in Sweden for the penultimate round of the World Sports Car Championship, but after running one car (XKD606) as high as third with Archie Scott-Brown/John Lawrence, they faded to eighth and 12th (Sanderson/Fairman XKD603) with mechanical problems. However ENB's XKD573 netted fifth place and Jaguar ended up third in the championship, a good result in the circumstances.

This year was really the end of Jaguar's competitiveness in sports car racing at international level, although the D-type was still good for Le Mans. Instead, constructors like Brian Lister were winning with lighter, flimsier De Dion-axled cars in shorter events, but none of these Jaguar engined cars ever made the grade in long distance racing. They were hampered by the new regulations introduced in 1958 which limited the upper capacity to 3 litres, and the 3-litre XK engine in its various guises hardly ever survived a race.

Facetious telegram from Tony Rolt to Duncan Hamilton after his sixth place at Le Mans 1957. (Adrian Hamilton)

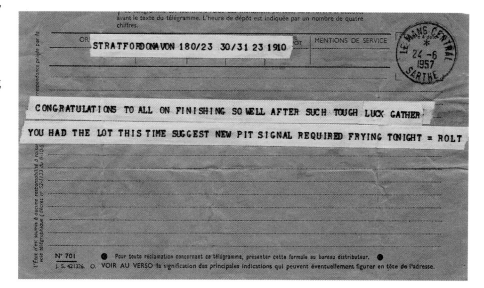

Chapter 9

1958 – Decline and fall

For 1958, sports car racing found itself burdened with a new set of rules aimed at tightening the specification of competing cars and limiting the largest class to 3 litres in an attempt to rein in speeds. This was in part a result of the fatalities at the Mille Miglia the previous year and the inevitable repercussions thereof. A new GT class was also introduced. Grand Prix racing suffered too with reduced race distances and the necessity to run on Avgas fuel (130 octane) that actually increased the fire hazard, rather than the more exotic brews of former years. Another bureaucratic master stroke.

All this nearly finished off a destitute Maserati which had invested a lot of money in the brutal 450S sports car, and whose 250F was now obsolete. Their continued presence in both forms of racing, almost exclusively by privateers, just made up the numbers. From world champions to also rans in a few short months. By contrast Ferrari benefited greatly, having been running a 3-litre V12 car in 1957 (the Testa Rossa). Aston Martin were in a similar position with their DBR1/300 and also stood to gain. In the face of such changes Jaguar remained unmoved although they had been quietly testing a new prototype production sports car fitted with a 2.4-litre XK engine in May 1957, now known as the E1A. Indeed, in January 1958, Ernest Rankin mentioned in a press release that the company had temporarily withdrawn from all forms of competitive motorsport. This was ultimately misleading.

Later in the year, on 10 July, Mike Hawthorn tested a modified version of the E1A at Silverstone using a purpose-built 3-litre all-alloy engine giving 260bhp at 6,750rpm lapping in 1min 49sec (compared with his fastest D-type lap in 1956 of 1min 47sec). The development of this car

A letter from 'Lofty' England dated 9 January 1958 discussing Duncan Hamilton's Le Mans entry for 1958. (Adrian Hamilton)

Opposite above: Duncan Hamilton with pipe and very well presented XKD601 awaits scrutineering for Le Mans 1958. Long-time Jaguar mechanic Ted Brookes looks on. (Photo Lafay)

Opposite below: The ex-Ecurie Ecosse XKD502 of Maurice Charles that was to be comprehensively smashed up after a collision during the early stages of the race. (Collection Bernard Viart/Paul Skilleter)

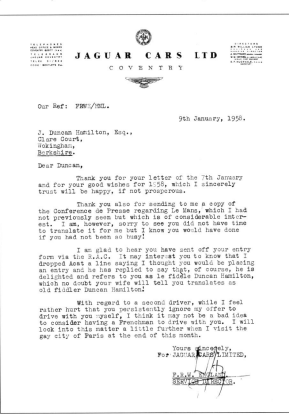

Letter:

TELEPHONES
HEAD OFFICE & WORKS
COVENTRY 62877 (10 LINES)
TELEGRAMS
JAGUAR COVENTRY
TELEX 31/808
CODE: BENTLEY'S 2nd.

JAGUAR CARS LTD
COVENTRY

DIRECTORS
SIR WILLIAM LYONS
...

Our Ref: FRWE/HML.

9th January, 1958.

J. Duncan Hamilton, Esq.,
Clare Court,
Wokingham,
Berkshire.

Dear Duncan,

Thank you for your letter of the 7th January and for your good wishes for 1958, which I sincerely trust will be happy, if not prosperous.

Thank you also for sending to me a copy of the Conference de Presse regarding Le Mans, which I had not previously seen but which is of considerable interest. I am, however, sorry to see you did not have time to translate it for me but I know you would have done if you had not been so busy!

I am glad to hear you have sent off your entry form via the R.A.C. It may interest you to know that I dropped Acat a line saying I thought you would be placing an entry and he has replied to say that, of course, he is delighted and refers to you as le fidèle Duncan Hamilton, which no doubt your wife will tell you translates as old fiddler Duncan Hamilton!

With regard to a second driver, while I feel rather hurt that you persistently ignore my offer to drive with you myself, I think it may not be a bad idea to consider having a Frenchman to drive with you. I will look into this matter a little further when I visit the gay city of Paris at the end of this month.

Yours sincerely,
For JAGUAR CARS LIMITED,

F.R.W. ENGLAND.
SERVICE DIRECTOR.

continued but it was never intended for racing and was eventually broken up on Bill Heynes's orders. For now Jaguar had only the ancient – by racing standards – D-type in short and long-nose form and the latest Lister variant to contest the major races including Le Mans. All of these were run by non-factory teams which were using a smaller capacity version of the XK engine supplied by Jaguar. (See sidebar.)

The 3-litre engines were not reliable and by the time Le Mans arrived Jaguar-powered cars had scored no points in any of the championship rounds, either in D-types or Listers. There had been evidence of valve trouble and, more usually, piston failure although one Ecosse car survived to finish ninth at the Nürburgring 1,000km. This was using Ecosse's own earlier Mk VII-based unit. In the unlimited national racing the new 'knobbly' Lister was continuing its predecessor's 1957 domination using the 3.8-litre engine. Tragically, in May, Scott-Brown crashed and was fatally burned at Spa and Lister never fully recovered

3-litre Jaguars

The Jaguar 3-litre engines were never a success, although they might have been had they received proper development. There were four versions with the final type appearing in four different variations, the last for E2A at Le Mans in 1960. The first 3-litre Jaguar XK type was developed by 'Wilkie' Wilkinson for Ecurie Ecosse and was raced in 1958 at Spa and the Nürburgring. Stan Sproat of Ecurie Ecosse recalled that it was built up from a de-stroked Mk VII production engine. The capacity was 2,954cc (83 x 91mm) and on test at Jaguar in November 1957, produced 234bhp at 6,100rpm using Weber 45DC03 carburettors.

Jaguar's 1958 customer engine was also a de-stroked 3.4, but was slightly larger being 2,987cc (83 x 92mm) and more powerful with 254bhp at 6,300rpm, again with Weber carburettors and employing the 35/40 wide-angle head. During 1958, Jaguar also tested E1A with an all-alloy engine at Silverstone driven by Mike Hawthorn, this measuring 85 x 88mm (2,997cc) and giving 260bhp. By December, using a cast-iron block and the ubiquitous Webers it was producing 272bhp at 6,750rpm on the Jaguar test bed. In 1959 this so-called short-stroke engine made its race debut in the Cunningham Listers at Sebring being rated at 258bhp at 6,000rpm, the lower maximum power now produced at significantly less rpm. Presumably this was in the interests of reliability, although this was to prove unattainable. The ultimate evolution was used in E2A for Le Mans 1960 with the alloy block and Lucas fuel injection, for which 294bhp at 6,750rpm was recorded. The engine owed its origins to Bill Nicholson, who was BSA's development engineer and works rider and responsible for the famous BSA Goldstar 500 single-cylinder motorcycle engine that also measured 85 x 88mm. Later, in the 1960s and '70s, he successfully raced MGBs. He persuaded Bill Heynes to build the engine using titanium conrods, but it would only produce the necessary power at high rpm at which point it had a limited life. Nevertheless it was by far the most powerful 3-litre Jaguar engine ever made and at nearly 100bhp per litre was on a par with the Ferrari V12 – not bad going for a twin-cam six over 40 years ago.

The remaining engine type was another 'Wilkie' Wilkinson special which was used in the Tojeiro at Le Mans in 1959 and XKD606 in 1960. Unlike the other engines this was a square unit (86 x 86mm) based on the 2.4-litre production unit with a purpose-made Laystall crank. Stan Sproat recalls that it was very smooth and powerful (about 270bhp) but disagreed with 'Wilkie's' high compression ratio specification. It blew out water under load on test and essentially, none of these engines succeeded, although the two Ecosse variants were not used sufficiently to prove anything worthwhile. The first one was not powerful enough, while the second was never properly developed. The two Jaguar efforts were also less than impressive. Their original de-stroked 3.4 suffered typically from piston failure, especially at Le Mans, but there was always some doubt about the quality of the fuel supplied at the Sarthe. The later short-stroke motor appeared to have a basic design flaw and broke its conrods, although at Le Mans 1960 it failed due to injection pipe failures leading to a weak mixture which burnt out pistons, and the head gasket failed through the associated overheating.

from his loss. Archie was irreplaceable. For Le Mans the factory supplied seven of its 3-litre XK engines for five D-types and two Listers. Duncan Hamilton was in the wars again at Jaguar for making public his favourable terms with Browns Lane, resulting in Bill Heynes writing to the effect that: 'You will have to mind your Ps and Qs in future.'

The 26th Le Mans, held on 21/22 June 1958, featured full works participation from Aston Martin and Ferrari, but the Jaguar contingent was numerous and varied.

Le Mans 1958

As already stated there were five D-types and two Lister-Jaguars, as follows:

No. 6 Jack Fairman/Masten Gregory XKD603. Engine EE1207-10. Reg RSF 303. (Ecurie Ecosse)
No. 7 Ninian Sanderson/John Lawrence XKD504. Engine E4007-10 (this is the same engine number as fitted to XKD603 in 1957 in 3.4-litre form). Reg RSF 302. (Ecurie Ecosse)
No. 8 Duncan Hamilton/Ivor Bueb XKD601. Engine EE1202-10. Reg 2 CPG. (Duncan Hamilton)
No. 11 'Mary' (Jean Brousselet)/André Guelfi XKD513. Engine EE1208-10. Reg G478 AT 69. (Henri Peignaux)
No. 57 Maurice Charles/John Young Jaguar D-type XKD502. Engine E2010-9. Reg MWS 302 (the original Ecurie Ecosse registration number from 1955). (Maurice Charles)

All the D-types had the 35/40 wide-angle head except XKD502 which was the ex-Ecurie Ecosse car of 1955. Additionally just before Le Mans XKD603 had received a new front frame, bonnet and suspension, excluding the stub axle carriers and a rear end rebuild at Browns Lane as well as the new engine. Also running were two Listers, thus:

No. 9 Freddy Rouselle/Claude Dubois Lister-Jaguar BHL105. Engine EE1204-10. (Equipe Nationale Belge)

No. 10 Bruce Halford/Brian Naylor Lister-Jaguar
 BHL5. Engine EE1205-10. Reg HCH 736
 (Bruce Halford)

The Belgian Lister was a 1958 'knobbly' customer
car (see sidebar) while the other was an early type
known colloquially as the 'Flat Iron' due to its body
style. Unlike the distinctive 'knobbly' whose bodies
were built by Williams & Pritchard, this car was
clothed by Maurice Gomm. All the works-built
engines developed between 247 and 251bhp at
6,000 or 6,250rpm, the very slight drop in peak
power caused by the Le Mans supplied fuel.

Ranged against the Jaguars were three works
Aston Martin DBR1/300s for Moss/Brabham,
Brooks/Trintignant and Salvadori/Lewis-Evans,
plus the old ex-works DB3S registration 62 EMU
for Graham and Peter Whitehead and no less than
10 Testa Rossa Ferraris. Three of these were works
entries for Hawthorn/Collins, P. Hill/Gendebien
and von Trips/Seidel, two were from ENB, two
from Luigi Chinetti's NART (North American

The Henri Peignaux-entered
XKD513 that finished third in
1957 had acquired a tailfin for
the 1958 race. Sadly the car
never ran properly and poor
Jean Brousselet ('Mary') was
killed when a Ferrari hit him
after he had crashed the
D-type. (Collection Bernard
Viart/Paul Skilleter)

XKD603 on the weighbridge.
Both this and the other Ecurie
Ecosse car (XKD504) lasted only
minutes in the race, a complete
and total reversal of their
1956/57 triumphs. Standing
behind the D-type is legendary
American lensman Jesse
Alexander. (Collection Bernard
Viart/Paul Skilleter)

Racing Team) and three from private owners. Unlike their Jaguar counterparts the non-factory cars were somewhat slower than their works brethren. The DBR1 Aston and the Jaguar wide-angle head engines were fairly evenly matched, 246bhp against a quoted 254bhp respectively, while Ferrari were claiming 300bhp but probably had a little less. Certainly they were no quicker than the factory Aston Martins as practice revealed. There was one Maserati 300S for Godia-Sales/Bonnier but otherwise the remarkably quick Porsche RSKs represented the best of the rest, although the 2-litre Lotus of Allison was very rapid if rather fragile.

With practice held in the evening and always with wear and tear in mind, times did not accurately reflect the true potential of the cars, except perhaps the factory Astons. Moss set fastest

Renowned American author and authority Karl Ludvigsen catches Duncan Hamilton and old Jaguar team-mate Peter Whitehead (who was to finish second with his half brother Graham in their venerable Aston Martin DB3S) sharing a joke with Peter Blond. In the background can be seen XKD504 with the Scottish saltire on its flank. Duncan is wearing his lucky Swiss red scarf, a present from his wife Angela. (Karl Ludvigsen/Ludvigsen Library)

Five of the Jaguar starters were slow away in 1958 with Sanderson in XKD504 and Halford in the 'Flat Iron' Lister already gone. Jack Fairman is in No. 6, Bueb is in No. 8 and just about to kiss the ENB Lister-Jaguar No. 9 with Maurice Charles No. 57 well on his way and the French D-type No. 11 still not moving. (Collection Bernard Viart/Paul Skilleter)

time with 4min 7.3sec, with team-mates Brooks and Salvadori second and third. Hawthorn's Ferrari and Fairman's Jaguar both recorded a 4min 13sec lap, a time beaten by Allison's (or Graham Hill depending upon which report you believe) Lotus (4min 12.7sec). Hawthorn complained of lack of top speed on Mulsanne (a fact borne out by Dubois's experience in the Lister during practice), noting in his book *Champion Year* that the Ferrari struggled to exceed 160mph (257kph). Pre-race form left Aston Martin as favourites with Ferrari and Jaguar next in line according to the pundits, which just proves how wrong some people can be.

In stark contrast to the almost guaranteed success of past years, Le Mans 1958 was an unmitigated disaster for Jaguar. Ninian Sanderson in XKD504 was out of the race after only minutes with a recurrence of piston trouble that they had

The old Maurice Gomm-bodied 'Flat Iron' Lister of Halford/ Naylor was the only 3-litre Jaguar-engined car ever to complete a 24-hour race, although it did break a camshaft, amongst other things, en route to its lowly 15th place. Nevertheless like the Duncan Hamilton D-type and unlike the other five Jaguar-powered cars, it did not suffer from piston failure. This Karl Ludvigsen photograph shows Bruce Halford in the Esses late on Saturday afternoon. (Karl Ludvigsen/Ludvigsen Library)

Despite starting on a warm and sunny day Le Mans soon degenerated into the all-too-familiar wet and miserable conditions that seem to haunt the Sarthe. Ivor Bueb turns into Arnage with the water streaming off XKD601. (Photo Lafay)

Ivor Bueb about to set out to sea as Len Hayden checks the offside bonnet strap while the official at the rear of the car holding a fire extinguisher must wonder what he is doing there in such wet weather. A small Union Jack adorns the top rear edge of the tailfin. Thanks to its competitive drivers, Hamilton of course excelling in the wet as usual, the D-type was running second at the time of its accident caused by a backmarker stopped in the road. Le Mans has always suffered from wildly varying driving standards. (Collection Bernard Viart/Paul Skilleter)

suffered in practice. Not long afterwards the other Ecosse car retired with the same problem. In his book 'Wilkie' stated he had built a short-stroke engine based on the 2.4-litre block with sodium-cooled exhaust valves. It had proved strong and unburstable on Robin Jackson's dynamometer and Jaguar took a keen interest in it. However, he was having problems getting a suitable crankshaft made and asked for Jaguar's help. They offered him their de-stroked 3.4 unit. These were used at Le Mans and he stated: 'One retired on the second lap, the other on the seventh, both from broken pistons caused by valve-gear trouble.' However in Graham Gauld's book *Ecurie Ecosse*, it is said that: 'Wilkie suspected the problem with the Ecosse cars and the other Jaguars was caused by fuel supplied at the circuit causing detonation and eventual piston failure but this was never proven.' Whatever the

ultimate cause, the end result was the same. Also in trouble in practice, and in effect only running for the starting money, was the ENB Lister, although this lasted a little longer at a reduced pace. It too had apparently suffered piston troubles and retired in the fourth hour from 15th position with a loss of oil pressure.

Also gone but due to an accident rather than mechanical failure was Maurice Charles in XKD502 who had collided with a Lotus and one of the tiny Panhards after White House on the approach to the pits. Charles was injured in the crash and the D-type finished up in three pieces. Jaguar's hopes were resting on the Hamilton/Bueb car and it lay sixth after one hour with Moss leading and pulling away from the two Ferraris of Hawthorn and von Trips. Shortly before 6pm the rain started just as Hawthorn set

the fastest lap of the race in 4min 8sec. Then suddenly Moss was out with engine failure and the first pit stops fell due. By 7.30pm wet weather maestro Hamilton had advanced to fourth and Collins in the Hawthorn Ferrari was suffering from clutch slip and stopped for 20 minutes in the pits. Having lost their number one car Aston Martin now lost another as Lewis-Evans spun the third car and wiped off the nearside front headlamp, without which the regulations meant retirement. The Hawthorn/Collins Ferrari began to slip down the field with a clutch problem although the car kept going until the 11th hour, so Maranello was also in the wars. At 8pm, according to race records, Hill/Gendebien led from their team-mates von Trips/Seidel, then came Hamilton in the Jaguar followed by the surviving Brooks/ Trintignant Aston. The Gurney/Kessler private Testa Rossa was a splendid fifth followed by the first of the works Porsches of Behra/Herrmann. In ninth place was the 'Flat Iron' Lister and the French D-type was way back in 39th having spent practice and the race so far misfiring. The weather was atrocious.

Then more disaster as 'Mary' (Jean Brousselet or Brussin, according to Andrew Whyte) crashed XKD513 just past the Dunlop bridge beyond the pits and was hit by Kessler's Ferrari. Tragically the Frenchman died (he remains the only Jaguar driver to have died at Le Mans) but Kessler survived. This American pairing (with Dan Gurney in his first Le Mans) had been lying fifth only a lap behind the leaders. In *Touch Wood* Duncan Hamilton comments: 'Cars were crashing all around the circuit, and J. Brousselet, better known by his pseudonym of Mary, was killed when his Jaguar crashed and an American-driven Ferrari ran into his car and over him. I nearly joined the pile up, and had it not been for a Frenchman who threw his hat on the road in front of me I would have done so. This Frenchman – and I have never been able to find out who he was – saved my life.' Leading up to midnight Hamilton had not only passed the von Trips/Seidel Ferrari but also briefly took the lead in the appalling, rain-soaked conditions. The other surviving Jaguar-powered car, Halford's Lister, was circulating steadily in seventh place. Aston Martin were lying fourth with their remaining car followed

ENB Lister-Jaguar

In 1999, I was able to drive the ENB Lister-Jaguar at Goodwood twice, thanks to the generosity of owner Chris Lunn and a chance meeting with Claude Dubois at the London offices of motor industry guru and authority Karl Ludvigsen. The reason for my involvement was that my father had owned the car in the late 1960s (purchased from hill-climb and sprint racer Ken Wilson in 1966 for £1,250!) and I was able to track test it for *Jaguar World* magazine. At the same time I had arranged for Claude to have a go and he turned up from France with eager anticipation. Like other Continental sports car racers of his time, Claude had driven all and sundry in races and hill-climbs all over Europe and had competed at Le Mans from 1957 to 1972 in a variety of cars. Claude's memories of Le Mans 1958 were of a very wet practice and race. He told me how during a downpour in practice he had overtaken Hawthorn's Ferrari Testa Rossa on Mulsanne and then realised that perhaps he was driving too fast in the torrential conditions. Another incident remembered was of sitting in the pits waiting to go out, while a mechanic checked the steering arms, a problem which affected the 1958 Listers. He also recalled that Pierre Stasse ran ENB on a shoestring, with only expenses and hotel bills paid. More than 40 years later, Claude drove the Lister at Goodwood beautifully and I have never seen anyone with such a wide smile on their face afterwards. It was a wonderful occasion.

The list of personnel and suppliers including their duties and accommodation for the Hamilton equipe at Le Mans 1958. (Adrian Hamilton)

In 1997 I accompanied Chris Keith-Lucas to Switzerland to retrieve the old 1958 Le Mans ENB Lister-Jaguar (BHL 105) back to Lynx Motors International where it was rebuilt for its new owner. I was able to reunite its 1958 driver Claude Dubois with the car at Goodwood in 1999. Left to right: the author, owner Chris Lunn and Chris Keith-Lucas in blue overalls with Claude in the car. (Derry Gibb)

by the Behra Porsche and the Whitehead's old Aston Martin DB3S. At half distance the Ferrari had re-established itself in the lead, Gendebien one lap in front of Bueb, the Ferrari faster on the drying road. The other works Testa Rossa, driven by Seidel, had slid off the road at Arnage, so now there was only one factory Ferrari left. As night faded into a wet and miserable dawn the Jaguar was catching up again, but the Lister had been delayed by 90 minutes through having a broken camshaft replaced. Despite this it was still in eighth place, an indication of just how spread out the field had become.

At 6am the last works Aston Martin was out

and by 8am Gendebien was leading Hamilton by just over a lap who handed back to Bueb, and it was raining again, having stopped briefly earlier on. At 10.30am Hamilton was back at the wheel but the Ferrari was now nearly two laps in front and in fact Phil Hill sat about 100 metres behind Duncan on the track, headlamps ablaze. Hamilton recorded in *Touch Wood* that just before midday: 'I was crowding on the pace because it was now (after 20 hours of racing) that I wanted Hill and Gendebien to use their drum brakes to the full in order to maintain their lead. There was every chance that their brakes would not last, particularily if the rain stopped. Suddenly I drove

into a cloudburst. A Panhard saloon had stopped, not only in the middle of the storm, but in the middle of the road. I tried to miss him, but in doing so got a wheel on the grass and the car spun. For a moment I was conscious of trying to steer the car while travelling backwards and then all went blank. I woke up briefly in the ambulance and a woman said: "vous n'êtes pas mort". Then I passed out again.'

Hamilton had ended up in a ditch with the car on top of him and had suffered head and leg injuries that were more serious than they had at first appeared. Given the relative lack of medical knowledge and facilities then extant, he was lucky to survive. Speaking to Duncan's widow Angela Hamilton just before Christmas 2000 confirmed that Hamilton had had to visit hospital for a considerable time afterwards suffering from terrible headaches which required constant treatment. He only drove in one more race, the 1958 TT at Goodwood with Peter Blond in the rebuilt XKD601 and they finished seventh. This was an unfortunate end to Hamilton's Le Mans and racing career although he would probably have retired about that time anyway, not being a fan of the much lighter and smaller machines that were beginning to dominate all forms of racing.

Meanwhile the Halford/Naylor Lister had

Claude was understandably overjoyed and it was a wonderfully nostalgic and moving occasion, and here he is blasting away from the Goodwood chicane on a beautiful sunny day. Note the small horizontal slits in the bonnet, a feature unique to this particular car. Since 1998 the Lister has raced each year at the Goodwood Revival meeting, driven by Tiff Needell. (Michael Cooper)

Claude Dubois in 1999. (Paul Parker)

Miracuously some tools appeared out of thin air and Brian Naylor was able to find top gear and somehow got the car rolling and back to the pits. Not content with this poor old HCH 736 then lost its rear brakes but the crippled car finally made it to the finish in 15th place. This was one of the worst Le Mans on record not only for Jaguar, but also for the weather and the Ferrari's winning average speed of 106.2mph (170.9kph) was astonishing, given the conditions. It also reflected the competitiveness of the Hamilton/Bueb Jaguar that had pushed the Ferrari hard for 20 hours. Almost as meritorious was the second place achieved by the Whiteheads in their old DB3S Aston Martin, albeit 100 miles (160km) behind the winning car.

1958 result

15th Bruce Halford/Brian Naylor Lister-Jaguar BHL 5
241 laps, 2,009.856 miles (3,233.858km),
83.743mph (134.742kph).

For Jaguar aficionados Le Mans 1958 was significant for two reasons. The first was that Bruce Halford's Lister remains the only 3-litre Jaguar-engined car ever to complete a 24-hour race, even if it did need a new camshaft. The second is that Duncan Hamilton's car did not suffer any apparent engine problems, despite being driven much harder for far longer than any of the other Jaguar runners. There was no sign of piston problems or any other related troubles but why, is now lost for ever in the ether of eternity, but it does make one wonder, especially as future races would continue the dismal record of fragility with Jaguar's 3-litre engines.

An already sad year with the loss of Scott-Brown, Musso and Collins was made worse when Peter Whitehead was killed while travelling as a passenger with his half brother Graham on the Tour de France. Later on Stuart Lewis-Evans was fatally burned in Morocco and then, on 22 January 1959, Mike Hawthorn died in a road accident driving his racing modified Jaguar 3.4 Mk 1. The all-too-frequently used analogy of Second World War fighter pilots and racing drivers of this period seems horribly true with hindsight.

developed transmission problems and Naylor was stuck out on the circuit past Mulsanne with a jammed gearbox. Eventually some mechanics arrived and they proffered advice as to what to do, the regulations barring any outside assistance.

Chapter 10

1959 – Le Mans

By the late 1950s, Jaguar had lost ground in sports car racing but had gained ascendancy in saloon car racing with their 3.4 Mk 1, that evolved into the famous 3.8 Mk 2. Even so Ecurie Ecosse were still running D-types and both Briggs Cunningham and Brian Lister had entered the championship fray with the Cambridge concern's cars.

At Sebring, Moss had actually led the race in a Cunningham Lister before running out of fuel due to a miscalculation, and had then been disqualified for outside assistance. This was a bitter

The unique square (86 x 86) 'Wilkie' Wilkinson Jaguar XK engine based on a bored-out 2.4 production block as fitted in the brand-new purpose-built Ecurie Ecosse Tojeiro. (Paul Skilleter)

'Wilkie' checking out his baby before the start. In the background the local gendarmes are looking menacing. (Edward Eves/Ludvigsen Library)

Stirling Moss in the Aston Martin DBR1/300-3 leads away with the two Ecosse cars of Innes Ireland in XKD603 (3) and Ron Flockhart in the Tojeiro (8) followed by the works Costin Lister (1) of Ivor Bueb. (LAT Photographic)

disappointment for Brian Lister and might otherwise have given Jaguar a win for their 3-litre engine. In Germany at the 'Ring Ecurie Ecosse had raced their 1958 Lister and Tojeiro but both had retired with suspension problems, rather than engine related troubles, so reliability was still an unknown for Le Mans.

There was only one actual Jaguar at Le Mans in 1959, old faithful XKD603, entered by Ecurie Ecosse who also had a brand-new, purpose-built Tojeiro-Jaguar. Brian Lister had entered two of his latest Costin-bodied devices making four Jaguar-engined cars in total.

Le Mans 1959

The Jaguar line-up was:

No. 1 Ivor Bueb/Bruce Halford Lister-Jaguar
   BHL2.59. Engine EE1305-9. Reg MVE 303.
   (Brian Lister)
No. 2 Walt Hansgen/Peter Blond Lister-Jaguar
   BHL3.59. Engine EE1302-9 (reserve engine
   EE1304-9). Reg VPP 9. (Brian Lister)

(Both cars had a Mr McDonnell listed as reserve driver, he being in reality Mike McDowell, sales manager of John Coombs's Jaguar dealership and a friend of Ivor Bueb.)

No. 3 Innes Ireland/Masten Gregory Jaguar D-type
XKD603. Engine EE1303-9. Reg RSF 303.
(Ecurie Ecosse)
No. 8 Ron Flockhart/John Lawrence Tojeiro-
Jaguar TAD1/59. Engine number unknown. Reg RSF 301. (Ecurie Ecosse)

They were all using the works Jaguar-supplied short-stroke 85 x 88mm 2,997cc engines except the Tojeiro that had 'Wilkie' Wilkinson's square 86 x 86mm unit. Lister had experimented with an

aerofoil air brake but after testing this was abandoned as not being worth the extra complexity and problems it caused. The two Ecosse cars were quite different but well matched. One was the old warhorse XKD603, prepared at Browns Lane for the last time but still competitive, and the other was a new car from John Tojeiro, styled by Cavendish Morton, that looked vaguely similar to Costin's Listers, and sporting a very small fin on the rear headrest. Like the Listers it had a De Dion rear end.

Yet again, the race for overall honours was going to rest with Aston Martin, Ferrari and Jaguar. Astons running their DBR1/300s for the third year, were now well developed and with slightly more power. There were three works cars to be driven by

Early in the race Ivor Bueb in the Costin bodied Lister (BHL 2.59) is pursued by Roy Salvadori in the winning Aston Martin DBR1/300-2 and the tiny Stanguellini 750 Sport of Roger Delageneste. The Lister lasted 121 laps before the engine threw a rod. (Ludvigsen Library)

The other Lister of Hansgen/ Blond, pictured here by renowned photographer Edward Eves, was the first Jaguar-powered car to retire, after 52 laps with a blown engine. (Edward Eves/Ludvigsen Library)

Opposite: *The Ecurie Ecosse Tojeiro with Ron Flockhart aboard races past a Stanguellini just after the Dunlop bridge. The 'Wilkie' square engine was considerably lower than the usual tall XK engine, hence the flat bonnet line. It lasted for 137 laps having reached fourth before retiring after the engine lost all its water and literally fused its innards together!* (Edward Eves/Ludvigsen Library)

Innes Ireland (3) in XKD603 and Ron Flockhart in the Tojeiro enjoy a dice while lapping one of the twin-cam MGAs of Lund/Escott as they round Mulsanne Corner pursued by Roy Salvadori in the Aston Martin DBR1/300. (LAT Photographic)

Moss/Fairman, Salvadori/Shelby and Frère/ Trintignant plus a private entry from Graham Whitehead who was sharing with Brian Naylor. A new DB4GT was also in attendance with an experimental 3-litre engine for Patthey/Calderari for the GT class but it was very slow. Ferrari too were using a familiar car, their well-tried Testa Rossa now with a Fantuzzi body and driven by P. Hill/Gendebien, Behra/Gurney and Allison/Da

Silva Ramos. Three older style 1958 customer cars complimented the Maranello entry but they were not of any great significance, although there was a strong contingent of 250GTs, the GT class now being a well-established feature of endurance racing. For the first time there had been an official practice in April and Phil Hill had recorded a meteoric 3min 59.3sec lap in the factory Testa Rossa that nobody else came close to. Only 19 cars took part, with no Jaguars present.

Pre-race practice was again dominated by Ferrari with Gurney (or Behra according to other sources) quickest on Thursday with 4min 3.3sec. Aston Martin by contrast were cruising but Gregory in XKD603 lapped in 4min 9.7sec, while the Hansgen Lister had managed 4min 12.2sec in the first session on Wednesday. The Tojeiro had suffered a breakage on its De Dion rear axle and parts had to be collected by Ron Flockhart and John Tojeiro using Flockhart's Auster plane from Namur in Belgium where the team's transporter had broken down en route. Not a good way to start the weekend. Race day was hot and humid with the threat of thunderstorms, but the weather held and Stirling Moss was first away at the Le Mans start, although Ireland had reached his Ecosse Jaguar just in front. (See sidebar.)

With Moss leading at the end of lap one, there followed the Ferraris of Gendebien, da Silva Ramos, then Ireland's Jaguar, Trintignant's Aston Martin and Flockhart (Tojeiro), and Bueb Lister. The third works Ferrari was temporarily stuck in mid-field after Behra had stalled his car at the start. Stirling continued to lead by a gradually increasing margin, although Behra was going quicker than anybody and gradually catching up, reaching third place after one hour. At this point Ireland was fifth, Flockhart sixth, Bueb 10th and Hansgen 11th. Ultimately Behra would catch and pass Moss, the superior power of the Ferrari (300bhp against approximately 250bhp) being decisive on such a fast course.

At three hours the Ferrari led from the Aston Martin with Gendebien/Hill next up then the two Ecurie Ecosse cars, the D-type leading the new Tojeiro. Bueb/Halford in the first of the Listers were ninth and the sister car lay 11th. Soon after, on its 52nd lap, the second Lister retired with a

blown engine as a rod ventilated the block. Don Moore, Lister's resident engine maestro was not happy about using Jaguar's short-stroke unit, as he explained to Doug Nye in *Powered by Jaguar*: 'The works 3-litres we had at Le Mans in 1959 had too short a stroke: halfway down the bore the con-rod angle was very acute and it was just overstressed. I think we blew two engines in practice …' Don Moore also commented it was noticeable that despite the supposedly aerodynamic Costin bodywork with its trick inflatable tonneau, the old D-type was quicker, as indeed was the Tojeiro. Bruce Halford realised that although he had 30bhp more than in 1958 when he had raced his old 'Flat Iron' Lister, the new car was no faster in a straight line, reaching 165mph (265kph). Another problem for the Listers was that under full fuel load their halfshafts were at too steep an angle and there could be transmission power loss to add to their other woes.

Innes Ireland and the Le Mans start

In his suitably outrageous autobiography *All Arms and Elbows,* Innes Ireland told how he had become proficient at the traditional Le Mans type start: 'Some days before leaving for France, I had gone to the works and tried this "leaping in and starting" business, by running across the works yard and vaulting into the Jaguar over the windscreen. I was in the act of doing this for the third time when the Ecurie Ecosse chief mechanic, a big burly Scot by the name of Sandy ('Sandy' Arthur), came across to me with an expression of absolute ferocity on his face. "What the hell do you think you're doing?" he roared. I explained a bit sheepishly that I was only trying out the Le Mans start, but he brushed all that aside. "All you'll do is break the bloody windscreen. Now be off with you."' Thus castigated Innes wisely decided to desist from his acrobatics.

With Moss dropping out and the Ferraris temporarily ruling the roost the Ireland/Gregory Jaguar was now second with the remaining Lister and the Ecosse Tojeiro in fifth and sixth. Inevitably

perhaps, another Jaguar engine failed and out went XKD603 after a very convincing display at around 11pm when, according to Innes Ireland, it threw a connecting-rod and spun on its own oil. Gregor Grant's *Autosport* race report gave valve troubles as the reason, as no doubt it did have, with a blown engine. The other Lister departed with similar travails on lap 121 having reached fourth by midnight while the Tojeiro was gone at around 3am. It too had briefly occupied fourth place but was losing water, a problem already noted by Stan Sproat during bench testing. He thought the compression ratio was too high and it was blowing out water. In the race it had leaked after a pit stop but regulations forbade water replenishment for a minimum number of laps between stops. He recalled in *Powered by Jaguar* that: 'After it ran out of water they just drove it into the ground – its insides melted, the head distorted, the pistons fused, the bottom end seized … it was the worst-damaged engine I ever saw. Nothing was salvaged

as I recall.' Later at Goodwood for the TT, the unfortunate car was destroyed in a huge accident at Woodcote after Masten Gregory famously jumped out when his steering apparently failed, although others thought he had simply dropped it.

So that was the end of Jaguar's adventures at Le Mans in the 1950s. Even though the last two years had been a big disappointment, the D-types had remained a front-running car at the Sarthe. They might even have picked up second place in 1958 but for an accident, and reliability problems had stopped a similar result, if not a possible win, in 1959. It was the end of Brian Lister's official participation in championship racing too, the final withdrawal hastened by the death of Ivor Bueb after crashing in an F2 race at Clermont Ferrand in late July. However 'what if' means very little and it was Aston Martin who finally won at Le Mans after the works Ferraris had broken one by one, just failing to beat Jaguar's 1957 speed and distance records.

Chapter 11

1960 – E for Effort

The start of a new decade saw the brief ascendancy of a new star, the 'Birdcage' Maserati, built mainly for the American market, but finding favour throughout Europe. Aston Martin had joined Jaguar in retiring from racing, unable to afford the cost and time required for developing a new car. Like Jaguar, private owners would race the DBR1/300s and achieve some worthy results. A half-hearted, too late Aston F1 effort was also about to expire. Ferrari were now almost omnipotent in the upper echelons of sports car racing, and the only factory team racing in the largest class.

Not content with their previous regulatory changes, the FIA introduced Appendix C regulations that decreed that windscreens were to be a minimum of 250mm (9.8in) high with an operable luggage compartment. This resulted in the cars looking very strange and in some cases downright ugly, the previously sleek and beautiful D-type acquiring a hideous high screen and strange hump on the rear deck for the supposed luggage. Apparently the idea was to promote the development of road-going vehicles out of the sports prototypes. It achieved nothing except raising costs and further compromised the whole concept of sports car racing.

Jaguar or indeed any Jaguar-engined cars were notable by their absence at the championship rounds preceding Le Mans, even Sebring was a 'cat-free zone'. However, there was something going on at Coventry that Jaguar quickly denied was in any way an official return to racing. The cause of the excitement was E2A, the one-off competition car built for Briggs Cunningham and featuring the short-stroke 85 x 88mm engine with an alloy block and Lucas fuel injection. Construction of E2A commenced on 1 January 1960 (not a public holiday then) and was completed on 27 February. The very next day, a Sunday, it was tested by Bill Heynes on the local roads and thence to Lindley (MIRA) on the 29th. Subsequently the engine (EE1310-10) was replaced and the gearbox removed as it could not pull the 2.93:1 final drive adequately. Another engine (EE1307-10) was fitted with a new type of dry-

The unpainted E2A at the Le Mans trials in April 1960 where American sports car ace and Cunningham driver Walt Hansgen lapped in 4min 09.1sec. At this stage it is still finless. Hansgen had won many races in Jaguar-powered machinery during the late 1950s and was a real racer. As with so many he finally perished, ironically six years later at the Le Mans trials, driving a Ford Mk II. (Paul Skilleter)

sump arrangement and in this form it appeared at the Le Mans test day on 9 April. Walt Hansgen drove it, posting a 4min 9.1sec lap but then had yet another blow-up when a connecting-rod failed. The car was geared to achieve 200mph (322kph) at 7,000rpm, and Jaguar designer Malcolm Sayer told Roger Woodley that it had actually pulled 6,800rpm in top. Thereafter the original engine was refitted but it burnt a piston during testing later that month. Alas the experimental five-speed gearbox was abandoned after problems and replaced with a four-speed syncromesh unit. At this stage the car was unpainted and had not acquired the trademark tailfin, and was registered VKV 752.

In appearance it looked like a smoothed out D-type with an E-type front end, a road-type framed windscreen and very high tail, doubtless as a result of those silly regulations. It also seemed to have excessive ground clearance as contemporary pictures show. Gone was the D-type's crude live rear axle, replaced by a fully independent rear end with inboard brakes and the bodywork was notable for its exposed riveted panel work, looking very aeronautical as a result. The kerb weight was estimated to be 1,925lb (873kg). Engine power was quoted as 294bhp at 6,750rpm prior to Le Mans on the Jaguar test bed, nearly a 20 per cent increase on the previous figures, and at 750rpm higher.

Pictured at the factory, E2A displays its heavily riveted but very clean lines and the very tall tailfin. Although there is a side exhaust in evidence, the up-on-stilts stance suggests that there is no engine fitted. I wonder. (Paul Skilleter)

Autocar stated the final drive ratio as 3.31:1. As presented for the race it now had the tailfin and was painted in the Briggs Cunningham livery of white with two parallel vertical blue stripes.

Amazingly, Ecurie Ecosse, now on their fifth Le Mans, had entered D-type XKD606 again, the sterling old warrior looking very strange with its high screen and ugly luggage container tail. (They had originally intended to run their Cooper-Monaco but Cooper were unhappy with the new screen regulations and the fitting of quick-change centre lock hubs was not possible in time for the race.) The *Autocar* race preview noted that it was fitted with one of 'Wilkie' Wilkinson's square 86 x 86mm engines based on the 2.4 unit, as per the Tojeiro in 1959. These were the only two Jaguars entered for Le Mans 1960, thus:

No. 5 Ron Flockhart/Bruce Halford Jaguar D-type XKD606. Engine BB8648-8 (this is a production 2.4 block number and the last figure which normally denotes compression ratio is meaningless in this application). Reg RSF 301. (Ecurie Ecosse)

No. 6 Walt Hansgen/Dan Gurney Jaguar E2A. Engine EE1308-10. (Briggs Cunningham)

Ranged against them was the full might of the Ferrari works team with P. Hill/von Trips, Frère/Gendebien and Mairesse/Ginther plus a NART entry for André Pilette and Ricardo Rodriguez, all in the latest TR60 version. Additionally seven of the increasingly rapid 250GTs were running. Happily Maserati had returned, fresh from their Nürburgring 1,000km triumph won by the Moss/Gurney car, with three of their new 'Birdcage' Tipo 61s, the fastest of which was driven by Gregory/Daigh, entered by Camoradi. Stirling Moss was not racing after crashing badly during practice for the Belgian Grand Prix at Spa. His Rob Walker Lotus 18 had lost a wheel and the resultant injuries kept him out of racing for two months. In an attempt to foil the aerodynamic drag caused by the latest windscreen height requirements the 'Birdcage' screen started halfway down the bonnet! The other possible challengers were the two privately entered Aston Martin DBR1/300s for Jim Clark/Roy Salvadori (Border

Looking absolutely immaculate, E2A awaits the fray as the man in the blazer tries to impress his companion about something in the Jaguar's cockpit. Note the small aerodynamic tweak on the single windscreen wiper. Car No. 1 is the Cunningham entered Corvette of Briggs Cunningham himself, Bill Kimberley and Richard Thompson. (Archives Serge Pozzoli)

Reivers) and Major Ian Baillie/Jack Fairman (Ian Baillie).

Pre-race practice began badly for the Cunningham Jaguar when it collided with Fritz D'Orey's Ferrari 250GT and had to have its nose repaired. Well-known American photographer and journalist Jesse Alexander reported in the respected American journal *Car and Driver* that Gurney took the repaired car out but could not better 4min 20sec due apparently to unequal braking, too soft suspension and instability on the Mulsanne Straight. This was Thursday night and practice was now over. Late on Friday both drivers were testing the car on public roads after some adjustments to improve the handling had been made. Elsewhere other reports suggest that Gurney set the fastest practice lap of 4min 4.5sec,

despite the car's apparent problems. Also doubtful was the very high top speed (about 190mph/300kph) claimed for this car, given that 165–170mph (265–274kph) was the absolute tops for the Maserati with its trick windscreen. (See sidebar.)

The race began in overcast conditions and the new Jaguar was quickly in trouble with Hansgen pitting on lap three with an injection pipe problem, something which seems to have dogged Jaguar at Le Mans. Ever the hare Gregory was leading by 70 seconds in the 'Birdcage' 'Maser' at 5pm from five Ferraris and the Ecosse Jaguar, and then soon after 6pm came torrential rain. It was to remain wet for the rest of the night but Sunday was to be hot and dry. Already the leading Maserati had hit trouble refusing to start after its first refuelling stop at around 5.49pm, losing 55 minutes in the process. Ferrari meanwhile had lost one of their works Testa Rossas when von Trips ran out of fuel at Tertre Rouge followed 15 minutes later by the NART entry with the same problem. Both cars were victims of fuel consumption miscalculation exacerbated by the latest FIA regulations limiting tank capacity to 29.5 gallons (134 litres). By 8pm three Ferraris led from the Ecurie Ecosse D-type,

Walt Hansgen in E2A leads the Lloyd Casner-entered Lilley/Gamble/Said Chevrolet Corvette through the Esses on Saturday afternoon. (LAT Photographic)

Given more time E2A could have been a winner. It should have been running in 1959 and really needed another year of intensive chassis and engine development to succeed, but by 1960 it was too late. (LAT Photographic)

the Border Reivers Aston Martin and the first of the very quick GT Ferraris with the Cunningham E2A running 10th. In the fifth hour the new Jaguar gained one more place but it was only running on five cylinders and the combination of a weak fuel mixture which in turn led to overheating, a burned piston and head gasket failure, spelt *finis* at 1.40am having dropped to 20th position on 89 laps.

With the Maserati challenge gone Ferrari enjoyed a two-lap advantage after eight hours, Gendebien leading on 101 laps from his team-mate Ginther. However the next three cars were all very close with the Scottish Aston just in front of the NART Ferrari of Rodriguez/Pilette and the Ecosse Jaguar, second through to fifth, all on 99 laps. Two hours later and the old D-type had risen to third but at half distance (4am) it was back to fourth but still well in touch with the leaders. Sadly, at 5.30am when running fourth on 168 laps, the crankshaft broke and the last ever D-type to race at Le Mans was out, having acquitted itself honourably against much newer cars. Interestingly it had been only marginally slower than the works Ferraris and was more than a match for the Aston Martin DBR1/300, a tribute to its original designers and the performance of the 'square' XK engine.

Maximum speeds recorded on Mulsanne make for interesting reading but should be treated with circumspection; the Maserati 'Birdcage' achieving 169mph (272kph), the best Ferrari Testa Rossa 162mph (261kph), the Ecosse D-type 157mph (253kph) and E2A only 153mph (246kph). Slower still was the Border Reivers Aston Martin DBR1/300 which struggled to 149mph (240kph), a direct result of the increase in frontal area and aerodynamic drag caused by the new high windscreens. So Ferrari won their fourth Le Mans (since 1949) with Paul Frère/Olivier Gendebien leading home the NART entry of Ricardo Rodriguez/André Pilette with Roy Salvadori/Jim Clark third in the Border Reivers Aston Martin. Fastest race lap was credited to Dan Gurney in E2A at 4min 04.0sec.

After its Le Mans travails E2A was off to America (it was on loan to Cunningham for the rest of the year) where Walt Hansgen won a race at Bridghampton against some reasonable opposition prior to a 500-mile race at Elkhart Lake. The car

Dan Gurney and E2A

Some 40 years after the event, Dan Gurney was to tell Adam Cooper in *Motor Sport* magazine: 'I don't want to upset people, but up until we got them to change it, I'd say the worst car I drove was the prototype E-type I shared with Walter Hansgen at Le Mans in 1960.' Further on he explained that, 'For whatever reason, they insisted on running it with toe-out in the rear wheels. It was exceedingly difficult, especially if you were in a passing move or got into any kind of side wind configuration.' After an incident during practice when he ran into a rain squall approaching White House at about 165mph (265kph) he commented: 'This car didn't want to be manhandled at all ...' He managed to avoid the wreckage of three cars that had crashed but had to fight the car's wayward directional stability. 'Finally they decided to put a little toe-in before the race, and that transformed it into a fine car.'

was now using a cut down windscreen and the special 3-litre engine had been replaced with a 3.8 unit (EE5028-10). There he finished third but was outpaced by the winning Maserati and the second-placed Ferrari. In October, Cunningham entered the car at Riverside where Jack Brabham struggled to qualify for the main race and finished an unimpressive 10th, one lap behind the winning 'Birdcage' Maserati. Walt Hansgen noted that E2A

Bill Heynes, upper right, looks on unhappily as futile efforts are made to combat the fuel injection problems that wrecked E2A's engine. Walt Hansgen squats on the pit counter and Dan Gurney in a plastic mac and holding a camera stands to his right. (Paul Skilleter)

was braking very early and lifting a rear wheel
thereby losing traction, so those Le Mans handling
woes suffered by Gurney were apparently still in
evidence. Following this, Bruce McLaren drove it
at Laguna Seca, finishing 12th and 17th in his two
heats for which he received $200! This was at least
better than Brabham who pocketed only $100 for
his Riverside efforts. Cunningham's resident
engineering genius Alfred Momo remarked that it
was too big and heavy. Building and developing a
race-winning or even fully competitive and reliable
car in just six months was no longer possible. Away
from the long distance endurance events sports car
racing was now increasingly dominated by lighter,
more fragile cars. The rear-engined Cooper
Monaco and Lotus 19 (Monte Carlo) were

unbeatable in sprint races and even the 'Birdcage'
Maserati and Testa Rossa Ferraris were outclassed.
The old order had changed, at least away from the
classic championship arenas.

Thereafter E2A was used briefly for testing the
Maxaret anti-skid braking system and later as a
decoy during testing of the XJ13. Painted dark
green and without its distinctive tail fin it was also
used in comparison testing against the new
production E-type, driven by David Hobbs.
Happily this unique car survived and was
purchased by ex-Jaguar apprentice Roger Woodley
on behalf of his well-known father-in-law,
photographer Guy Griffiths, during the late 1960s
and it still resides with his daughter Penny all these
years later.

Chapter 12

1962 – Privateers star

Notwithstanding the official stance, it was impossible for Jaguar to avoid the racing connection given that their image was so closely bound by association with Le Mans and many other competition triumphs. It was inevitable that the sensational introduction of the production E-type in early 1961 would immediately rekindle old passions. Only weeks after its debut two cars entered by Tommy Sopwith's Equipe Endeavour and John Coombs at Oulton Park for Graham Hill and Roy Salvadori respectively, finished first and third in a 25-lap race against Aston Martin and Ferrari opposition. However, despite the best efforts of Hill and Salvadori and occasionally Mike Parkes and others, it was obvious that the E-type was too heavy and too much of a production car to beat the well-developed Ferraris. As the British season progressed the Ferrari 250GTs driven by Moss and Parkes were just too fast, although the Jaguar was only marginally slower. For the first time since 1950 there were no Jaguars at Le Mans, and no E-types raced at Goodwood for the Tourist Trophy. It was left to Aston Martin to unsuccessfully challenge the Italian machines in the increasingly important GT class.

Jaguar's backdoor involvement continued, developing the E-type for racing under John Coombs's umbrella. After Roy Salvadori crashed the original Coombs car (BUY 1) at the Easter Goodwood meeting in 1962 it was rebuilt with a lighter gauge steel body and in time acquired the optional hard top and later still, D-type pattern wheels. It was re-registered 4 WPD and driven almost exclusively by Graham Hill. Much effort was put into reducing its weight and improving the handling but even with a full racing spec engine it was still too slow against the new 250GTO Ferrari that was proving invincible. Jaguar themselves had built a low-drag coupé that was supposed to be the first of a batch of four or six cars but in the end it remained a solo effort and stayed put in Coventry until Dick Protheroe was allowed to buy it in June 1963.

With the Coombs car notching up second and third places in national racing an intrepid pair of semi-professional racers decided that they wanted to do some serious racing instead of 20-minute sprints around the usual British venues. Peter Sargent was already a seasoned Jaguar competitor

The Peter Sargent E-type (850009) in its early modified guise at the Le Mans April trials where it lapped in 4min 22.9sec. The car's rather messy embryonic appearance and production chrome trim soon disappeared along with the wire wheels and front bumpers. Note the Roadster windscreen that was significantly lower than the FHC equivalent. Peter Lumsden is wearing the helmet and behind him, with his back to the camera is Brian Playford. (Paul Skilleter)

having raced XK120s, C-types, a D-type long-nose and now a very early E-type Roadster. This car, 898 BYR, was to be transformed into a very effective Le Mans racer. The other half of the duo was Peter Lumsden, a successful Lotus Elite driver whose cars were prepared by Brian and John Playford who also fettled Sargent's Jaguars. They met at the Playford's Croydon works and plans were formulated for a Le Mans bid. (See sidebar.)

The car travelled to Le Mans for the April test days where it managed a 4min 22.9sec lap and

898 BYR

Peter Sargent had acquired his Roadster E-type registered 898 BYR in 1961, taking delivery before Jaguar dealer Henleys got their London Piccadilly demonstrator, causing some ruffled feathers as a result. The car was immediately stripped out and prepared for a GT support race at the 1961 German Grand Prix. Sargent remembers that it understeered horrendously and had ineffective brakes. Speaking to Brian Playford at his Surrey home in November 2000 he related that his brother John was given a leather jacket by the two Peters as a present for driving the E-type to Germany and back!

By the time of Le Mans 1962 the car had been totally rebuilt and re-engineered, particularily at the rear, by Brian and John Playford. The original roadster screen was retained and an aluminium roof and tail section added, all much lower than the standard FHC body. It had a pump and radiator to keep the oil cool in the rear axle, over which sat a purpose-made fuel tank. There were also ducts to extract the hot air from the inboard-mounted rear brakes, while the fronts used the larger discs from the big Mk IX production saloon. Brian Playford also used a much bigger brake servo and altered the interior, creating a proper driver's footwell and scooping out the rear bulkhead to provide more legroom, something that Jaguar said could not be done. The aluminium bonnet had been made using a former over an original steel version, which explained its slightly more bulbous appearance. The original production engine had been replaced, Brian Playford recalled, by a wide-angle 3.8 dry-sump engine and D-type gearbox that came from Peter Mould's 'knobbly' Lister-Jaguar (BHL 120).

Speaking to the the two Peters, Sargent and Lumsden in 2000, Sargent remembered the smell of cooking that permeated the car as he approached the Esses during the race and the merry-go-round which was easily visible from the track. Lumsden recalled that, until the last hour, the car had behaved impeccably and it would pull 6,000rpm in top. Both men occasionally felt brave enough to take the Mulsanne kink 'flat', but it was normally just a momentary lift through there. Peter Sargent opined that White House, a notorious combination bend before the pits, was the most important on the circuit, a good exit speed giving an advantage all the way past the start/finish area and around the Dunlop Curve and up the hill towards the Esses.

recorded 155mph (249kph) on the Mulsanne Straight, although it looked rather cobbled together at this stage. Dunlop provided some Stabilia radial tyres with a racing tread pattern, but these were much too hard and made the car very twitchy, causing Lumsden to spin, as Brian Playford recalled in 2000. A purpose-made coupé hardtop was added to the body while retaining its roadster style windscreen that was noticeably lower than the production version. This lowered the frontal area and improved the aerodynamic drag factor. By the time of the Nürburgring 1,000km race in May (where the car retired) it was looking much smarter and had been developed to the point that it was no longer just a modified production E-type. It was joined by two others, a works-prepared FHC for Briggs Cunningham and another FHC entered by Maurice Charles.

Charles had raced a 3-litre D-type (the old Ecurie Ecosse 1955 XKD502) at Le Mans in 1958 but crashed after colliding with a Lotus that strayed into his path and ending up in hospital. Happily he recovered and in 1962 his entry for an E-type at Le Mans was accepted. Talking to Paul Skilleter in *Jaguar World* in 1998, Maurice recalled that he did not have a car so he bought a new opalescent dark blue FHC that arrived at the supplier on 11 May 1962, giving him only six weeks to prepare for the race. An engine was built up using spare D-type parts, the clutch and gearbox were also D-type and the brakes were changed using the bigger Mk IX calipers/discs on the front and larger, Jaguar-provided units at the rear. Alloy doors, tailgate and bonnet supplied by Ken Baker's company (who later successfully raced his own E-type 7 CXW) completed the transformation. Ken was supposed to be one of the *pilotes* but ultimately he did not drive the car.

Co-driver for the race was John Coundley, a well-known British circuit racer of D-types and Listers with his mechanic John Pearson in attendance for the race only. Now renowned in the racing world as the Jaguar preparation specialist *par excellence*, John described his time at Le Mans 1962 as: 'The most miserable experience of my life!' Working conditions were stressed and unpleasant and the accommodation even worse. It was indeed an unhappy weekend and Jaguar's Mike McDowell, reporting to Bill Heynes post race commented: 'The Charles/Coundley car [in comparison with the other E-types] however, gave considerable trouble due almost entirely to poor preparation.'

McDowell, on hand for the other two Jaguar entries, reported that during practice the E-type suffered from low oil pressure that was traced to a faulty oil pump. There was considerable swarf left in the engine on assembly and on Thursday evening the engine dropped a valve. Another problem with the front suspension was sorted out by Jaguar's Frank Rainbow and Bob Penney. Jaguar then lent Maurice Charles a spare engine for the race, but only reluctantly, relations between Charles and McDowell being somewhat fraught. This had led to 'Lofty' England's typically understated aside, 'Mr Charles, please put Mr McDowell down.' In the race the new engine failed and later Bill Heynes accused Charles of over revving it. Charles denied the charge and so it proved as there had been bearing failure caused by bits of metal left in the oil cooler from the first engine failure, despite flushing with petrol and blowing through with an airline. Bill Heynes apologised.

Le Mans 1962

The Jaguar entries were:

No. 8 Maurice Charles/John Coundley Jaguar E-type 860458. Engine R5910-9 (Jaguar's spare loaned to Charles for the race). Reg 503 BBO.
No. 9 Peter Sargent/Peter Lumsden Jaguar E-type 850009. Engine R1035-9. Reg 898 BYR.
No. 10 Roy Salvadori/Briggs Cunningham Jaguar E-type 860630. Engine R5909-9. Reg 1337 VC.

Cunningham's entry was a standard steel-bodied FHC comprehensively modified by Jaguar's experimental department, with an aluminium bonnet and the old non-syncro bottom gear Moss gearbox. Unlike the Sargent/Lumsden car it had rear exiting tail pipes. The works-built engine developed 296bhp at 5,750rpm. It was driven to Le Mans by Mike McDowell and handed over to Briggs Cunningham who had not even seen it before, let alone driven it! Reg 898 BYR was running a dry sump specification and was

marginally more powerful (299.5bhp at the same rpm). This had also been assembled at Coventry. Both cars had 15-inch diameter D-type pattern wheels. The third car, owned by Maurice Charles, was another FHC and was running with an engine borrowed from Jaguar after its own had dropped a valve in practice. Unlike the other E-types it ran on competition wire wheels.

Ranged against the Jaguars in the GT class were six Ferrari 250GTOs and two Aston Martin DB4GT Zagatos plus an Austin-Healey 3000. Of these one of the Astons, the British-entered Salmon/Baillie car was reasonably competitive, otherwise it was Coventry versus Maranello. The winner of the race was certain to come from the prototype class and the main competitors here were Ferrari, Maserati and Aston Martin with their new Project 212. Practice was dominated by the quickest prototypes while the best Jaguar time was achieved by Salvadori in the Cunningham E-type recording 4min 16sec, somewhat adrift of the quickest GTO Ferraris but this was not unexpected. Peter Lumsden had noted a squeak somewhere within 898 BYR that was not identified, a warning sign that was to cost them dearly.

A warm sunny day greeted the starters for the 30th *Vingt-Quatre Heures du Mans* on 23 June 1962. The heat was sufficient to cause the alloy hardtop on the Sargent/Lumsden car to settle nearly an

Three E-types raced at Le Mans 1962, including this entry from Maurice Charles (860458), which he was to share with John Coundley. During practice the car's original engine failed and Charles was lent a works unit, but this also failed early in the event, so co-driver Coundley never got to drive it in the race. (Collection Bernard Viart/Paul Skilleter)

Now looking much smarter and considerably more developed, the Sargent/Lumsden 850009 before the off. This picture shows the car's rather bulbous bonnet, the NACA duct and the side air outlet. The tall man in dark glasses and hat is Eric Brown, sometime chairman of the Jaguar Drivers' Club and owner of a famous XK120DHC (1 ALL) that was raced in 1964 by Jackie Stewart. (Collection Bernard Viart/Paul Skilleter)

inch lower into its rubber mounting! Graham Hill led away in the new Aston and stayed there for just over a lap before Gendebien passed him in the Ferrari 330LM. Maurice Charles had made a brilliant start but quickly fell back into the ruck, the car slowly drifting down the field before a conrod exited the block just before 7pm. The remaining E-types were outside of the top ten with the British entry in 12th place and the Cunningham car 18th at 8pm. By this time the leading Ferrari GTO was holding down sixth position. By midnight the two Jaguars had reversed their positions in 13th and 14th but behind the Salmon/Baillie Zagato Aston with the GTOs now running well ahead. The Sargent/Lumsden car had been delayed by brake pad problems but now began to speed up again and at 1am the Jaguars occupied ninth and tenth with

the Zagato Aston now misfiring. The new Project 212 Aston Martin had long since departed and the big Maserati 151s were faltering leaving Ferraris in the first six places.

Half distance saw Peter Sargent in 10th place, a lap ahead of the Cunningham E-type and a race of attrition now developed with the British Jaguar slowly advancing up the field. Salvadori's progress was perhaps hampered by his co-driver's more leisurely pace and they lost ground to their British counterparts. Four hours later the two Jaguars had advanced to sixth and seventh positions, the leading GTO Ferrari now in third place overall (Noblet/Guichet), but the next one, driven by 'Eldé'/'Beurlys', was within reach. As the morning wore on the second-placed prototype Ferrari of Baghetti/Scarfiotti retired and Sargent /Lumsden were now fifth and catching the second GTO Ferrari with the Cunningham entry two laps behind in sixth place. By midday the British Jaguar was just under a lap behind the fourth placed Ferrari and gaining 13 seconds a lap but a serious problem was about to spoil the party. With less than two hours to go Lumsden suddenly found himself without any gears as he exited Arnage with the car rattling and shaking and smoke coming out of the gearbox. He came into the pits and Peter Sargent took over for the last hour having managed to coax the car out of the pits. As he recalled to the author in 2000, 'The gearbox began to scream and I could not use more than 3,000rpm in top gear. So I went round the circuit for the last hour stuck in top gear doing about 90mph. With less than 30 minutes to go Roy Salvadori in the Cunningham car passed me. We should have finished third.'

A post-race examination showed that a reversible gasket in the pressure-fed D-type gearbox which had an oil feed hole, had been put on the wrong way round at Jaguar during

Roy Salvadori in the Briggs Cunningham E-type FHC (860630) that looks positively upright compared with the British car with its lower roof line. Note the air intake mounted spotlight and the small Perspex screen mounted on the bonnet on the driver's side that was meant to deflect bugs, a typical period 'mod'. (LAT Photographic)

The rear of 850009 showing its multitude of air outlets for brake and cockpit cooling that were made even more necessary by the very hot weather. (Collection Bernard Viart/Paul Skilleter)

Opposite: *Peter Sargent cruises over the line, stuck in top gear, one arm resting on the open window and doubtless feeling pretty fed up. In the second picture Brian Playford (left) and brother John accompany the E-type as it trickles back to the paddock.* (Collection Bernard Viart/Paul Skilleter)

Peter Lumsden rounds Mulsanne Corner past the abandoned Ferrari of Fulp/Ryan that is stuck in one of the notorious Le Mans sandbanks. Once in you could rarely get out, and although many tried, few ever succeeded. (LAT Photographic)

preparation, thus starving the unit of oil. That it survived nearly 23 hours plus practice was a miracle, but this was the source of the squeak that Peter Lumsden had heard in practice. Worse still the task had been assigned to someone unfamiliar with the D-type box. Many years later Peter Sargent was to reflect that Jaguar's attitude toward their privately funded Le Mans attempts and the development of the cars was less than helpful.

Frustratingly so close to capturing third place, Sargent/Lumsden had to settle for fifth but they had otherwise enjoyed an impressive run. The car had performed extremely well, lapping in 4min 13sec and being timed at 168mph (270kph) on the Mulsanne Straight. Another problem that escaped mention at the time was that the D-type-pattern spun magnesium alloy wheels of 15-inch diameter (the original design was 16-inch) were splitting around the steel centre. Meanwhile the Cunningham car gained a place but it should have been Jaguar third and fifth instead of fourth and fifth.

1962 results

1st Phil Hill/Olivier Gendebien Ferrari 330LM (0808) 331 laps, 2,765.876 miles (4,450.294km), 115.244mph (185.428kph).

2nd Jean Guichet/Pierre Noblet Ferrari 250GTO (3705 GT) 326 laps, 2,724.169 miles (4,383.188km), 113.507mph (182.632kph).

3rd 'Eldé (Leon Dernier)/'Beurlys' (Jean Blaton) Ferrari 250GTO (3757 GT) 314 laps, 2,618.375 miles (4,212.965km), 109.720mph (176.539kph).

4th Roy Salvadori/Briggs Cunningham Jaguar E-type 860630 310 laps, 2,589.010 miles (4,165.717km), 107.875mph (173.571kph).

5th Peter Sargent/Peter Lumsden Jaguar E-type 850009 310 laps, 2,587.022 miles (4,162.518km), 107.792mph (173.437kph).

Ironically this was to be the E-type's finest hour at Le Mans even though a much lighter all-alloy version was on the horizon.

Chapter 13

1963 – 'Lightweight' letdown

The Briggs Cunningham 'lightweight' E-type line-up at Le Mans 1963 with the fastest car of Hansgen/Pabst (850664) nearest the camera. In the background behind the furthest E-type and standing next to the woman in the striped jumper is Peter Lumsden with sun hat and bow tie. (Collection Bernard Viart/Paul Skilleter)

Opposite above: The induction side of the fuel injection 'lightweight' E-type engine in one of the Cunningham cars with its characteristically long trumpets. (LAT Photographic)

Opposite below: Brian Playford in sombrero standing by the unique coupé space-frame Lister-Jaguar of Peters Sargent and Lumsden. This picture shows the high opening doors and the Zagato like roofline of the Frank Costin-designed body. (LAT Photographic)

In early 1963 Jaguar announced the 'Competition E' although it quickly gained the soubriquet 'Lightweight E-type'. The first was built around John Coombs's 4 WPD and this car's relatively successful British racing activities and the development work carried out by Jaguar in 1961/62 undoubtedly promoted the whole concept. (It should be remembered that Jaguar had already built the low-drag coupé, but that used a steel monocoque and was to remain a one-off.)

Subsequently, 12 'lightweights' were constructed, three for Briggs Cunningham, the rest for assorted private owners. Jaguar had been rather clever in overcoming the homologation rules that demanded at least 100 cars of the type were to be built by stating that the aluminium cars were 'standard' and that the steel-bodied production versions were the 'lightweights'! Because body profile was free Ferrari had managed to homologate its GTO on the basis of their 250GT road car, so the rules were not only highly flexible but completely meaningless. Later Aston Martin and Carroll Shelby would take similar liberties with the regulations. It has to be said however that the E type, even in full 'lightweight' mode was much nearer to its productions origins than any of its rivals.

The basic specification of the new car was broadly similar to the late 1962 Coombs car but now with an aluminium monocoque, alloy block and Lucas fuel injection. To begin with a close ratio four-speed gearbox was used although a five-speed ZF unit appeared later. Power from the wide-angle head (35/40) 3.8-litre engine was still around 300bhp at 5,500rpm although the shorter British events allowed a higher state of tune. The most significant factor was the loss of weight, Jaguar claiming a figure of 2,028lb (920kg), lighter than the GTO Ferraris, although this now looks slightly optimistic.

Two such cars travelled to Sebring, one for Briggs Cunningham that finished a delayed eighth and the other, entered by Kjell Qvale, finished seventh and won its class. This car was raced once more then effectively disappeared until it was discovered under a pile of junk in a Florida garage in 1999! Subsequently sympathetically restored by Lynx Motors International in Hastings, England this remarkably original car is now raced occasionally by Lynx chairman John Mayston-Taylor in selected historic events. In Britain the Coombs and Tommy Atkins 'lightweight' E-types quickly established themselves as Ferrari beaters with Graham Hill winning at Snetterton, Goodwood, Silverstone and Mallory Park before defecting to Maranello Concessionaires and Ferrari for the Goodwood TT. Abroad the two Peters, Sargent and Lumsden, took their new

Space-frame Lister

Although it had already been decided to purchase a 'lightweight' E-type, Peter Sargent had bought the unique space-frame Lister chassis and suspension *sans* engine from John Coundley for the 1963 Le Mans. It was the brainchild of Frank Costin and is not fondly remembered by Brian Playford who prepared and engineered all the Sargent/Lumsden cars, together with his brother John. It was purchased because it was supposedly a very light sprint car, but the necessary strengthening for endurance racing made it somewhat heavier.

Sargent recalled that it had rear-wheel steer, a fact confirmed by Brian Playford who told the author that there was a serious design flaw in the rear suspension which caused the rear wheels to toe out, an alarming trait at 170mph (275kph)! Sargent was adamant the suspension was too soft and Frank Costin did admit to them that suspension was not his forté. It had side-mounted fuel tanks and a quick-release windscreen, a feature developed by Brian Playford that he was to later incorporate in their 'lightweight' E-type.

The coupé body designed by Frank Costin was made by Williams & Pritchard who had built the 'knobbly' Lister bodies in 1958 and had the doors set into the roof. At high speed Peter Sargent noticed that a huge gap opened up at the top of the doors, although when stationary, they were quite secure. A retaining bolt modification took care of the problem, but there was obviously a lot of air pressure building up somewhere in or on the body.

After Le Mans the car was not used again in any serious racing during 1963, but returned to race in the 1964 Nüburgring 1,000km driven by John Coundley and Jack Fairman where it retired with suspension troubles. At this point the car was still in its original ownership but was sold shortly afterwards to David Harvey. During the early 1970s it turned up in historic racing, now without a roof, and was very successfully raced by Gerry Marshall for London car dealers Hexagon of Highgate. More recently it has been rebuilt with its coupé body again and will be prepared and run in selected events by Don and Justin Law for its new owner.

'lightweight' (S850663) to the Nürburgring 1,000km where Lumsden had a huge accident and effectively wrote off the car, after a very encouraging run. An even better show was provided by Peter Lindner in his new 'lightweight' (S850662) leading the race briefly, setting fastest GT lap (9min 38.0sec) before retiring with engine failure.

For Le Mans 1963 there was eager anticipation amongst Jaguar fans as to whether the 'lightweight' E-type could successfully challenge the formerly omnipotent GTO Ferraris. Much was expected after the surprisingly effective challenge in 1962 and three of the all-alloy E-types were on hand courtesy of Briggs Cunningham. Peter Lindner's

car (who was Jaguar's German distributor) was not entered as he, with regular partner Peter Nöcker, were busy winning the Nürburgring six-hour touring car race in their 3.8 Mk 2, the third consecutive victory for Jaguar in that event. Neither was the Sargent/Lumsden car attending as, apart from still being *hors de combat* after its German adventures, the intrepid duo had entered a special coupé Lister-Jaguar. (See sidebar.) It was taken to the Le Mans test days in April where Peter Sargent recorded a respectable lap of 4min 16.3sec despite a Watts linkage failure, and in May, raced at Silverstone in the traditional *Daily Express* Trophy meeting. The body had to be altered at the rear to admit the all important regulatory luggage box.

Le Mans 1963

Jaguar entries for the 31st Le Mans 24-hour race were:

No. 14 Walt Hansgen/Augie Pabst Jaguar 'lightweight' E-type 850664. Engine RA1349-9S. Reg 5114 WK.
No. 15 Briggs Cunningham/Bob Grossman Jaguar 'lightweight' E-type 850659. Engine RA1345-9S. Reg 5115 WK.
No. 16 Roy Salvadori/Paul Richards Jaguar 'lightweight' E-type 850665. Engine RA1350-9S.
No. 17 Peter Sargent/Peter Lumsden Lister Jaguar. Engine R1035-9. Reg WTM 446 (used only for customs purposes; the car did not have an actual road registration).

The E-types were running in the GT class, whereas the Lister was a *bona fide* prototype and up against much quicker and more formidable competition. There were only four GTO Ferraris this year, but Aston Martin had brought two new Project 214 cars plus the bigger engined 215 Prototype version. Additionally Jean Kerguen entered his old DB4GT Zagato for the last time, while an unknown quantity were the two roadster AC Cobras, one of which was shared by 1956 winner Ninian Sanderson. Overall winner was almost guaranteed to be one of the works Ferrari prototypes and a special but unclassified entry was the Rover-BRM gas turbine to be driven by World Champion Graham Hill and his BRM team-mate Richie Ginther. The quickest GT cars in practice were the new Project 214 Astons, with the Ferrari GTOs and E-types well matched. The best time of each make was as follows:

Aston Martin Project 214 (0195/R)
  McLaren/Ireland 4min 00.7sec.
Ferrari 250GTO (4757 GT) Abate/Tavano 4min
  05.5sec.
Jaguar 'lightweight' E-type Hansgen/Pabst 4min
  06.9sec (Salvadori/Richards 4min 09.1sec and
  Cunninghan/Grossman 4min 11.5sec).
AC Cobra (CS2131) Sanderson/Bolton 4min
  12.4sec.

For comparative purposes the Sargent/Lumsden Lister recorded 4min 13.4sec and the old Zagato Aston a very worthy 4min 10.7sec. Fastest time was claimed by the NART 4-litre Ferrari 330LM with 3min 50.9sec although the works Ferraris and the 215 Aston (3min 52.0sec) were all very close. Only now, six years on, were the sports racers significantly quicker than their 1957 counterparts. The Jaguars were lacking straight line speed, which was not surprising given the addition of two extra lights set into the bonnet which must surely have increased aerodynamic drag. Even without this added factor the roadster-style E-type with its small hardtop was not as slippery as it looked and suffered from front end lift, a common factor with many front-engined cars of the pre-spoiler period.

Sadly Le Mans 1963 was not a *tour de force* for Jaguar, rather a bad day at the races. Within the first hour Hansgen was out with the quickest E-type suffering gearbox problems, the Cunningham cars using prototype versions of Jaguar's own four-speed all-syncromesh unit which would be used on the 4.2 production E-types in 1964. According to Roy Salvadori all the cars had suffered lower gears seizing up in practice. At 4.30pm one of the small French René Bonnets had crashed and overturned approaching the Esses and Peter Sargent had lightly damaged the nose of the Lister avoiding the wreckage. It was running in 16th place at 6pm but was doomed to retire early when its clutch bolts

sheared, caused by a faulty batch from the manufacturers. Once again the Peters had been let down by the failure of a component part beyond their control. By now the second Cunningham E-type of Salvadori/Richards was also suffering gearbox maladies and had slipped from 14th to 36th position by 8pm.

The fates had not finished with Jaguar yet as Bruce McLaren suffered a 180mph (290kph) blow-up in his works Aston Martin 214 dumping a sump full of oil on Mulsanne and, although Grossman only got his windscreen splashed with oil in the third E-type (also now suffering gearbox

With the nose removed the rather strange looking unequal length wishbone front suspension of the Lister is revealed. Peter Sargent complained to the author in 2000 that the suspension was far too soft and after Le Mans substantially thicker springs were fitted, but neither Peter raced it again. (Paul Skilleter)

problems), Salvadori had a major accident. Going at over 160mph (258kph) he almost held the ensuing slide on the oil slick but just dropped a wheel on to the grass verge and the car went out of control. During a previous stop he had been unable to fasten his seat belt and now, as the car hit the bank he was thrown out through the rear perspex window. Lying on the side of the road, soaked in petrol with another driver beside him, he was only able to drag himself away from the track by digging his fingernails into the dirt and grass on the verge and hauling himself to relative safety. While the fire fighters tried to extinguish the now burning Jaguar, its horn blowing forlornly, an Alpine driven by B. Heinz had also crashed and the unfortunate driver was fatally burned. The Jaguar was destroyed, the only 'lightweight' not to survive out of the original 12 cars. Sanderson had a number of lurid spins in the British-entered Cobra without

damage to himself or the car. Although only battered and bruised Roy Salvadori was in such pain afterwards that he was virtually immobile for two weeks.

With just four and a half hours gone only one Jaguar was left in the race, the Cunningham/ Grossman car that was lying 18th, rising to 14th by midnight and eighth by half distance (4am). Four hours later they had gained another place and were now two places ahead of the Sanderson/Bolton Cobra but there were three GTO Ferraris in front, one of them now in third place overall. As the morning progressed Bob Grossman suffered total brake failure on Mulsanne at maximum velocity approaching the bottom gear Mulsanne Corner at the end of the long straight. A brake pedal pin had sheared and Grossman had to ram the straw bales in the escape road to stop the errant Jaguar with predictable results. After finding a phone

The Salvadori/Richards 'lightweight' E-type chassis 850665 with gearbox trouble. The already suspect aerodynamics were not helped by the twin spotlights, while the obligatory bug deflector placed just in front of the louvres has obviously been doing its job. The car has a UK tax disc mid-screen reading AUG 63. Note the third windscreen wiper has been removed leaving the spindle poking out of the scuttle. This was the only 'lightweight' to be officially written off after burning out in Salvadori's accident on Mulsanne. (Paul Skilleter)

and ringing in to the pits, Grossman drove the battered car back with the front completely stoved in and the front tyres flat. This took over 30 minutes and then having spoken to the organisers they were allowed to cannabilise the Hansgen car and use its radiator and bonnet front to rebuild the E-type. Unfortunately the regulations forbade exchanging bonnets, so they had to cut the front off the donor car's bonnet and marry it up with the rear section of the crashed one. All this took over 90 minutes and the Jaguar resumed in 10th position.

One advantage of having a very sturdy car is that it can survive such an incident, certainly no Ferrari, Aston or Cobra would have been driveable after a shunt of these proportions. The car was now driven to the finish and it came home ninth the accident having dropped it behind the Cobra. Ferrari, of course, won with the works 250P of Scarfiotti/

Bandini some 134 miles ahead of the second placed Ferrari 250GTO ('Beurlys'/Langlois) with the other GTOs fourth and sixth.

1963 result

9th Bob Grossman/Briggs Cunningham Jaguar 'lightweight' E-type. 283 laps, 2,372.446 miles (3,817.266km), 98.851mph (159.051kph).

After Le Mans the 'lightweights' continued to do well in national events, and the German car won a GT race at the Avus in Germany. The five-speed ZF gearbox was supposed to be in common use but this proved to be something of a liability. Not only did it absorb more power than the four-speed box (55bhp as compared with 25bhp), but it added 88lb (40kg) to the weight of the car thereby almost negating the weight saved by the alloy block. A

Peter Sargent races the Lister in bright sunshine late on Saturday afternoon before the clutch bolts sheared. (LAT Photographic)

further complication was that the alloy block was not stiff enough to cope with the extra weight of the ZF unit, the old XK engine having been designed with a cast-iron block. Cylinder head gasket failure and cracking, the crankshaft bearings running out of true and block flexing and splitting were all side effects, exacerbated by the compromised design of the aluminium crankcase.

Brian Playford has explained that originally there was only one five-speed ZF gearbox in use which was swopped between the Coombs car and Peter Lindner's German car! He also noted that Jaguar mounted the gearbox too far back using a 4in (102mm) spacer. This exacerbated the flexing problems with the alloy crankcase, whereas on the rebuilt 49 FXN he had moved the unit 3in (76mm) closer thus alleviating the trouble.

By the time of the TT at Goodwood Graham Hill had stopped racing the Coombs car, preferring the Ferrari 250GTO and already the frontline career of the 'lightweight' was beginning to falter. An exception was the brilliant performance by Dick Protheroe at Reims in the supporting sports/GT race for the French Grand Prix. He finished second overall vanquishing all the GTO Ferraris in the low-drag coupé, although this was not as already noted, a true 'lightweight'. The two surviving Cunningham E-types finished third and fourth at the Bridghampton 500 in America behind two Cobras, the much lighter and very powerful Anglo-American cars being better developed than their British circuit contemporaries.

Chapter 14

1964 – Last orders for the XK engine

Despite the gloomy prognosis there were four regular E-type competitors in international racing during 1964 and the Coombs car was still active on British circuits along with some of its brethren. Those four were Dick Protheroe in his low-drag coupé (EC 1001) plus the 'lightweights' of Peter Lindner, Sargent/Lumsden and Peter

Sutcliffe. These four cars between them raced at Spa, Nürburgring, Le Mans, Reims and Montlhéry, but only the four Peters, two German and two British, Sargent and Lumsden, went to the Sarthe.

In April, Lindner/Nöcker and Sargent/Lumsden had turned up for the annual Le Mans test days with both cars now sporting very dramatic coupé

The incredibly sleek lines of the Samir Klat-developed and Brian Playford-engineered Sargent/ Lumsden 'lightweight' E-type (850663) during the Le Mans trials on 18 April 1964. (LAT Photographic)

The rear view of 850663 showing how much lower it was than the German 'lightweight' and its much flatter rear deck. Peter Lumsden rounds Tertre Rouge with a noticeable degree of negative rear camber in company with the Bianchi/Blaton Ferrari 250GTO (5575), the Dewez/Kerguen Porsche 904GTS (041) and the Piot/Marnat Triumph Spitfire (X937). (Michael Cooper)

style bodywork. Lindner's version was similar to the Protheroe car in shape but finished in silver with heavily riveted rear panels. It had been specially constructed by Jaguar and was to enjoy works engines and preparation. The British car by contrast was a purely private effort and was stunningly beautiful. It sat very low, had a long Vanwall-style nose with a NACA duct on the bonnet and flush screens. The bodywork was designed by Dr Samir Klat with reference to Frank Costin's philosophy, and the engine was tested at Imperial College in London. Much research and hard work had gone into this car by Brian and John Playford who built it, and Dr Klat and Harry Watson who were the boffins. They were not content with the basic specification and conducted all sorts of experiments, but found Jaguar basically sceptical and unhelpful. Both cars recorded identical lap times of 4min 7.3sec but reports vary as to how fast they were on Mulsanne, 168–9mph (272kph) being typical estimates. Lindner's engine was reputed to

deliver 322bhp at 6,000rpm. The new Daytona Cobra coupé was five seconds quicker over the lap.

Le Mans 1964 was notable for the challenge to Ferrari supremacy by the new Ford GT40, although Dearborn reliability was still suspect. In the GT class the two Daytona Cobras with their coupé bodies had power and driver advantages while AC had entered their own fastback version and the fourth car was a privately entered French roadster. Otherwise four of the ubiquitous GTO Ferraris, all sporting the 1964 LM style bodywork, appeared plus a lone Aston Martin Project 214 car, now owned and driven by Mike Salmon.

Le Mans 1964

The two Jaguar entries lined up as follows:

No. 16 Peter Lindner/Peter Nöcker Jaguar 'lightweight' E-type 850662. Engine RA1347-9S. Reg 4868 WK.

No. 17 Peter Sargent/Peter Lumsden Jaguar 'lightweight' E-type 850663. Engine RA1348-9S. Reg 49 FXN.

The engine in the British Jaguar was the renumbered RA1345-9S that had finished ninth at Le Mans in 1963. Lindner's engine had started off as RA1358-9S and was changed to its race designation RA1347-9S prior to installation on 3 June 1964. Both cars used the ZF five-speed gearbox.

Lap times for the GT cars in practice proved just how fast were the Daytona Cobras, and the lone Aston Martin. Once again the GTO Ferraris and E-types were on par but somewhat slower than their rivals. The best GT times for each marque were:

Gurney/Bondurant Daytona Cobra (CSX2299) 3min 56.1sec.
Salmon/Sutcliffe Aston Martin DP214 (0194/R) 3min 58.6sec.

Bianchi/Blaton ('Beurlys') Ferrari 250GTO (5575 GT) 4min 3.4sec.
Lindner/Nöcker Jaguar 'lightweight' E-type (850662) 4min 5.9sec.

The British Jaguar had recorded a leisurely 4min 16sec but was capable of going much faster. Lindner's time reveals just how little had been gained in the nine years that had passed since Hawthorn had lapped in 4min 06.6sec with XKD505 during his duel with Fangio's Mercedes 300SLR in 1955. Obviously the E-type was heavier, but it had shown a sustained 344bhp on test courtesy of a special exhaust system, had much wider and stickier tyres, modern brakes and Le Mans as a track was faster. Driver potential makes a difference, but even allowing for Hawthorn's brilliance, the E-type time was very disappointing. It was not very quick in a straight line in practice either despite the special engine but went faster in the race (about 176mph/283kph). An obvious

Peter Lindner in 850662 chases Innes Ireland in the Maranello Concessionaires Ferrari 250GTO (4399 GT) early in the race as they begin the long thrash up the Mulsanne Straight. (Michael Cooper)

49 FXN's low ground clearance

Amongst the myriad of modifications to 49 FXN was the very low ground clearance. It was 4in (102mm) lower than the standard 'lightweight' E-type. This had been achieved by remounting the steering rack and lowering the inside pick-up for the upper front wishbone arms to achieve the desired degree of negative camber at the front that increased grip and eliminated the E-type's excessive bump steer tendencies. Brian Playford remembered Lindner shouting from the pit counter at the Le Mans trials in April, wanting to know why his new car did not look like 49 FXN. As already noted, the British car also benefited from its repositioned gearbox.

feature of the car was the very high ground clearance, typical of the E-type but hardly suitable for Le Mans. Photographs taken at the Nürburgring before Le Mans show a very pronounced front-end lift, a characteristic of the Protheroe low-drag car and must surely have dramatically increased its frontal area and drag at high speed. No such problems afflicted the Sargent/Lumsden machine which was a much better car dynamically, even without the benefit of a factory support. (See sidebar.)

Drama was supplied by Piper's Ferrari 250LM losing all its oil at the start, causing plenty of sliding around. The two Jaguars ran 19th and 20th during the first three hours, the German car in front, but by 9pm, the British Jaguar had risen to 12th while the other had fallen to 21st. It was losing water and despite Frank Rainbow and Bob Penney changing a head gasket in record time the problem returned, and it dropped further and further behind, eventually retiring early Sunday morning after completing 149 laps and having spent three hours in the pits. This would appear to have been caused by too high internal cylinder head pressures, a phenomenon noted by Samir Klat and Harry Watson during their own engine development. Klat's opinion of Jaguar went down another notch as a result, especially when they declined to discuss his engine's power curves and potential. Happily he had somewhat better relations with Jaguar's aerodynamicist Malcolm Sayer, who always took an interest in anything new. It was the last XK-engined car to race in the Le Mans 24-Hours. Meanwhile, having reached fifth in class, 49 FXN was running into gearbox trouble and it fell to 34th place, retiring before midnight after 80 laps. The car had been timed at 174mph (280kph) with more to come. Although a purely privately run and funded team Klat, Watson and the Playfords had produced a very good car and had applied proper scientific thinking to its development and performance. Dr Klat had even photographed pit stops so as to eliminate any unnecessary delay and improve the efficiency of the operation. This was thought rather strange at the time, but of course he was decades ahead of the game. So that was that, or to put it in the words of a contemporary pop song, 'Its all over now'. *Après*

Le Mans a report from Derrick White (a South African engineer formerly with Connaught before joining Jaguar) on the German car made less than happy reading, its main points being that the E-type was too heavy and did not have enough power. He also complained of the amount of time lost during practice in changing the final-drive ratio, a huge job on the E-type where individual gears could not be swapped.

In the meantime Jackie Stewart was using the John Coombs 'lightweight' to good effect in British racing and Dick Protheroe won his class at the Reims 12-hour race in the low-drag coupé. Thereafter 49 FXN raced at Goodwood for the TT and Lindner's car also came. However, during practice it could not be persuaded to go fast enough, and Peter Sutcliffe was asked to try it. He was only a little quicker and crashed at Woodcote, caught out by the wayward handling and inconsistent brakes. The car was rebuilt in time for the 1,000km race at Montlhéry where tragedy

struck as Lindner collided with an Abarth, killing both drivers and three officials. The car was impounded by the French authorities for many years and was not reconstructed until the 1980s by the original Lynx Engineering. Later it was rebuilt again because the roof line was wrongly shaped.

As for 49 FXN, it survived the rigours of club racing and then a long spell in America, but is now thankfully back in the UK, fully restored and racing again for Sir Anthony Bamford who also owns XKD603. Peter Sargent stopped racing in 1964 after a domestic accident left him with a serious neck injury. His partner Peter Lumsden continued to use the car and scored several wins in British events before the E-type expired during the 1965 Guards Trophy at Brands Hatch. It was now very fast indeed, Klat and Watson's engine work producing 348bhp on the test bed. However the big front-engined GT cars had nearly reached the end of their days at international level and there were to be no more Jaguars at Le Mans for 20 years.

Opposite: Another view of the German 'lightweight' that highlights its extraordinarily high ground clearance. What were Jaguar thinking of? (LAT Photographic)

Peter Sargent negotiates Mulsanne Corner, with the Mulsanne escape road in the background. This view illustrates perfectly the very Vanwall-like nose of 850663, the small bonnet-mounted 'bug' deflector and the NACA duct. Note that Sargent, like Lumsden, is wearing sunglasses as the early evening sun strikes the car. (Archives Serge Pozzoli)

Chapter 15

1984 – The Americans are back

During the intervening years, before any Jaguar-powered cars returned to Le Mans, the world had changed. Even Ferrari, who for so long dominated sports car racing, had won their last Le Mans in 1965 and had pulled out of Prototype/GT racing to concentrate on F1 during the early 1970s. Motor racing had become much more focused and specialised, cars were now purpose-built purely for racing and could never be driven on the road. Technology had bred huge power, but more importantly, aerodynamic downforce, wide, sticky tyres and enormous grip allied to fantastic braking. Two decades had passed, Malcolm Sayer had died prematurely in 1970 and Jaguar had resolutely stayed out of racing, although there had been the XJ13 in the mid-1960s.

This was really Bill Heynes's pet project, but Jaguar chief William Lyons was not interested. It was a mid-engined 5-litre four-cam V12 and had beautifully rounded lines that belied its overweight construction, suspect aerodynamics, poor handling and brakes. Originally started in the early 1960 it eventually produced a peak power of 502bhp but the relentless advances in technology had already rendered it obsolete for competition use. The four-cam V12 engine which was two XK heads on a common block was largely the work of Claude Baily. Had they managed to build and race it by 1965 it might have succeeded. In January 1971, as a prelude to the launch of their new V12 production engine Jaguar tester, Norman Dewis (who had driven at Le Mans in 1953 and 1955) was demonstrating the XJ13 at Lindley for the press.

On his last lap the XJ13 suffered a wheel or tyre failure and crashed at high speed, severely damaging the unique car, but happily not Mr Dewis. Fortunately its centre section survived intact and the car was subsequently rebuilt and shown in public for the first time in 1973.

Jaguar themselves had slipped into the clutches of BMC in July 1966 which quickly evolved into the even worse mess that was to become British Leyland. It was a miracle that Jaguar survived the attentions of Sir Donald Stokes and others including the ever-present industrial unrest and political meddling, suffering continual problems with build quality and reliability that dogged it for nearly 20 years. On the credit side there had been some light relief. The E-type had prospered in British mod-sports racing for several years, using much hacked about and modified production cars on ever wider tyres. By the early 1970s, 1950s sports racing cars were appearing in historic racing and the Jaguar XK engined C, D, and Lister variants became famous all over again. Willie Green, driving Sir Anthony Bamford's XKD603, returned to Le Mans in 1973 and won the special historic race there.

The need to boost flagging sales had encouraged Jaguar in America to race the now almost moribund E-type, and in 1974 Joe Huffaker and Bob Tullius's Group 44 Inc was chosen to run the V12 E-type against the all-conquering Corvettes. Huffaker, who had previous Jaguar racing experience, was the West Coast representative, while Group 44 from Winchester, Virginia covered

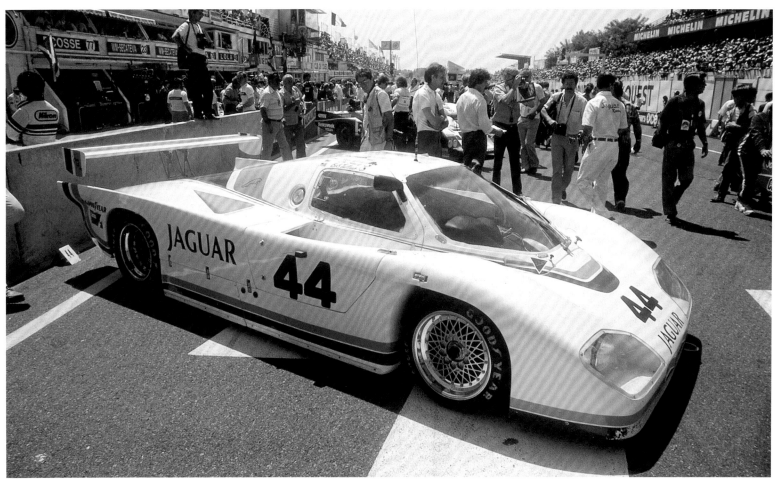

the East Coast. Tullius had formed his now famous team with Brian Fuerstenau after successfully campaigning a Triumph TR3 and a TR4 in the 1960s. The V12 E-types were a great success in 1974/75 culminating in Tullius winning the national championship in 1975. Thereafter plans to race the XJS began and this produced spectacular results for Tullius who won back-to-back championships in the Trans Am series of 1977/78. XJS wins continued as late as 1981 when Tullius had three victories and finished runner-up in the championship. In England a rather less well thought out plan to race the XJ12 coupé in the European Touring Car Championship against the omnipotent BMW 635CSI provided two years of ever growing frustration. Announced in 1976 to much acclaim and general flag waving, the cars were unready and underfunded. Poor Ralph

Broad, famous and successful Mini and Ford entrant found himself without adequate factory support and grappling with assorted mechanical problems and fragility that constantly hobbled the cars. Second place at the Nürburgring in 1977 was their best result and after failing to win the TT at Silverstone, the plug was pulled. Frustratingly the car, which had always been faster than its BMW rival, was on the verge of finally coming good. However, internal politics and even the choice of model (they should have used the XJS that was much more amenable to racing as the Americans had proved) doomed the project almost from the start.

Nil desperandum however, and in 1981, Bob Tullius, Mike Dale and Lee Dykstra (see sidebar) met to discuss the future of Jaguar racing in the States. In Coventry John Egan had taken over and

The Group 44 XJR-5 of Tullius/Redman/Bundy (006) before the race, displaying its immaculate preparation and sparkling turnout. (LAT Photographic)

a more positive pro-active approach was set in motion to overcome the ossification and stagnation of the BL years. Things were looking up and on 7 January 1982 a new Jaguar IMSA GTP Coupé was announced to promote the quality of Jaguar engineering and provide a powerful marketing tool. It was to be designed, built, prepared and raced by Group 44, the main movers in this project being Mike Dale, Lee Dykstra, Bob Tullius and crew chief Lawton 'Lanky' Foushee. MG and Triumph had already faded away in 1980/81 and Jaguar sales had suffered. Designed by Dykstra using the Jaguar V12 engine, it was a mid-engined ground effects racing car designed for the American IMSA GTP series. To begin with it had a standard sized V12 on six Weber carburettors, which grew to 6 litres later on and the chassis was an aluminium honeycomb floor with steel bulkheads. The body was semi-monocoque with glass fibre panels and the whole ensemble was finished in immaculate white with two-tone green stripes outlining the cockpit area and all around the base of the body. It weighed 2,090lb (950kg) as per the IMSA rules and made its delayed debut at the Road America 500-mile race in August netting third place for Tullius/Adam. Derek Bell tested the car known as the XJR-5 at Silverstone in July 1973,

The sister car of Adamowicz/ Watson/Ballot-Lena (008) during a pit stop in the race, its formerly pristine finish now grimy and chipped from the ultra high speeds. It retired after crashing due to a deflating tyre. (Sutton)

describing the engine as fantastic. The Jaguar was a regular front runner against the hordes of Porsches and won four races during 1983. However tentative plans to enter Le Mans were dropped due to reliability and technical problems. For 1984 two new, much modified and developed cars were on hand and one finished third at the Daytona 24-hour race followed up by a 1, 2 victory at the Miami Grand Prix. By April a decision had been taken to race at Le Mans and plans were announced by Jaguar supremo John Egan for a two-car team.

Meanwhile, the ever shifting sands of FISA rule changes favoured the IMSA specification cars in 1984, but different regulations proposed for 1985 suited nobody and Porsche boycotted Le Mans as a result. Ultimately, Group C rules were used in 1984, but the works Porsches stayed away, although this made little difference as they had many of their latest cars entered with private teams (there were 16 956/962 variants in all). Ferrari might be gone but Italy was represented by Lancia, albeit with only three cars and they were to prove enormously fast. Other interesting runners included three French-constructed Rondeau Cosworths, using a sports car version of the legendary F1 engine, two WM-Peugeots, two works Mazdas with rotary engines and an old rival, Aston Martin. These were the two Nimrod cars powered by Aston's 5.3-litre V8. Jaguar had wisely decided to keep a low profile concerning the two Group 44 XJR-5s, but French newspapers were not so coy, proclaiming: *'Le Retour de Jaguar!'* It was also the return of the Americans 21 years on from Briggs Cunningham's final sortie with the 'lightweight' E-types. Inevitably the two XJR-5s became the centre of attention, somewhat irritating for Lancia who had entered officially with factory cars.

Le Mans 1984

The two Group 44 cars lined up thus:

No. 40 Tony Adamowicz/John Watson/Claude Ballot-Lena Jaguar XJR-5 (008).
No. 44 Bob Tullius/Brian Redman/Doc Bundy Jaguar XJR-5 (006).

The drivers were a mix of successful American racers plus two veteran Brits and Le Mans and rally specialist Claude Ballot-Lena. The Frenchman was an accomplished all-rounder who first drove at Le Mans in 1966 (racing here every year up to and including 1986) and had driven all and sundry during his career. Bob Tullius was of course team principal while Polish-American Tony Adamowicz had begun competing in 1963, and first partnered Tullius in 1966. Three years later he was the SCCA Formula 5000 champion and raced Ferrari 512s at Le Mans in 1970 and 1971 (finishing third). He drove a variety of machinery successfully over the years and had enjoyed a three-year stint racing Nissan 280ZX turbos. 'Doc' Bundy started his career in 1973 preparing cars for Peter Gregg's Brumos Porsche Racing but did not compete until 1980. He had already appeared at Le

Mans in 1981 winning his class with a Porsche 924 Turbo, joining Group 44 in 1983. Brian Redman was a throwback to the 1960s, having driven for John Wyer, Porsche and Ferrari amongst others as well as for a brief stint in F1 with McLaren and a very successful career in F5000 in America during the 1970s. He joined Group 44 in 1983. He was still very fast, while John Watson had been a leading F1 driver for many years for Surtees, Roger Penske, Brabham and McLaren as well as having sports car experience with Porsche. The XJR-5s had about 600bhp available from their 6-litre Jaguar V12 engines, but the turbocharged Porsches and Lancias had much more, at least for qualifying.

Qualifying was predictably a turbo boost orgy with Lancia claiming the two top slots, followed by five Porsches. Le Mans had inevitably altered with the years since Jaguar had last appeared here and the track now measured 8.467 miles (13.627km). The leading times for each of the major contenders were:

Bob Wollek/Sandro Nannini Lancia LC2-84 (005). 3min 17.11sec.
Stefan Johansson/Jean Louis-Schlesser/Mauricio Narvaez Porsche 956 (104). 3min 26.1sec.
Roger Dorchy/Alain Couderc/Gerard Patte WM-Peugeot P83B. 3min 30.01sec.
Ray Mallock/Drake Olson Nimrod Aston Martin C-2B (005). 3min 33.12sec.
Brian Redman/Doc Bundy/Bob Tullius Jaguar XJR-5 (006). 3min 35.33sec (the other car recorded 3min 39.16sec).

Both the immaculate, gleaming Jaguars were driven conservatively to strict orders in practice but in race trim the gap between them and the Porsches and the Lancias was not so marked. Random recorded speeds on the Mulsanne Straight had the best Lancia reaching 219mph (352kph), Porsche 219mph (352kph), WM-Peugeot 226mph (364kph), Nimrod 212mph (341kph) and Jaguar 211mph (339kph). The XJR-5s were limited to 6,450rpm on Mulsanne and the drivers were told not to put the car in a situation where an accident could occur. Despite this Bundy lost his 'nose' at the Ford chicane and the second car driven by Watson needed an engine change after water was found in the cylinders. A further hiccup was caused by the Micos electronics mismanaging the ignition timing.

No longer did the Le Mans 24-hour race start at 4pm, now it was an hour earlier and the traditional run and jump in start had been abandoned in 1970, instead a rolling start was employed. Wollek's Lancia took the lead, only to be overtaken on Mulsanne by Dorchy's WM, these French cars being specially adapted for very high straightline speed. After swapping places in the first two laps Dorchy suddenly had an off caused by braking problems and had to pit for repairs. At 4pm the two Jaguars were running in 15th (No. 40) and 19th

No. 006 rounds Mulsanne on a sunny day. The gearbox broke on Sunday morning ending a very impressive debut. Note the very long radio aerial on the roof. (LAT Photographic)

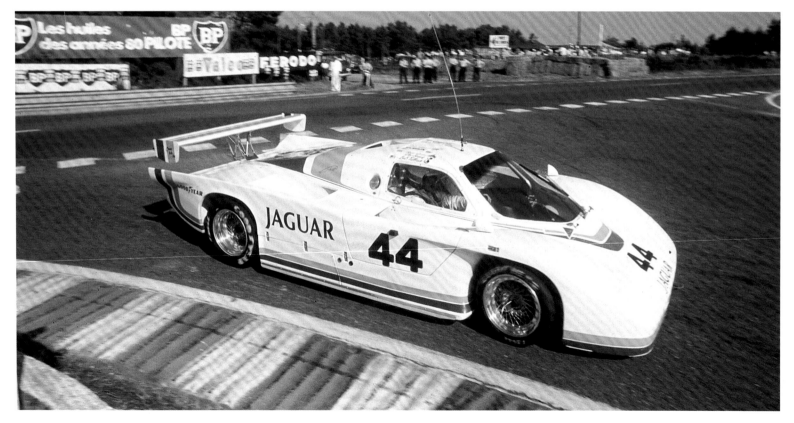

and were the last of the quicker cars to refuel, briefly holding first and third while the others stopped. By 5pm Porsche were 1, 2 with Lancia third and the Watson Jaguar was sixth with the other car 12th. With four hours gone the leading Jaguar remained in sixth place, now pursued by the Mallock/Olson Nimrod and the Redman/Tullius/Bundy car was up to 10th. Of more note perhaps was that by 8pm only two cars had retired, a far cry from the 'good old days'. The Lancia of Wollek/Nannini continued to lead, now by a lap, followed by a Porsche, Lancia and two more Porsches and then the first Jaguar.

Sadly, at around 9.15pm, John Sheldon driving one of the Nimrod-Aston Martins crashed on the Mulsanne kink at over 190mph (306kph) the car hitting the barriers on the left before crossing the road and hitting the barriers on the right. It exploded into a fireball of such ferocity that it set the nearby trees alight. Jonathan Palmer in the Canon Porsche 956, who was about to lap Sheldon, braked heavily to avoid the accident and Sheldon's team-mate Drake Olson, who was unsighted, sped by. Palmer watched in horror as a piece of Sheldon's disintegrating car landed in the road causing Olson to crash as he swerved to avoid it. Luckily Olson was unharmed and Sheldon survived, albeit with some very bad burns but tragically a marshal was killed and another seriously injured. So both Nimrods were out at the same time, a blow from which the team never recovered and the whole project subsequently folded.

Group 44's first unscheduled stop in nine hours of racing occurred when Adamowicz stopped to replace the nearside rear tyre that had lost some of its carcass, dropping them back a place. The Lancias remained in the lead and by 2am they were followed by three Porsches, two Jaguars (both on the same lap) and six more Porsches! However, during the 13th hour disaster struck for the Italians when one Lancia lost fifth gear and spent 45 minutes in the pits having it replaced, dropping to 14th. Meanwhile the first seven cars were separated by only three laps. Then the almost metronomic regularity of the Jaguars was disrupted as Ballot-Lena stopped with a broken throttle cable at Arnage. He managed to jury rig a repair

The XJR-5

Brian Redman remembers the XJR-5 with affection, recalling that it was a pleasant car to drive with no obvious vices. He had already enjoyed some success with it in the States, winning the Miami Grand Prix, but felt that the gearbox probably would not last 24 hours, as previous breakages had occurred. Additionally, while it had been one of the quickest cars in the IMSA series, at Le Mans it was not so competitive against the European Porsches. Seventeen years on he also recalled how beautifully finished and prepared it was and felt that the team was always struggling against the sheer numerical supremacy of Porsche, a problem other teams would discover in time.

and returned to the pits where eight laps were lost making a repair, but only one place was dropped. This car was doomed not to last however as Adamowicz crashed at Tertre Rouge at around 6am, caused by a deflating tyre. He managed to get the car back to the pits but damage to the oil tank was terminal so it was out. Less than an hour later and only 25 minutes into his stint, Redman pitted the remaining Jaguar with no third gear that took 45 minutes to replace, dropping from fifth to 10th in the process. Subsequently the car reached sixth position but at 11.30am on Sunday morning the gearbox broke and that was the end of Jaguar's Le Mans renaissance. (See sidebar.)

With one Lancia out and the remaining one battling with mechanical woes, the race was a Porsche walkover, the German cars taking the top seven places led by Henri Pescarolo/Klaus Ludwig in the Joest Racing entry. Group 44 and Jaguar however could be well satisfied with their showing although the Hewland gearbox was deemed marginal now that the engine was developing 600bhp. The No. 40 car (008) was timed at 212mph (341kph) and the No. 44 car (006) at 216mph (348kph) on the Mulsanne Straight and one had actually led the race on lap 14 during the first fuel stops. The remainder of Group 44's domestic season in America netted four second and three third place finishes against Porsche and March-Chevrolet and they finished third overall in the IMSA chassis and engine manufacturer's championship. It was a consistent season and with a little more luck they could have won more races against the very strong and numerous opposition.

Chapter 16

1985 – No progress

The Group 44 pit with the Redman/Adams/Haywood XJR-5 No. 40 (006) and the Tullius/ Robinson/Ballot-Lena No. 44 (008). (Sutton)

Early in 1985, Mike Dale of Jaguar America announced that he wanted Group 44 to return to Le Mans. The year had begun badly for the team with one car catching fire at Daytona after puncturing the oil tank and the other retiring with falling oil pressure. At Road Atlanta however Brian Redman and Hurley Haywood won from their team-mates Tullius/Robinson. Unlike 1984, Group 44 did not want to miss any of the American IMSA rounds because of Le Mans and the

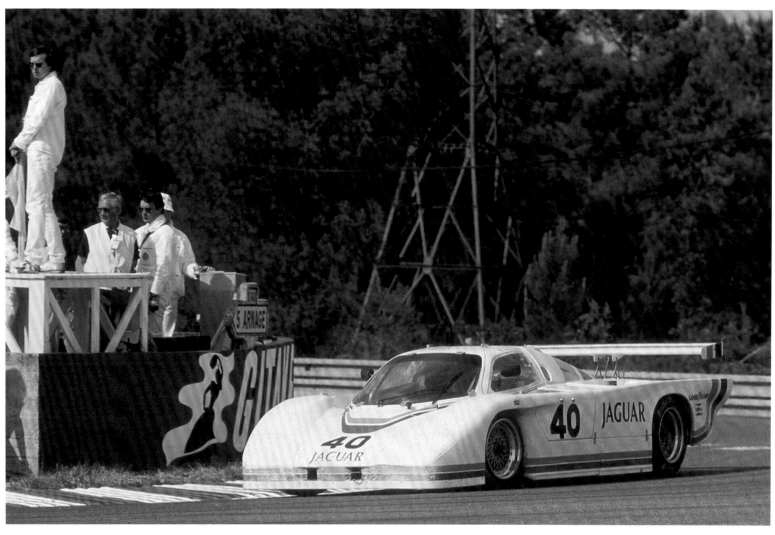

pressure was building up. They had two cars specifically for the French classic and then the provisional list showed that Jaguar itself had made three entries, but these unsurprisingly never materialised. Group 44's season continued with Redman leading at Riverside until he was pushed off, the other car finishing third. Laguna Seca, Charlotte and Lime Rock all produced second places, wins being forfeited at the last two due to a reluctant safety harness and oil on the screen respectively.

Le Mans 1985 was notable for the semi-official return of Mercedes-Benz whose engine was powering the new Sauber C8 while Porsche returned with three of their latest 962C models,

backed up by nine private cars. Lancia was trying again with two LC2-85s and Aston Martin power was used in Steve O'Rourke's Emka 84/1. There were also some Porsche-powered chassis (March and Cougar), but the other serious contenders were Group 44's two XJR-5s:

No. 40 Brian Redman/Jim Adams/Hurley
  Haywood Jaguar XJR-5 (006).
No. 44 Bob Tullius/Chip Robinson/Claude Ballot-
  Lena Jaguar XJR-5 (008).

Hurley Haywood was one of the most consistent and successful sports car drivers of his era, eventually going on to win Le Mans three times.

Unlike their first year at Le Mans, the Group 44 Jaguars were not so competitive in 1985. The No. 40 car (006) of Redman/Adams/Haywood, seen here at Mulsanne Corner, retired early on Sunday morning with a broken CV joint. (LAT Photographic)

Another view of 006 that accentuates the height of the relatively tall windscreen. The long roof-mounted 'whiplash' aerial of 1984 has been replaced by a much more modest device that is barely visible. In the background the assembled spectators and presumably 'officials' seem very vulnerable behind the rather inadequate looking Armco. (Sutton)

Chip Robinson hailed from American Super Vee racing, replacing Doc Bundy while Jim Adams was an experienced sports car racer and Group 44 regular.

Qualifying was dominated by the turbocharged Porsches and Lancias with the two Jaguars running at about the same pace as 1984. The best times for each of the leading contenders, with their weight and speed on Mulsanne were as follows:

Hans-Joachim Stuck Porsche 962C (003) 876kg (1,932lb), 3min 14.80sec, 219mph (352kph).
Alessandro Nannini Lancia LC2-85 (002) 891kg (1,965lb), 3min 15.95sec, 226mph (364kph).
Tiff Needell Emka-Aston Martin 84/1 (MC 02 84C) 3min 33.12sec, 216mph (348kph).
Chip Robinson Jaguar XJR-5 (008) 1,012kg (2,231lb), 3min 35.32sec, 209mph (336kph). (Haywood 997kg/2,198lb, 3min 37.29sec, 204mph/328kph).

It is to be noted how heavy the Jaguars were compared with their rivals, while the maximum recorded speed was down on 1984, if these figures are accurate.

Alas the new Sauber was a non-starter after it took off on the rise on the Mulsanne Straight, somersaulting twice backwards and landing back on its wheels before hitting the barriers. Driver John Nielsen was unhurt but it is a spooky coincidence that Mercedes-Benz should suffer two similar accidents 14 years apart. Speeds had risen dramatically over the years and the Sauber was timed at 221mph (356kph), so uncontrolled air flow getting under the cars was now very dangerous. For the record it had lapped in 3min 37.56sec in the first session. They would return.

The first hour of the race established a pattern of leading Porsches and Lancias interrupted by some judicious early refuelling by the Emka of Needell that saw the British car leading briefly. Interestingly it was the private Porsches that were dominating, while the works cars were off the pace due to their apparently heavy fuel consumption. The Jaguars occupied 12th and 14th places after two hours, separated by the Emka-Aston Martin and by 7pm they were 14th and 15th but running well. At this time three private Porsches led with one of the Lancias and two more Porsches completing the top six. Even after seven hours the top 13 were covered by only two laps, but both Jaguars had been delayed, Ballot-Lena with a misfire that required a new ignition box and the other car by a loose door. At midnight the two XJR-5s ran 15th and 16th in a field that had very few retirements, but before 2am the No. 40 car was out with a broken CV joint, stopping just beyond the pits. Unlike 1984, the opposition was proving rather more reliable and the heavy Jaguars were struggling with their fuel consumption as well; not a good combination given the restrictive fuel regulations (limited to 2,100 litres for the race). This had also affected reliability as running the cars for better consumption led to detonation and less power.

Through the night and into the morning the surviving XJR-5 and the Emka circulated just a minute or so apart, being 14th and 15th but then Tullius stopped with a misfire, necessitating a change of the Lucas/Micos management system which took 10 minutes. Two hours later it was back with the same problem plus it was using an excessive amount of fuel and once again the electronic brain was replaced, the whole business taking 30 minutes. By now the car was 15th but it was a V11 due to valve failure (contemporary reports suggest that a piston was rammed into the cylinder head) but the team would not give up. Having isolated the cylinder the XJR-5 struggled on to finish 13th, two places behind its well-matched British rival, the Emka. The winning Porsche of Ludwig/Barilla/Winter was the same car that had won in 1984, with the first works Porsche in third position.

1985 result

13th Bob Tullius/Chip Robinson/Claude Ballot-Lena
    Jaguar XJR-5 (008) 2,736.00 miles (4,402.22km),
    114.00mph (183.43kph).

Both Jaguars had lapped within a fraction of each other (No. 44 3min 36.6sec and No. 40 3min 36.7sec) but they had not been fully competitive due to the aforementioned fuel restrictions and associated problems. Nevertheless the desire to carry on was alive and well, but the status quo was about to change.

Despite running on only 11 cylinders, Tullius/Robinson/ Ballot-Lena brought home 008 to 13th place, followed here by two of the omnipresent Porsches. (LAT Photographic)

Chapter 17

1986 – The Scottish are back

Derek Warwick, Jean-Louis Schlesser and Eddie Cheever who drove the No. 51 XJR-6 (286) enjoy the parade lap at Le Mans on 31 May 1986. (Sutton)

Following the Jaguar XJC Group 2 debacle in 1976/77 a great deal of research was undertaken by Jaguar for Group 5 racing, but this petered out due to lack of money and the fact this category was deemed unsuitable. Then, in 1981, well-known Scottish touring car racer and team owner Tom Walkinshaw approached Jaguar to run the XJS in the new FIA Group A Touring Car Championship for 1982. This turned out to be as successful a partnership as the BL/Broadspeed one had been unsuccessful, finishing third in the championship in 1982, second in 1983 and winning in 1984. The XJS was the dominant car in this class and when the Group 44 cars appeared in 1982, Le Mans was never far from Jaguar's thoughts.

In February 1985, Sir William Lyons passed away leaving just a handful of survivors from the halcyon days of the 1950s. This was just months before the real resurgence of Jaguar's racing glories began, and it was a pity he did not live long enough to see it. Originally Jaguar had intended to run a Lee Dykstra-based car, but this was never a serious proposition even though an XJR-5 was painted in dark green and used for publicity purposes in the UK. Tom Walkinshaw had other ideas. In 1985, ex-BRM designer Tony Southgate (see sidebar) began work on the first TWR Jaguar, designated XJR-6. The use of this nomenclature as a continuation naturally upset Bob Tullius who had to call his new car XJR-7, and worse still he was to be eased out of Le Mans, Jaguar preferring him to concentrate on the American scene while TWR took on the World Endurance Championship. In hindsight it might have been better for Jaguar if it had allowed Tullius to continue with his Le Mans bid, there being safety in numbers as well as the positive advantages of diversity. The XJR-7 first competed at Daytona in December 1985 and had the last of its 28 races

there in February 1988, winning a total of three events in that time. There was also an evolution of the basic design that was designated XJR-8, but it was never raced. Southgate's car was completed and tested at Snetterton in June 1985 but did not race until August in the Budweiser 1000 at Mosport in Canada. Two 6.3-litre cars, finished in dark green and emblazoned with a large JAGUAR decal, were third and fifth in practice and one came third after the quicker Martin Brundle car suffered a front wheel bearing failure. At Spa, Brands Hatch and Fuji both cars retired but the season's end produced a second for Thackwell/Nielsen/Lammers. TWR finished joint seventh in the Team Championship and the beginning of what was to become Jaguar's most successful era in racing had begun. (See sidebar.)

Former F1 driver and mover Guy Edwards brokered a sponsorship deal with Gallaher in 1986 that resulted in the cars becoming known as the Silk Cut Jaguar Racing Team. The XJR-6s (now 6.5 litres) developed 690bhp and were entered in all the championship rounds. Pre-season testing was carried out in February at Paul Ricard on the original long circuit. (See sidebar.)

Round one of the Driver's Championship (a separate entity from the Manufacturer's Championship) at Monza for the Supersprint had Schlesser/Brancatelli third on distance but unclassified as it was not running at the finish. The Cheever/Warwick car retired with driveshaft failure, a problem that was to return in future races. Following this disappointing start at Silverstone came the first Jaguar victory in a world championship endurance race since Le Mans 1957 with Derek Warwick/Eddie Cheever beating the works Porsche of Bell/Ickx by two laps. Le Mans was drawing ever nearer and just as Jaguar had experienced all those years ago with the new D-type, expectations were high. Instead of its usual June date Le Mans this year was taking place somewhat earlier than normal being run on the 31 May/1 June. It was the first time in 30 years that an official Jaguar team would race at the Sarthe albeit run by TWR and not the factory. There was also a link with the past as Tom Walkinshaw had briefly driven for the reborn Ecurie Ecosse. The Scots were back. They had three cars and ranged against

them were the massed ranks of 2.6 turbo Porsches led by the works team, numbering 13 in all. Also in contention were two of the 5-litre Mercedes-Benz turbo-powered Sauber C8s plus an assortment of lesser entries that might benefit from retirements.

Brian Redman squinting in the sun before the start alongside Claude Ballot-Lena who drove the Group 44 Jaguars in 1984/85. (Sutton)

The XJR-6

Talking from his home near Silverstone in 2000, Tony Southgate recollected that Tom Walkinshaw had never intended to use the Group 44 car. Tony described it as a nice, low-tech well-developed car, but what was needed was something more advanced. The original XJR-6 was paid for totally by Tom Walkinshaw and in its original form had very flimsy gullwing type doors. It owed much to the stillborn Ford C100 project that Southgate had previously designed and built, but never raced. This first chassis was built at Jon Thompson's Prototypes workshop at Wellingborough, Northants. Walkinshaw's intention was to race in all the championship rounds and not just Le Mans.

For 1986 a redesigned body took care of the door problems, but TWR never expected this car to last the distance at Le Mans. It came in high-drag and low-drag configuration, the latter for Le Mans, although the low-drag long tails made access to the rear of the car very difficult. The gearbox could not cope with the huge torque and sustained extremely high speeds for hour after hour, a weakness that remained throughout the car's life. There were also hub bearing and CV joint failures, and the engine was very susceptible to over revving and dropped valves. Ironically it was fuel pump failure, broken drive shaft and suspension damage caused by a blown tyre that ended the car's Le Mans debut.

The No. 53 XJR-6 (385) of Brancatelli/Percy/Haywood, like its sister cars, was well in the running before a drive shaft failure at around 2am on Sunday morning ended its race, despite Win Percy's efforts to get it back to the pits, where it could have been repaired. (Sutton)

Nissan Motorsports had two of their March-based cars managed by the very capable Keith Greene, but their Japanese drivers would not obey the team manager and constantly tried to overrule his orders.

The rules stipulated just two classes for the sports prototypes, C1 for the larger cars and C2 for the lesser brigade.

Le Mans 1986

The Jaguars lined up thus:

No. 51 Derek Warwick/Eddie Cheever/Jean-Louis Schlesser Jaguar XJR-6 (286).
No. 52 Hans Heyer/Hurley Haywood/Brian Redman Jaguar XJR-6 (186).
No. 53 Gianfranco Brancatelli/Win Percy/Hurley Haywood Jaguar XJR-6 (385).

For Le Mans the cars had a longer tail and lower mounted wing to accommodate the very high speeds reached on the Mulsanne Straight. Once again the diktats of safety had caused some circuit changes and Le Mans now measured 8.406 miles

(13.528km). To accommodate TWR's first 24-hour sports car race, approximately 25 tons of spares accompanied the team which found the garage/pit facilities somewhat inadequate. After some considerable effort by chief truckie Keith Partridge and the pit crew, a fascia board was erected and the pits organised into something more acceptable.

As speeds rose over the years the associated increase in physical effort and stress grew and three drivers per car became the norm, but not compulsory, the third driver being effectively a reserve. It is worth noting that both Redman and Haywood were on loan from Group 44 and that the driver line-up was very talented. Warwick and Cheever were F1 drivers, Schlesser (nephew of the late Jo Schlesser) was a press-on racer with a wide experience including F3 and F2 and he had finished second at Le Mans in 1981. In 1983 he was test driver for Williams and had raced the original XJR-6 in Canada in 1985. Heyer and Brancatelli were top drawer touring car drivers, while the very talented but underrated Win Percy had a very impressive record in touring cars and was good in anything he drove.

There had been a pre-race testing session held in May where Cheever and Schlesser were quickest recording 3min 21.89sec and 3min 22.24sec respectively to head all the Porsches. Actual race qualifying however, was a question of how far

Win Percy

At the time there was a reluctance at TWR to use touring car drivers for the sports car team, but Tom Walkinshaw gave Win Percy the chance to have a go at Paul Ricard. Eventually, when it was his turn, Win found hmself sitting in the car wondering, 'what am I doing here?' Walkinshaw assured Win that if he did not like it there was no disgrace, he could just stop and there would be no harm done. In fact, Percy had never driven a ground-effect racing car before and after just two laps he loved it. Everybody's times were well-matched and Eddie Cheever, who had been watching Win out on the circuit, was very impressed and asked afterwards: 'Where have you been all this time?'

When Win got to Le Mans he found himself driving down the legendary Mulsanne Straight at over 200mph for the first time and trying not to worry about the sustained mega velocities. During this he was aware for several seconds of another car that had drawn level with him, and when he felt comfortable he looked across to see Derek Warwick smiling and waving at him! Talking to Win many years later he remembered that team manager Roger Silman was still not happy about using touring car drivers, but that during the race Tom Walkinshaw was very proud of his saloon car men who were doing so well.

could you turn up the screw for the turbo cars and nobody doubted that Porsche would claim pole. So it turned out, the fastest times, weight and speed on the Mulsanne Straight per marque being:

Jochen Mass Porsche 962C (004). 879kg (1,938lb), 3min 15.99sec, 218mph (351kph).

Hans Heyer, Hurley Haywood and Brian Redman shared this XJR-6 (186). It was the first Jaguar to retire, on lap 53, with fuel pump failure. This shot shows designer Tony Southgate's low-drag long-tail to good effect. (Sutton)

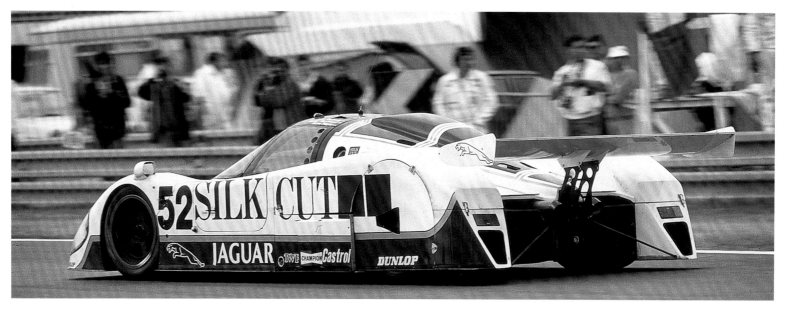

Eddie Cheever Jaguar XJR-6 (286). 871kg (1,920lb)), 3min 21.60sec, 221mph (356kph) (Heyer 3min 24.95sec, 221mph/356kph, Brancatelli 3min 29.24sec, 218mph/351kph). Christian Danner Sauber-Mercedes C8 877kg (1,934lb), 3min 26.69sec, 207mph (333kph).

The Jaguars lined up fifth, seventh and 14th and they were much lighter than their Group 44 IMSA spec predecessors. Highest recorded speed of all on Mulsanne was 232mph (373kph) by one of the Joest Porsches, an older 956 version. It is worth mentioning again that the official recorded speeds were not necessarily the highest and Tony Southgate reckoned the Jaguars were reaching 230mph. The track had been very slightly revised for this year and should have been faster but in reality speeds were down from 1985. Porsche had the advantage of using special 3-litre qualifying engines, so race pace would be more realistic to the benefit of the Jaguars.

Jaguar attracted a very large contingent of

A frantic night pit stop. Note the 'vent' man on the far side of the Jaguar as it is refuelled. It was the failure of this procedure which caused Win Percy's car to suffer a split monocoque. (Sutton)

British fans for the 1986 Le Mans, many of them falling foul of the *gendarmerie* en route who indulged in savage on-the-spot speeding fines. They were very much in evidence amongst the huge crowds opposite the pits and elsewhere around the circuit. From the start Klaus Ludwig led away in the Joest Porsche ahead of the works cars but by the end of the Mulsanne Straight Warwick had got the Jaguar into second spot. Warwick held on for three laps before Stuck and Wollek passed him in the factory 962Cs, but the

Saubers were already in the wars. Pescarolo stopped with a holed oil cooler and spent a long time getting back to the pits, while team-mate Nielsen pitted on lap 10 with handling problems. The bigger cars managed approximately 45 minutes between fuel stops, so race order see-sawed back and forth as they stopped to replenish their tanks. During the second hour the Porsches established themselves in the leading positions but all the Jaguars were running strongly in fourth, fifth and seventh positions, led by the No. 51 car.

The Warwick/Schlesser/Cheever XJR-6 races on into the night. It lasted the longest of the three Jaguars and ultimately retired with suspension damage caused by a blown tyre on Sunday morning. (Sutton)

Win Percy suffers a fuelling problem

The ever friendly and modest Win Percy recollected that prior to his retirement with drive shaft failure at 2am he had been in the pits refuelling. As he sat in the car he received a tremendous blow in the back that nearly winded him and caused him to shout out. When it happened a second time he wanted to get out but was told to stay put. Then, with refuelling complete, Tom Walkinshaw waved him back into the race angrily, only to be contacted on the radio by his pit crew to ask him if everything was OK. Yes it was he replied, and then they radioed him again and again, so Win asked what the problem was as the car felt fine. They did not say anything other than they would talk about it later. Some time afterwards the drive shaft failure occurred ending the car's race despite Win's efforts to bodge it so it could be driven back to the pits. Then the racing was stopped due to poor Jo Gartner's fatal accident on Mulsanne.

(Earlier in the night Percy had been duelling with Gartner, the two of them taking it in turns to slipstream each other. He noticed that if he sat directly behind the German car at over 200mph/322kph a cushion of air stopped him from getting too close, but if he pulled out even slightly he could then go by without too much effort.)

Still puzzling over what had caused the mystery thumps in the back he discovered that during refuelling, the man on the other side who vented the surplus air from the tank during refuelling, had not been connected up to the release valve properly. The two painful blows were caused by the tank expanding under pressure while refuelling and too much fuel had gone in (118 litres instead of 100). The tank had been overfilled and the monocoque had split directly behind Win's back (he was sitting directly on the tub without a seat), hence the blows! They could not risk a fire by trying to extract the surplus and instead, sent him back into the race to quickly use up the fuel. No wonder Walkinshaw was so agitated!

This promising state of affairs was not to last however for when Heyer stopped at Indianapolis with a suspected fuel pump failure the car was out on lap 53.

With night falling the three leading Porsches led by a lap from the two remaining Jaguars and the rest of the field. Both Saubers were now gone and only Porsche or Jaguar could win this race, the Germans having a large numeric advantage despite losing several of their cars. Schlesser was leading Brancatelli by 54 seconds when he took to an escape road briefly, allowing the sister car to close up. By midnight No. 53 was running fourth while the lead Jaguar had fallen to sixth after both cars had been delayed by

battery and headlight problems respectively. At around about 2am, Win Percy suffered a driveshaft failure and, despite all his efforts to effect a temporary repair out on the circuit, the car was stranded and that was two Jaguars out. (See sidebar.) Just after 3pm, Mike Wilds in the C2 class Ecosse spun on oil at the Porsche Curves and was then hit by the third-placed Porsche of Jochen Mass who had also lost it. Exit another Porsche. Disaster then struck when Jo Gartner crashed on Mulsanne and his Porsche caught fire which brought out the pace car for over an hour. Poor Gartner had been killed. When the leading Porsche (the incredibly fast privately entered Joest 956 that had won in 1984 and 1985) retired at around half distance the surviving Jaguar was up to second place, albeit eight laps adrift of the leader.

The status quo was maintained until 8.35am when, after 239 laps, Schlesser had his right rear tyre blow out on Mulsanne which comprehensively damaged the suspension and rear bodywork. Schlesser briefly left the road, but despite taking 10 minutes to nurse the Jaguar back to the pits, the rear suspension pulled itself apart. Thus ended an impressive Le Mans debut for the new Jaguars, and before they left TWR crewman Keith Partridge sprayed a message on the wall for the fans that read: 'Thanks for coming, we'll be back.' So Porsche won (Stuck/Bell/Holbert) as was to be expected, but at last there was some serious opposition to the all-conquering German marque. Ludwig had set fastest lap at 3min 23.3sec but Cheever had been in the 3min 26/27sec bracket, so the Jags were well on the pace.

For TWR the remainder of 1986 brought mixed results. They finished second and third at the Nuremberg Supersprint, fourth and sixth at the Brands Hatch 1,000km, third at the Jarama Supersprint, two DNFs and one DNS at the Nürburgring 1,000km, second and fifth at the Spa-Francorchamps 1,000km and second at the Fuji 1,000km. So, TWR was joint third in the Team Championship and Jaguar were second highest manufacturer. Derek Warwick and Eddie Cheever were third and fifth in the driver standings.

Chapter 18

1987 – Triumph and failure

Development continued in 1987 with the TWR XJR-6 evolving into the XJR-8, concentrating on reliability and weight. Engine size had increased to 6,995cc giving 720bhp with overall weight at scrutineering reduced to the regulation minimum of 850kg (1,874lb). (The original 1971 production engine had given 272bhp from 5.3 litres.) Including raising the engines at the rear to reduce driveshaft angles, quick release fuel pumps, redesigned starter motors, tyre temperature sensors and some minor bodywork changes, 64 modifications had been made. The new cars were completed in February followed by an extensive testing programme at the Paul Ricard circuit in France. Another engine variation was tried later in the year using a four-cam head and, although it was more powerful (about 750bhp), the extra weight and complexity made the car slower in testing at Silverstone.

Round one of the World Sports Prototype Championship was the Jarama Supersprint on 22 March 1987 and it was duly won by the TWR XJR-8 of Lammers/Watson with Cheever/Boesel third. One week later, at the Jerez 1,000km, Cheever/Boesel triumphed but the other Jaguar retired. Off to Monza in April and Lammers/Watson beat the works Porsche with the other car fourth but not classified as it was off the road. The 100 per cent record of victories continued at Silverstone in May where Cheever/Boesel led home Lammers/Watson for TWR's first 1, 2 in the series. A third car for Brundle/Nielsen was running third until a collision with a Porsche caused its retirement. One week

after this an official test session was held at Le Mans and the Jaguars were quickest (Boesel) with 3min 24.38sec and team-mate Lammers third split by Wollek's Porsche with the third XJR-8 fifth. There was now a whole month before the next round at Le Mans on 13/14 June.

If expectations had been high in previous years, then they were off the graph following TWR's domination of the 1987 season thus far. Furthermore it was 30 years since the Ecurie

Pretty girls and cigarette advertising. How non-pc! Silk Cut's presence on the Jaguars was well promoted elsewhere, but thanks to British television's total apathy toward sports car racing and TWR's great success, the team did not receive the public acclaim and kudos in its own country that it deserved. (Sutton)

Ecosse Jaguars had led home a 1, 2, 3, 4, 6 at the Sarthe. For 1987 TWR faced not only the massed ranks of Porsches, as ever, but also a much more effective Sauber-Mercedes team using their new C9. The Japanese continued their fascination for Le Mans with both Nissan and Toyota joining the incredibly noisy rotary-engined Mazdas, but their day was yet to come. TWR ran three cars (see sidebar) designated XJR-8LM (for Le Mans) and the driver/car combinations were:

No. 4 Eddie Cheever/Raul Boesel/Jan Lammers Jaguar XJR-8LM (387).
No. 5 Jan Lammers/John Watson/Win Percy Jaguar XJR-8LM (286).
No. 6 Martin Brundle/John Nielsen Jaguar XJR-8LM (186).

For 1987, Tony Southgate had managed to develop a conventional short tail that was just as effective and saved all the complexities and inconvenience of the 1986 long-tail design. The Dunlop tyres were now radial, and there were better and stronger hub bearings and CV joints.

Once again the circuit had changed, a lap now covering 8.410 miles (13.535km). A new chicane had been added at the Dunlop Curve that added four to five seconds per lap for a typical C1 car; essentially the track was becoming slower as the years progressed in an attempt to curb the terrifyingly high speeds. TWR's drivers were a mixed bunch of F1 and ex-F1 with a couple of sports car chargers for good measure. The TWR newcomers for Le Mans were American Eddie Cheever who had driven for many F1 teams (Theodore, Osella, Tyrrell, Ligier, Renault, Alfa Romeo, and by 1987, had arrived at Arrows), his potential largely wasted on unreliable or uncompetitive cars. Dutchman Jan Lammers was another whose F1 career was compromised by mediocre machinery, while Martin Brundle had spent three years at Tyrrell before joining the West Zakspeed team, another F1 graveyard for any driver's F1 ambitions. All three were well matched in terms of speed with Brundle having just a slight edge. Raul Boesel, who had joined the team almost by chance, had left F1 in 1984 and taken up Indy car racing. His subsequent successes with TWR greatly enhanced his reputation. Dane John Nielsen was normally Brundle's partner and his varied background included karts, Danish Formula Ford (1975 champion), European Super Vee (champion 1979/80/81), German F3 (champion 1983), European F3 (championship runner-up 1984) and F3000 (1985–87). Third drivers were effectively reserves and not always used in the race.

Twelve Porsche 962 derivatives appeared, the three works cars having bigger, 3-litre engines, but one of these crashed in practice and did not start. Additionally there was a French-entered Cougar with Porsche power that was a potential winner, so Porsche had strength in numbers once again. The Saubers were fast, but had only two works cars, and although the Nissans were still not quick enough, the two Toyota Team Toms had more speed as well as being closely matched. Also in the running were the two French WM-Peugeots that had very high top speeds but suspect durability. Unsurprisingly the two works Porsches headed the grid. Best

qualifying times plus speed on Mulsanne for each marque were as follows:

Bob Wollek Porsche 962C (008) 3min 21.09sec 220mph (354kph).
Eddie Cheever Jaguar XJR-8LM (387) 3min 24.36sec, 219mph (352kph), (Brundle 3min 24.68sec, 219mph/352kph, Lammers 3min 24.98sec, 220mph/354kph).
Pierre-Henri Raphanel Cougar-Porsche C20 (01) 3min 26.21sec, 223mph (359kph).
Johnny Dumfries Sauber-Mercedes C9 (02) 3min 26.58sec, 214mph (344kph).
Jean-Daniel Roulet WM-Peugeot P86 3min 33.92sec, 227mph (365kph). (Dorchy's newer P87 was timed at 238mph/383kph!)
Alan Jones Toyota 87C Dome (003) 3min 34.45sec, 198mph (319kph).

All three Jaguars qualified within 0.62 of a second of each other in third, fourth and fifth positions just as team manager Roger Silman had predicted.

Opposite above: TWR supremo Tom Walkinshaw is not giving anything away as he listens to the enemy! Although TWR failed to win Le Mans in 1987 they won all the other championship rounds that year and, of course, the championship itself. (Sutton)

Opposite below: John Watson is trying to convey some esoteric point to an unconvinced Tony Southgate, designer of the TWR Jaguars. Note Watson's creased face that is bearing the marks of his recently removed helmet. (Sutton)

After various dramas and travails the Cheever/Boesel/Lammers XJR-8 (387) finished fifth, the only Jaguar to survive at Le Mans 1987. (LAT Photographic)

The true maximum velocity of the Jaguars was estimated to be 240mph. Otherwise the pace of the little Toyotas was notable given their relative lack of straightline speed.

Le Mans had returned to its traditional 4pm start but constant drizzle and an extra pace lap to check conditions meant that it was just past 4.5pm before the race began. Many cars were on wet rubber but now the rain passed on and the track started drying. The two works Porsches completed lap one ahead of Brundle while Lammers lost fourth place to a hard-charging Dumfries in the Sauber C9. The leading trio had started on intermediate rubber that suited the conditions perfectly but Porsche were in for a nasty shock. The fuel as supplied by the organisers was not compatible with the Bosch Motronic control system that these cars used and within seven laps three of the privately entered 962s were out followed a short while later by Mass's works machine. After the first three had stopped with piston failure, each car was recalled to the pits to have its ignition retarded by 1.5°, but they were too late to save Mass. Echoes of 3-litre D-types 29 years on.

This left Stuck embroiled in a battle with Brundle which continued when Bell and Nielsen took over, the two cars being nose to tail with the Jaguar leading the Porsche. During this early stage and in the chaos of everybody stopping to refuel for the second time the Jaguars briefly ran 1, 2 and 3 to the joy of the assembled Brits. At 8pm Holbert now led in the 962C from the three Jaguars and the privately run BLR/Liqui Moly Porsche. Sadly for Jaguar this promising state of affairs could not last and Cheever pitted with first a puncture and then a broken throttle linkage that lost the XJR-8LM two laps. Then the rain returned and as night fell both Saubers went out and it was two Jaguars versus two works and one privately entered Porsche. Gradually Cheever reeled in the Liqui Moly 962C which was running third, but he was spared the trouble when that car caught fire at Mulsanne Corner and was burnt out. Luckily driver James Weaver escaped unharmed. As a result the race was run under a yellow flag for 30 minutes while the mess was cleared up. Meanwhile the leading Stuck/Bell/Holbert Porsche had finally pulled out enough of a gap so that it did not lose its lead during refuelling.

With nine hours gone the Jaguars were occupying second, third and fourth positions but the Lammers/Watson/Percy car lost its rear bodywork on Mulsanne which was retrieved and had to pit, losing third place to the Cheever/Boesel car. Then third driver Win Percy took over and had a huge accident when a tyre failed on the Mulsanne kink at over 200mph (322kph). The ensuing smash left just the front of the car including the cockpit relatively intact but the doors, most of the engine, rear suspension, wheels and gearbox were all gone. Win was completely unharmed and quite sanguine

about it all, but Tom Walkinshaw was considerably shaken. (See sidebar.) As a precaution the remaining Jaguars had their radial tyres switched back to the Dunlop crossplies.

Despite this, Jaguar was running 2, 3 and the leading Porsche looked to be within reach again although Boesel had caused slight frontal damage sliding off at Arnage which meant a pit stop for repairs. Then, more drama as Nielsen having taken over from Brundle, returned to the pits with a vibration problem which required two stops and a complete change of tyres to cure it. Worse still the Cheever car had a holed gearbox, Eddie apparently having hooked reverse and this was plugged and

Opposite: Jan Lammers driving 286 before its dramatic Mulsanne accident caused by tyre failure after Win Percy had replaced John Watson. (LAT Photographic)

Survival cell. Tony Southgate's design undoubtedly saved Win Percy's life after the car crashed at over 200mph (322kph) on the Mulsanne Straight after a tyre failure. This is the tub of 286 back at the TWR factory. (Win Percy)

Walkinshaw's premonition

When confirming the details for Le Mans 1987 Tom Walkinshaw had told Win Percy that he would be qualifying but probably not racing. This was not good news but Walkinshaw declined to discuss it until after the race. Win was sharing his car with Jan Lammers and John Watson and during Saturday night Lammers did a double stint because Watson was off the pace and did not want to drive in the dark. So Win was woken up and told to take over from the Dutchman at the next stop. When the time came Percy sat in the Jaguar for a very long time while they sorted out a brake pad problem and eventually got going, feeling quite nervous.

That year's cars had tyre sensors which had worked perfectly in testing, giving an onboard flashing warning if tyre temperature became too high. However after many hours of high speed racing they had become covered in rubber debris and muck and were no longer functioning properly. A marshall had seen sparks coming from the tail of Win's car as he exited Tertre Rouge on to the Mulsanne Straight. Travelling at over 200mph (322kph) and just 500 metres to the kink, the Jaguar began to vibrate and at 300 metres a rear tyre exploded. From inside the car Win only had time to register that the car was becoming airborne from the rear and thinking 'you're going flying Win' and he then let go of the wheel into a tuck position and closed his eyes briefly. When he opened them all he could see was the night sky, then some tree tops! The first impact was massive, the second less so and miracuously the car gradually shed its speed, sliding down the road on its side, wearing a hole in Win's helmet. 'I could feel my head getting hot with the friction', he told me in 2000. When the car came to a halt most of the rear and much else was gone including the driver's door, leaving the centre section with Win still strapped to it.

Some Toyota team personnel who had been hiding in the trees trackside gave Win a lift back to the pits, where a white-faced Tom Walkinshaw was at pains to make sure that Win was really uninjured. In fact Percy was completely unharmed and apart from his helmet was unmarked bar a small black mark on his overalls where his knee had been wedged against the underside of the dashboard! Later on the remains of the car and tyres were retrieved and immediately the Dunlop tyre technician admitted that a rear tyre had delaminated and failed, tearing off the rear bodywork that caused the crash. The tub of the car was still intact, a testament to its strength and durability and Tony Southgate told the author that it could still have been used with some repairs to its corners. Had Win been in anything else he would have died and the grateful driver wrote a letter of thanks to the designer for saving his life, along with the triple barrier Armco. (In 1986 there had only been two layers where Gartner was killed.)

As for Tom Walkinshaw's ghost like palour, it transpired that before Le Mans he had experienced a premonition that one of his drivers was going to die at the race. This explained his reluctance to let Win drive as he was not otherwise a regular on the sports car team.

the car sent on its way again (see sidebar).

Now with the typical Le Mans early morning mist clearing TWR suffered another blow as the Brundle/Nielsen car retired with a cracked cylinder head after 16 hours. Then Cheever was back, the rear of the car trailing flames; oil weeping from the gearbox had ignited. Amazingly the TWR mechanics changed the gearset in 20 minutes! Just before 9am a crash at Indianapolis brought out the pace car and everybody trailed around for an hour while the barriers were repaired. The gremlins had really got their teeth into Jaguar and within a lap of the restart Boesel was stopped on the Mulsanne Straight with no fuel pressure. His radio would not function at this part of the circuit, being in a blind spot, but he switched to the auxilliary fuel system and set off only to lose the rear bodywork that had not been properly secured! A new one was fitted at the pits but after Cheever took over the car stopped again on Mulsanne. Once more the recalcitrant machine was coaxed back to the pits for repairs and then with less than two hours to go a suspension strut had to be replaced. Finally the race was over and the Jaguar came home fifth, bloody but unbowed, and those damn Porsches won again, Derek Bell scoring his fifth Le Mans victory.

1987 results

1st Hans-Joachim Stuck/Derek Bell/Al Holbert Porsche 962C (006) 355 laps, 2,977.477 miles (4,791.777km), 124.062mph (199.657kph).
2nd Jurgen Laessig/Pierre Yver/Bernard de Dryver Porsche 962C (130) 335 laps.
3rd Pierre-Henri Raphanel/Hervé Regout/Yves Courage Cougar-Porsche C20 (01) 332 laps.
4th George Fouche/Franz Konrad/Wayne Taylor Porsche 962C (118) 327 laps.
5th Eddie Cheever/Raul Boesel/Jan Lammers Jaguar XJR-8LM (387) 325 laps, 2,730.91 miles (4,394.03km), 113.79mph (183.09kph).

More than anything else Le Mans 1987 proved just how difficult it was to beat Porsche in a 24-hour race. Certainly the TWR Jaguars had proved superior in the shorter events, but the long, increasingly flat out blind that Le Mans had become exposed their relative lack of durability in comparison with their rivals. The German company had been involved in motorsport constantly for 36 years and enjoyed an insuperable advantage in terms of experience and continuity. Their 962C was the latest in a long line of development and had a very reliable and powerful turbocharged engine, even though the chassis was crude by the TWR Jaguar standards. Certainly they were not so strong or safe in the event of a big accident, but they were, odd mishaps apart, virtually bombproof. Of course, they were driven by some of the world's greatest endurance racers, a formidable combination of speed allied to experience. Additionally the works cars were backed up by a large and very competitive 'customer' second string, some of whom were nearly as fast as the factory cars.

The rest of TWR's season proved the point with a first and third at the Brands Hatch 1,000km, a

Overheated starter motors

Amongst the problems of running a very big and relatively heavy V12 engine at racing speeds for hour after hour is heat soak. Kevin Lee, then chief mechanic, explained that the cars would be reluctant to restart after stopping due to overheated starter motors. To overcome this a 6in (150mm) hole was cut in the bodywork adjacent to the offending unit and sprayed with fire extinguisher foam to cool it down. This worked quite well, but it also caused a degree of white smoke as the car left the pits, misleading onlookers into believing that the engine was about to fail.

first at the Nürburgring 1,000km and a brace of 1, 2 victories at the Spa and Fuji 1,000km races. TWR Silk Cut Jaguar were the World Sports Prototype Champions and Raul Boesel was Champion Driver. So Jaguar had won every round of the championship except the one they really wanted above all else, but 1988 would take care of that.

The long-tail configuration was dropped in 1987 as illustrated here by the Brundle/Nielsen XJR-8 (186) which retired with a cracked cylinder head at around 8am on Sunday morning. (LAT Photographic)

Chapter 19

1988 – At long last

British fans at Le Mans 1988
make their presence felt and
this time they really had
something to celebrate.
(Sutton)

The year began with an announcement by the Daimler-Benz board at Stuttgart on 12 January formally confirming their official support for Peter Sauber's Group C team and in true Mercedes fashion they won the first

British fans at Le Mans 1988 make their presence felt and this time they really had something to celebrate. (Sutton)

championship round at Jerez. The drivers were Jean-Louis Schlesser (ex-TWR), Mauro Baldi and Jochen Mass. It was a close run thing however because the TWR Jaguar XJR-9 of John Nielsen/Andy Wallace and John Watson finished only 24.51 seconds adrift after over five hours of racing.

For round two at Jarama Jaguar responded with a victory for Eddie Cheever/Martin Brundle but again the margin was slim, just 19.273 seconds, albeit in a shorter race. Sauber however were second with Schlesser/Baldi while the Nielsen/Watson Jaguar was third. Schlesser set fastest lap and TWR had a real fight on their hands, the 5-litre turbocharged Mercedes-Benz-powered Sauber more than a match for the normally aspirated 7-litre Jaguar. The next race at Monza gave TWR another win with Martin Brundle/Eddie Cheever beating Schlesser/Baldi/Mass in the Sauber, this time by a lap after nearly five hours. The home turf at Silverstone in May was yet another triumph for TWR Jaguar and again it was Brundle/Cheever who beat the two Saubers of Schlesser/Mass and Baldi/Weaver, the winning margin a slender 35.61 seconds. So as Le Mans approached TWR Jaguar had won every round bar one, but Sauber was a real threat despite running only two cars. However Le Mans above all else was the race that all the teams wanted to win and the opposition was cranked up a notch or three, Porsche in particular being keen to retain their Sarthe domination.

It was the 56th *Vingt-Quatre Heures du Mans* and

31 years since the last Jaguar victory. The pressure to succeed was extreme after the disappointments of the previous years. This was all relative of course, bearing in mind that they had won both the manufacturers and drivers titles in 1987, but Le Mans had remained elusive. Taking a leaf out of Porsche's book, TWR were seeking safety in numbers running five cars with two separate pit crews, numbers 1, 2 and 3 by the regular team and numbers 21 and 22 by the TWR IMSA team. There were three drivers per car excepting their quickest which was driven by Martin Brundle and John Nielsen. All the cars were 'sprint' chassis adapted to LM specification, fitted with rear wheel covers, small wings behind the rear wheels, the engine now angled differently to lower the centre of gravity and a new underbody. Tyre size was down from 19-inch in 1987 to 17-inch.

TWR entered the five XJR-9LMs with 14 drivers, split into two teams, the European team was overseen by Roger Silman, and they were:

No. 1 Martin Brundle/John Nielsen XJR-9LM-588 896kg (1,976lb). (Alistair McQueen)

No. 2 Jan Lammers/Johnny Dumfries/Andy Wallace XJR-9LM-488 894kg (1,971lb). (Eddie Hinckley)

No. 3 Raul Boesel/John Watson/Henri Pescarolo XJR-9LM-287 913kg (2,103lb). (Ken Page)

The IMSA crews were controlled by Tony Dowe and they were:

No. 21 Danny Sullivan/Davy Jones/Price Cobb XJR-9LM-186 917kg (2,022lb). (Ian Reed)

No. 22 Derek Daly/Larry Perkins/Kevin Cogan XJR-9LM-188 914kg (2,015lb). (Dave Benbow)

This was a massive undertaking with a mountain of spares, tools and assorted equipment (see sidebar). On the driver front there were some new faces. Ex-Williams F1 and Le Mans veteran Henri Pescarolo, ex-Lotus F1 man Johnny Dumfries, sports car specialist Andy Wallace, ex-Tyrrell F1 racer Derek Daly and three Americans and one Australian – all successful regulars on the American scene.

Against them were ranged 11 Porsches 962Cs: three works cars (Stuck/Ludwig/Bell, Wollek/Schuppan/van der Merwe and Mario Andretti/Mike Andretti/John Andretti), two each from Brun

The fastest Jaguar in practice of Brundle/Nielsen (588) was hobbled by handling problems during the race but ultimately retired at 9am on Sunday morning with cylinder head failure caused by overheating due to a holed radiator. John Nielsen is rather too close for comfort to Sigala's Porsche 962C early in the race. (LAT Photographic)

Five cars and 14 drivers

Twelve years later I visited the Arrows Grand Prix base near Witney in Oxfordshire where Kevin Lee (chief mechanic until 1989), Jeff Wilson (No. 1 mechanic on No. 1 car and then chief mechanic in 1990) and Keith Partridge (chief truckie) recalled their Le Mans experiences.

They explained the sheer scale of the operation needed to cope with five cars and 14 drivers, each of whom had their own separate caravan for rest periods between driving stints. Each one had to be shepherded through the paperwork (licences, medicals etc.), and each had to qualify their respective car. In all, over 120 people constituted the team, movements and associated personnel necessary for the race, including accommodation, catering and transportation.

During the race, running five cars meant that one of them was stopping every 10 minutes, so rest was not possible. Just how physical this had become for all concerned can be judged by the 14lb (6kg) in body weight that Andy Wallace lost during the 1988 race! The cars did not have power steering and the brake pad material was relatively hard for longevity, so strength and stamina were required. Some drivers collapsed after their stints, while others, like John Nielsen, were relatively unaffected.

As the race approached its final stages, everything that was no longer needed had to be removed, otherwise it would disappear into the invading crowds. Keith Partridge recalled seeing a whole nose cone bobbing through the masses one year, but this was retrieved. Pit security was always a problem.

Motorsport (Lechner/Hunkeler/Reuter and Sigala/Pareja/Schaefer), Joest Racing (Hobbs/Theys/Konrad and Dickens/Jelinski/'Winter') and Kremer (Giacomelli/Okada/Takahashi and Nissen/Fouche/Grohs), and one from Vern Schuppan, who was actually driving one of the works cars, (Redman/Jarier/Elgh) and finally the Primagaz/Obermaier entry (Wood/Yver/Laessig). The Porsche AG machines had the latest Bosch Motronics MP1.7 management system which gave them at least 50bhp advantage and better fuel consumption over the privately entered machines. Just as formidable on paper and winners of the season's opening round were the two works Sauber-Mercedes C9-88s for Acheson/Niedwiedz and Mass/Baldi/Weaver, but this was to be a let down as overheating rear tyres, possibly exacerbated by the new, abrasive road surface caused a blowout on the Mulsanne Straight during first practice. The ensuing moments conducted at 224mph (360kph) fortunately came under the control of Klaus Niedzwiedz, but after due consideration and bearing in mind similar tyre failures during testing at Monza, Sauber decided to withdraw. There was nothing left of the Michelin tyre to examine afterwards but the on-board telemetry told the story and Mercedes decided to withdraw, a move which was regretted by Porsche and Jaguar but widely applauded. Eleven years later they would adopt a different stance, fortunately escaping the consequences of aerodynamic problems. In 1988, was the memory of the 1955 catastrophe still potent enough to give them pause for thought?

The rest of the 48-car field were not potential winners except by default, although there were some promising machines amongst them. Japanese honour was upheld by the Toyota Team Toms Toyota 88Cs and the Nismo Nissan R88Cs, the Toyotas proving the more rapid. Nismo used Win Percy and Mike Wilds in one of their cars while Toyota fielded Tiff Needell and Geoff Lees in each of their entries. The Toyotas were very effective in practice with the Lees/Sekiya/Hoshino machine ninth fastest and the sister Barilla/Ogawa/Needell entry 11th quickest. The French Cougar-Porsche and WM/Secateva cars promised some excitement, the latter pulling 253mph (407kph) on the

Mulsanne Straight with its special low drag bodywork, but they were not especially fast over the whole lap. Practice seemed to indicate that Porsche had the edge with the works cars in the top three positions and the leading Jaguar in fourth spot. Confusingly the third Porsche was driven by father and son Mario and Mike Andretti with Mario's nephew John Andretti, which should give future historians some trouble! Father was the quickest of the family trio. However, Jaguar had been suffering some tyre and handling troubles of their own during qualifying and had set their times with less than perfect set-ups. A combination of the aforementioned new abrasive road surface and the ride height was causing the tyres to overheat on the Mulsanne Straight where velocities were exceeding 230mph (370kph)! This then caused handling problems on the twisty bits. Their best lap, by Martin Brundle, was achieved in near dark conditions despite having to cope with slower traffic. After this the drivers, engineers and designer Tony Southgate discussed the problems and adjusted ride heights, camber angles and spring rates which improved the balance and handling, although the fuel mixture was not yet dialled in properly.

The top qualifiers for each make were as follows:

Hans-Joachim Stuck Porsche 962C (010) 3min 15.64sec.
Martin Brundle Jaguar XJR9-LM (588) 3min 21.78s (Lammers 3min 23.74sec, Sullivan 3min 25.42sec, Daly 3min 26.78sec and Boesel 3min 27.33sec).
Geoff Lees Toyota 88C Dome (008) 3min 25.39sec.

Both Saubers had lapped in the 3min 30sec bracket before their withdrawal.

A vast gathering of over 200,000 spectators greeted the assembled grid at 3pm on Saturday, 11 June 1988, including thousands of British supporters hoping for a Jaguar victory. The Brits booed the German Porsches and the Germans booed the British Jaguars. The night before in true British fashion there had been some trouble with the French police which was sorted out by the use of CS gas. Aahh! *Entente Cordiale*! After all the

Raul Boesel, John Watson and veteran F1 and sports car racer Henri Pescarolo drove chassis 287 but it retired with transmission problems late on Saturday night. (LAT Photographic)

Opposite: All the drama and pent up emotion of a pit stop is evident as the winning Jaguar XJR-9LM (488) of Lammers/ Dumfries/ Warwick comes in. Note the overhead gantry with the TWR sign and the 'vent' man for clearing excess fuel, in white helmet and blue gloves. (LAT Photographic)

One of the two IMSA-spec XJR-9LMs of Sullivan/Jones/Cobb (186) that finally finished 16th after many problems. (LAT Photographic)

razzamatazz, the parade of near-naked Hawaiian Tropic girls, the playing of numerous national anthems and the arrival of many parachutists, the time had come. It was the practice to contact the drivers via the radio link at the start and when TWR's pit crew radioed Jan Lammers his response was: 'I'm out at the moment, please leave a message and I will contact you on my return'!

Hans Stuck assumed command for Porsche as the cars crossed the line from their rolling start, but by Mulsanne Corner Jan Lammers had his XJR9 up to third which quickly became second at Indianapolis. The end of lap one and Stuck swept past in the lead, Lammers still second with Bob Wollek and Mario Andretti in the other works Porsches right on his tail. Martin Brundle meanwhile was further back in the ruck and would quickly discover that his car was not handling very well, a consequence of removing the rear anti-roll bar, which the other cars retained. As already mentioned practice set-up had been disrupted by overheating tyres which had compromised handling and also fuel consumption rates. In an attempt to gain advantage Brundle and Nielsen had opted for a different set-up and now their car

was not fast enough on the Mulsanne Straight which meant it was being driven harder and in turn used more fuel. Not a good start for the team's number one pairing. However Jan Lammers was more than compensating and duly took the lead on lap six, but it was a tenuous one as he was relentlessly pursued by Stuck and Wollek. Andretti ran fourth ahead of Brundle while John Watson was dicing with the Joest Porsche of Stanley Dickens for sixth place and the remaining Jaguars of Sullivan and Daly followed on.

The first pit stops loomed and John Watson handed over his XJR9 to Raul Boesel followed by the other Jaguars, but the works Porsches stayed out rather longer. Then all three came in together, causing consternation in the ranks! When the dust settled it was seen that Johnny Dumfries had assumed the lead in the Lammers car from Stuck (still driving) and Vern Schuppan (replacing Wollek), and the status quo was restored. As the second stops fell due the works Porsches once again went further on their fuel, which briefly gave them 1, 2, 3 before they stopped in turn, handing the lead back to Dumfries. It was not all roses however for TWR as John Nielsen had spun the ill-handling Jaguar at Indianapolis, losing nearly two laps. Further drama was supplied by the fastest Porsche, now driven by Klaus Ludwig, almost running out of fuel having done one lap too many between stops. He barely coaxed it back to the pits, losing two laps in the process. Thus the leading Jaguar now had a breathing space, the second Porsche of Wollek having dropped back and the Andretti car was third but being caught by Boesel and Sullivan in their Jaguars. These five were the only cars on the same lap. Running sixth was the quicker Joest Porsche with the other two XJR9s seventh and eighth with Brundle/Nielsen rapidly making up lost ground.

At 7pm Wollek, who had speeded up and taken advantage of the Porsche's superior fuel consumption, had handed over to Vern Schuppan in the lead but the Australian was soon passed by Lammers (back in the Jaguar) and Mario Andretti. When the veteran American pitted Lammers and

Schuppan had a real go, the lead swapping to and fro, changing three times in one lap! Shortly afterwards a minor collision between the Lammers Jaguar and the Brun Porsche of Pareja caused the TWR car to be delayed by a minute or so while its tail was repaired. Consequently the leading Porsche, now driven by Sarel van der Merwe, consolidated its position ahead of the field. Later on, having run their car relatively gently, the Andrettis had fuel to spare and speeded up to briefly take the lead, but as darkness approached their car dropped back to third. Andy Wallace was now hammering along in the Lammers car and did a double stint stopping at 10pm. An hour later Lammers had closed to within half a minute of Wollek, but at 11.20pm TWR lost the Boesel car with transmission failure near Indianapolis. So far the race had been see-sawing back and forth between Jaguar and Porsche, and this was the first factory car to retire. Just before midnight Jaguar were in the lead again with the

This overhead view of the Daly/Perkins/Cogan IMSA car (188) shows the large central roof vent and the covered rear wheels. It finished in fourth place. (Sutton)

The filthy, bug-spattered winning car races on into the gloom and Porsche are beaten at last. (LAT Photographic)

Lammers/Dumfries/Wallace car while the Brundle/Nielsen Jaguar and Stuck/Bell/Ludwig Porsche were continuing their relentless climb back to the front. However more disappointment struck TWR when the Sullivan/Jones/Cobb XJR9 which had been third, developed a serious gearbox problem that delayed it sufficiently to end all hopes of a podium finish.

At the halfway mark Stuck had unlapped himself but Porsche had suffered their first major setback as the Wollek car was retired after a long stop with intercooler water pump failure. The constant grand prix pace had taken its toll. Nevertheless the quickest Porsche was still reeling in the leaders with Klaus Ludwig closing to within 25 seconds of the Jaguar during a double stint at the wheel. Also still closing in was the Brundle/Nielsen Jaguar in third while the Daly/Perkins/Cogan car had risen to fifth by 5am, with the Joest Porsche of Dickens/Jelinski/ 'Winter' splitting them. At this time the remaining American Jaguar was many, many laps behind, in 24th place. Porsche's number one car continued to creep up on the leading Jaguar, but the German team was concerned that this car might suffer a similar problem to the Wollek/Schuppan/van der Merwe machine. Briefly as dawn broke and pit stops disrupted the order,

Stuck led as Andy Wallace pitted the leading Jaguar, but normal service was resumed as Stuck made his scheduled stop. British hearts fluttered however when Lammers suddenly pulled in with a split windscreen at 6.35am which required replacing. Porsche then took the lead but their moment of glory was just that as it was decided to change the intercooler water pump which cost the Stuck/Bell/Ludwig car seven minutes. Jaguar were now back in front but then just before 9am the Brundle/Nielsen XJR9 was out. A small hole in the radiator caused by a stone led to water loss and overheating and adding much needed fluid caused the head to split. A sad end to a fine drive in a difficult car.

With less than six hours to go the Lammers/ Dumfries/Wallace Jaguar led the Stuck/Bell/ Ludwig Porsche and the weather which up to now had been dry, decided to dampen things down a bit. At first Stuck closed in on the Jaguar, but then on a part-dry part-wet track, which suited neither slicks nor intermediates, the gap stabilised. With five hours to go the Jaguar's lead was just 100 seconds, and the two oponents were still racing as fast as they dared. Behind this the Joest Porsche and the Daly/Cogan/Perkins Jaguar were third and fourth with the second Joest Porsche of

Hobbs/Theys/Konrad leading the crippled Andretti Porsche in sixth. This car had been running at a reduced pace since midnight and had suffered an intercooler problem which resulted in part of the pump being replaced. The other TWR Jaguar had now reached 16th which was where it finished. There was more excitement with two hours to go as Bell stopped the Porsche with fuel pump maladies dropping a lap, but these were quickly sorted out and Klaus Ludwig took over and soon unlapped himself. With both cars needing fuel stops the gap grew and reduced as the end approached, and finally after 24 hours and 31 years Jaguar had won Le Mans again by just 2min 36.85sec from the works Porsche. It was a fantastic race run almost flat out from the start and the Jaguar had beaten its great German rival fair and square. The Joest Porsches came in third and fifth separated by the second Jaguar, the crippled Andretti Porsche surviving to be sixth.

The whole place is about to erupt as Jan Lammers leads home the trio of XJR-9LMs to win Le Mans 1988. Sadly, British TV licence payers were denied this moment of triumph, and indeed any live coverage at all!
(LAT Photographic)

Thirty-one years after Jaguar had last won at Le Mans, a few friends and bystanders enjoy the moment! (LAT Photographic)

1988 results

1st Lammers/Dumfries/Wallace Jaguar XJR-9LM (588) 394 laps, 3,313.15 miles (5,330.86km), 137.72mph (221.59kph).
2nd Stuck/Bell/Ludwig Porsche 962C (010) 394 laps.
3rd Dickens/Jelinski/ 'Winter' Porsche 962C (004) 385 laps.
4th Daly/Perkins/Cogan Jaguar XJR-9LM (188) 383 laps.
5th Hobbs/Theys/Konrad Porsche 962C 380 laps.
6th Andretti/Andretti/Andretti Porsche 962C 375 laps.
16th Sullivan/Jones/Cobb Jaguar XJR-9LM (186) 331 laps.

Incredibly, there was no British live television coverage and precious little at all subsequently, a reflection not only of the attitudes of British broadcasters but also their reluctance to pay for the broadcasting rights. Everywhere else in the Western world Jaguar's triumph was writ large, but in the UK only enthusiasts and those involved knew what had been achieved. Tom Walkinshaw had warned back in 1986 that it would take three years to win

and it had. For Tom, team manager Roger Silman, designer Tony Southgate, the drivers, engineers and mechanics it was a wonderful triumph. Afterwards Peter Falk of Porsche congratulated Tom Walkinshaw, and Tony Southgate remembers their comment that they never thought a road-car engine would beat them. The rest of the season saw Sauber re-establish itself with a vengeance, winning at Brno (Schlesser/Mass), at the Nürburgring (Schlesser/Mass) and at Spa (Baldi/Johansson). TWR Jaguar however finished second at each of these events and won at Brands Hatch and Fujii to clinch the C1 title with 345 points to Sauber's 285. Triple points for winning Le Mans as per the FIA's new points system based on a distance coefficient made the difference. The driver's championship was won overall by Gordon Spice in the C2 category, while Martin Brundle beat Schlesser in C1.

Some sadness crept into 1988 with the deaths of Claude Baily in February and Harry Mundy in May, but the TWR Jaguar achievements of winning the championship and Le Mans guaranteed more sales and happy faces all round.

Chapter 20

1989 – German revenge

For 1989, TWR continued to use the big V12-engined XJR-9 while developing a new 3.5-litre turbo car (XJR-11) for future use. This utilised the basic costings of the engine in the Jaguar XJ220 road car, but totally re-engineered with all-new internals. The old car meanwhile had to undergo some revisions to accommodate an FIA diktat that no mechanical components were to be visible beyond the bodywork, even though it had raced like this in 1988. Another apparent problem was TWR's Dunlop tyre contract, the ever growing opposition now making use of Michelin, Goodyear and Bridgestone that were all improving rapidly.

As for the main opposition this was very definitely the Sauber-Mercedes operation, Porsche having officially withdrawn although they were still represented by many private owners. Some of these, notably Joest and Brun, were extremely competitive, especially at Le Mans, notwithstanding the Porsche 962 was now an old car, and age had already begun to tell on the shorter distance and sprint events. Mazda, Nissan and Toyota remained a potential threat however at Le Mans. The first big outing for TWR was the Daytona 24 hours in February where they scored a second place and two DNFs. They should have won but various problems delayed them sufficiently to let an American Porsche win. Sebring saw them outraced by the winning Nissan after brake troubles intruded but they still finished second. The first championship round proper, at Suzuka, set the tone for much of the season when Sauber triumphed with a 1, 2 and Jaguars were

handicapped by their fuel consumption, managing a fifth place only. Dijon was even worse with no finishers and off the pace, although the Saubers were beaten by a Joest Porsche into second and third.

Next up was Le Mans and until now the Jaguar effort had been looking less and less convincing. However they could expect to be more competitive on the long, fast Sarthe track and so it turned out. A small detail was that the organising club (*Automobile Club de l'Ouest*) had fallen out with the FIA and the race lost its championship status for the year, but in practice this made no difference to the entry. Le Mans could stand alone. Apart from the three works Saubers, a total of 17 privately entered Porsche 962s turned up, the best of which (Joest and Brun) were still potential winners. Also worthy of consideration was the Japanese contingent of Mazda, Nissan and Toyota, the first named having a record of durability. TWR's entry for 1989 was one less than the steamroller approach of the previous year and was:

No. 1 Jan Lammers/Patrick Tambay/Andrew Gilbert-Scott Jaguar XJR9-LM (588).
No. 2 John Nielsen/Andy Wallace/Price Cobb Jaguar XJR9-LM (688).
No. 3 Davey Jones/Derek Daly Jaguar XJR9-LM (288). (Reserve driver Jeff Kline not used for race.)
No. 4 Alain Ferté/Eliseo Salazar/Michel Ferté Jaguar XJR-9LM (287).

All the cars ran on 17-inch front and 18-inch rear diameter wheels on Dunlop crossplies. There were five drivers left over from 1988, the rest being Frenchman Patrick Tambay, ex-F1 for Renault and Ferrari, Englishman Andrew Gilbert-Scott, sometime F3 and F3000 racer, American sports car ace Davey Jones, former F1 driver Chilean Eliseo Salazar and the Ferté brothers, Alain and Michel. Brundle and Cheever had departed, returning to F1.

Qualifying was keenly contested, but as expected the 5-litre turbocharged Sauber-Mercedes were quickest, having taken over Porsche's traditional role. The track remained at the same length as 1988 and the best times for each team were:

Jean-Louis Schlesser 5.0T Sauber-Mercedes C9/88 (02) 3min 15.04sec.
Jan Lammers 7.0 Jaguar XJR-9LM (588) 3min 18.35sec (Jones 3min 19.48sec, Alain Ferté 3min 20.19sec, Nielsen 3min 20.65sec).

Hans-Joachim Stuck Joest 3.0T Porsche 962C (145) 3min 19.80sec.
Julian Bailey 3.5T Nissan R89C (01) 3min 24.09sec.
Takashi Yorino 1.3r Mazda 767B (002) 3min 25.45sec.
Geoff Lees 3.2T Toyota 89CV (08) 3min 25.60sec.

Note how well matched the Jaguars were and how much quicker they went compared with 1987/88, this being the third year that the track had retained its configuration so comparisons could be made. They were third, fourth, sixth and eighth fastest. Also worthy of comment was the speed of the tiny 1.3-litre rotary-engined Mazdas.

The beginning of the race caused immediate setbacks for TWR, when Lammers pitted at the end of lap one with a puncture followed a lap later by Alain Ferté with the same problem. In fact he had been misled by a faulty tyre sensor. So two

The start of Le Mans 1989 with the two Saubers leading away from the No. 1 XJR-9LM (588) of Jan Lammers and the No. 3 car (288) of Davey Jones with Alain Ferté in No. 4 (287), and John Nielsen in the fourth Jaguar (688) just behind him.
(LAT Photographic)

Jaguars were now last after just seven minutes! Happily both Jones and Nielsen were charging and by lap three they were 1, 2 ahead of Baldi's Sauber. Another fast starter was Bailey's Nissan and he climbed to third before clouting the back of Nielsen's Jaguar at Mulsanne Corner causing the Jaguar to pit for attention to its rear end. The Japanese car however had suffered suspension and monocoque damage and was out, no doubt making Bailey-san very popular. Jones continued in the lead now seven seconds ahead of Bob Wollek's Porsche 962C who had passed the Saubers of Baldi and Mass, while their team-mate Schlesser was dropping back with a car that would not rev like its sisters.

After the first pit stops Davey Jones had a lead of 20 seconds over the Mass Sauber with Jelinski and Stuck in Joest Porsches next. The other three delayed Jaguars were all charging up the field (Lammers, A. Ferté, Wallace) but the Toyota challenge was already in trouble with one car out after crashing. Mass and Stuck continued to scrap over second place while Jones eased away in front, 35 seconds ahead by the time of the second fuel stops on lap 25. Derek Daly took over and continued to pull away very gradually from the Joest Porsche, the Mass Sauber now driven by Manuel Reuter delayed by a stop to check for damage after running over exhaust debris on the Mulsanne Straight. By lap 38 Daly was 50 seconds in front and the other Jaguars were all well in contention, with Lammers having climbed to third and Ferté to sixth, although Price Cobb's progress was interrupted by a loose safety harness.

In the fourth hour Jaguar suddenly had a bad attack of the gremlins with the No. 1 car pitting with a broken exhaust, losing several places, while the leading Jaguar suffered gearbox problems. Daly stopped the car at the beginning of Mulsanne on lap 50 with no drive in fourth gear. His team radioed instructions to him and Derek had to take the back off the gearbox and try to locate a gear. Having done this and reassembled the box he discovered he had selected reverse! So the whole procedure was repeated and eventually he got the car back to the pits where a permanent repair to the selectors was completed but with 50 minutes lost in total. Up at the front the Porsche of

Stuck/Wollek continued to lead their German counterparts with the No. 4 Jaguar now 3rd ahead of the other Joest Porsche. Even this state of affairs could not last as later on Ferté suffered a broken exhaust, just as Lammers had done, probably caused by tyre vibration. It dropped to eighth and then had a repeat performance further into the evening.

By midnight the Stuck/Wollek Porsche was still leading with Jaguar No. 1 second and closing, but No. 3 had retired at 10.35pm with a dropped valve following its earlier gearbox maladies. The other two XJRs were seventh and eighth, and at 1.20am, the leading Porsche was stopped with overheating, caused by a cracked pipe, losing 15 minutes and the lead to Jaguar No. 1. Next came Baldi's Sauber with Nielsen now third in No. 2 Jaguar. At 3am, No. 1 Jaguar was a lap and three quarters ahead of Baldi's Sauber which was only 30 seconds clear of Stuck, Nielsen and Mass who were covered by just seven seconds. The pace was unrelenting and the first eight cars were all lapping in under 3min 30sec.

Lammers made an unscheduled stop with a slow puncture on lap 183, allowing the Sauber back on to the same lap, but then just past half-time (4am) Ferté was in the pits with a broken third gear and

The Lammers/Gilbert-Scott/ Tambay XJR-9LM (588) was the highest-placed Jaguar after many delays and problems, including a broken exhaust, puncture and gearbox oil seal failure that required a gearbox change. It had led for some time before the transmission problems, and finally finished fourth. (LAT Photographic)

debris floating around in the gearbox. Amazingly the pit crew replaced the gearbox in 70 minutes and the car returned in 16th place. The next casualty was the Nielsen/Wallace/Cobb car that had been sounding rough for a couple of hours, falling down the field and finally retiring at 5.20am with valve trouble. All the while No. 1 Jaguar remained in the lead until it suffered a failed gearbox oil seal and it stopped at 6.20am. Another mammoth gearbox change was required and in the early morning light the job was completed in 50 minutes! Of course, this dropped the car back to ninth, some 10 laps adrift of the leading Saubers. With everything to gain and not much to lose Walkinshaw unleashed his drivers and they drove flat out, almost coming to grief when Tambay spun at Tertre Rouge nearly taking Alain Ferté with him.

Such was their pace that on lap 246 Alain set the fastest lap of the race in 3min 21.27sec (150.436mph/242.051kph), a new lap record and remarkably close to its qualifying time. Still more trials and tribulations awaited TWR however when Michel Ferté collided with a Porsche, damaging an air intake that required a pit stop for repairs and then Lammers was in too because of a loose fire extinguisher rolling around the cockpit. Now it was a drive to the finish for the delayed third-place Porsche and the two surviving Jaguars being driven flat out to regain lost ground. Some excitement came at 2.45pm when the second-placed Sauber lost all but fifth gear, but it survived to the flag with no clutch. Also slowing with clutch problems was

Opposite: Any of the Jaguars could have won Le Mans 1989 but for their reliability problems and the Nielsen/Wallace/Cobb car (688) ran strongly but finally stopped with terminal engine problems at 5.20am on Sunday morning. (LAT Photographic)

Davey Jones also led in his XJR-9LM shared with Derek Daly, but it suffered first of all gearbox maladies and then a dropped valve that ended its race late on Saturday evening. (LAT Photographic)

Jaguar No. 4 was driven by the Ferté brothers, Alain and Michel together with Eliseo Salazar. After experiencing two broken exhausts and a gearbox change they came home eighth. (LAT Photographic)

the Stuck/Wollek Porsche but it too kept its position. So Sauber scored a perhaps lucky 1, 2, 5 with Porsche third and sixth and the Jaguars pitching up fourth and eighth despite the myriad of problems that had beset them. The Mazdas finished seventh and ninth. The German victory looked convincing, but the Jaguars in race trim were quicker and would undoubtedly have won given better luck and/or more reliability, although they had been troubled by very high oil consumption.

1989 results

1st Jochen Mass/Manuel Reuter/Stanley Dickens Sauber-Mercedes C9/88 (03). 389 laps, 3,271.74 miles (5,265.11km), 136.702mph (219.954kph).
2nd Mauro Baldi/Kenneth Acheson/Gianfranco Brancatelli Sauber-Mercedes C9/88 (04). 384 laps.

3rd Bob Wollek/Hans-Joachim Stuck Porsche 962C (0145). 382 laps.
4th Jan Lammers/Patrick Tambay/Andrew Gilbert-Scott Jaguar XJR-9LM (588). 380 laps.
8th Alain Ferté/Eliseo Salazar/Michel Ferté Jaguar XJR-9LM (287). 368 laps.

After this, the best Jaguar could manage was second place at the next round in Jarama. At Brands Hatch the new turbocharged XJR-11 appeared but it faded to fifth after starting on pole, and the last race of the season at Mexico saw the now uncompetitive XJR-9s reappear to finish fifth and sixth. Overall the season had been a real disappointment for TWR, not winning a single race while Sauber had cleaned up.

Another link with the origins of Jaguar was lost when Bill Heynes died in July. Good news for Jaguar however was that a bid to buy them by Ford had been accepted, guaranteeing them a real future and more racing in an increasingly hostile world.

Chapter 21

1990 – Seven up

By 1990, the World Sports Car Championship was beginning to decline, in no small part due to the continuing bureaucratic squabbles 'twixt the FIA and the *Automobile Club de l'Ouest* (ACO), who ran Le Mans. One serious bone of contention was the dictum that no track should have a single stretch longer than two kilometres. Le Man's famous Mulsanne Straight was nearly six kilometres, albeit with a right-hand kink within its length. Once again the race was denied championship status.

Not satisfied with this the FIA then threatened to suspend the licence of anybody competing at Le Mans. The ACO capitulated and agreed to install two chicanes on Mulsanne in the name of safety. Over the decades and especially more so latterly, there had been a number of high speed crashes on Mulsanne caused by tyre and engine failures. However the extra braking and acceleration caused by the chicanes would increase engine, brake and tyre wear and crucially fuel consumption. Another unwelcome consequence was that the trackside gravel traps would spread their contents liberally over the road when cars ran wide or spun off.

The knock-on effect of this dispute was to affect sponsorship, and the demotion of the sport's premier sports car event sent entirely the wrong message. Ticket prices, now under the control of the FIA, went up to F1 levels further damaging the category's public appeal. The public could choose to watch whatever they wanted especially given the rise of touring car racing and they did. In fairness it must be noted that all interested parties bar Aston Martin, had long ago (late 1988) agreed with the FIA over the new 3.5-litre free formula regulations. Popular sentiment saw this new category as a device to entice the engine manufacturers ultimately into F1, and many of the smaller C2

Jaguars get sunburnt too! The four XJR-12s lined up in the pits on a very hot day with their high-tec reflective covers. (LAT Photographic)

teams lacked the finance to make the change. To survive, some teams began hiring 'rent-a-drivers' and fields inevitably shrunk, while F1 prospered with the benefit of proper television coverage and all the wealthiest sponsors.

TWR were now racing their XJR-11 full time, except at Le Mans and the American venues of Daytona and Sebring which fell outside the official championship. There they ran the V12 cars, now designated XJR-12, and duly won at Daytona, finishing 1, 2. Running amongst the turbo cars, the big Jaguars were not the quickest in qualifying, but in race trim they were fast enough and reliable. Sebring produced a third place behind two of the new Nissan GTP-ZXTs and then the XJR-12s stood down while the XJR-11 contested the World Sports Car Championship. Round one at Suzuka was a disaster with both cars retiring, but the second race at Monza yielded a third and fourth behind the new Mercedes (née Sauber) C11s. Silverstone was a much happier hunting ground and the XJR-11s finished first and second, followed by second at Spa

Early in the race Davey Jones in his XJR-12 (190) is followed by Jan Lammers in 290. They are running sixth and seventh behind their team-mates. Ultimately the Jones/Ferté/Salazar car would retire with terminal engine problems at around noon on Sunday. (Paul Skilleter)

behind the Mercedes again. Now came Le Mans and disappointingly Mercedes-Benz withdrew, using the FIA/ACO dispute as their reason for not attending. They had won in 1989 and were quite content, having gained a substantial marketing boost.

Taking up the cudgels was Nissan who had eight of their 3.5 turbo cars, but they were still outnumbered by the Porsche 962s which totalled 19 cars! The two Joest entries were brand-new, virtually works cars with 3.2T (turbocharged) engines. Mazda and Toyota were trying again, somewhat overshadowed by their Nissan compatriots. Jaguars apart, the rest of the field comprised the smaller C2 category cars and assorted IMSA machines. TWR arrived with four XJR-12s and 11 drivers, the complete entry being:

No. 1 Martin Brundle/Alain Ferté/David Leslie
Jaguar XJR-12 (990).
No. 2 Jan Lammers/Andy Wallace/Franz Konrad
Jaguar XJR-12 (290).

No. 3 John Nielsen/Price Cobb/Martin Brundle
Jaguar XJR-12 (1090).
No. 4 Davy Jones/Michel Ferté/Eliseo Salazar
Jaguar XJR-12 (190).

The Jaguars were in effect IMSA spec cars running in Group C form with a high downforce set-up. Martin Brundle had returned for 1990 and the newcomers were Scottish touring car ace David Leslie and Austrian sports car driver Franz Konrad. Luis Perez-Sala was reserve driver but not used in the race.

Because of the two new chicanes (the first one was named Virage Nissan and the second Virage de la Carte S) on Mulsanne the track now measured 8.451 miles (13.600km) and was approximately 20 seconds slower per lap. Revised qualifying rules allowed the use of 'T' (testing) cars and Mark Blundell's Nissan set an untouchable time, although the car was not going to be raced. Porsche lost one front runner when Jonathan Palmer had a huge shunt when his car

unexpectedly turned left at 200mph (322kph), destroying the Joest 962C but luckily not Jonathan. Rear suspension failure was the likely culprit. TWR's practice times were nothing special, but the cars were superbly presented and set up with brakes and suspension strengthened to cope with the new chicanes. The drivers described their machines as 'perfection'. The fastest times for each of the leading makes were as follows:

Mark Blundell 3.5T Nissan R90C (Lola) (03) 3min 27.02sec.
Oscar Larrauri 3.0T Porsche 962C (160) 3min 33.06scc.
Davy Jones 7.0 Jaguar XJR-12 (190) 3min 36.10sec (Brundle 3min 36.55sec, Nielsen 3min 37.00sec, Lammers 3min 43.50sec).
Geoff Lees 3.2T Toyota 90CV (04) 3min 37.13sec.
Volker Weidler 1.3R Mazda 3min 43.04sec.

Blundell's time was courtesy of maximum turbo boost, minimal fuel, a nearly clear lap and a great

Martin Brundle, Alain Ferté and David Leslie drove 990 but it was delayed by various problems early on and finally retired with a cooked engine due to a detached water pump belt on Sunday. (LAT Photographic)

deal of skill and courage but was not indicative of the Nissan's race pace. Larrauri was second quickest but over six seconds slower than the Japanese rocket. The Jaguars lined up seventh, eighth, ninth and 17th, Lammers being quite content to save his car any unnecessary punishment. Despite the new chicanes the faster cars were still reaching 215mph (346kph).

Race day was hot and getting hotter, so everybody, especially the turbo brigade, were counselling caution. A happy atmosphere was encouraged by the TWR drivers saluting the crowds and all was well. Not so for Nissan however who lost Kenny Acheson's car on the formation lap with total brake failure, and then en route back to the pits the wretched car suffered a transmission failure, a legacy of previous travails. The rather spread out rolling start enabled Bailey (Nissan) and Larrauri (Porsche) to open up a 10-second gap within three laps from Hasemi's Nissan. By lap eight Hasemi was followed by a menacing troop of all four Jaguars (Brundle, Nielsen, Jones and

Lammers) and the first fuel stops began. Over the years the combination of turbocharging, restrictive tank capacity and limited consumption has meant cars have covered less and less distance between stops. Consumption was further increased by the need to brake and change down and then accelerate up through the gears at the two Mulsanne chicanes, so everybody was affected. The Jaguars stopped on laps 10 and 11, with no driver changes. At the second stop it was all change and Lammers briefly led while the leaders pitted, the constant refuelling being a nightmare for those keeping lap charts.

Three hours into the race and the Nissan was leading by 42 seconds from Ferté's Jaguar with the other XJR-12s in fourth, fifth and sixth positions. Porsche was suffering from high brake-pad wear, the Joest cars in particular. One hour later the Nissans led 1, 2 but then Brancatelli in the leading car collided with Aguri's Toyota, destroying the Toyota and forcing the Nissan to pit for repairs to a damaged nose and new tyres. This promoted No. 1

Jan Lammers, Franz Konrad and Andy Wallace drove their XJR-12 (290) to second place after an incident-filled race, inheriting the runner-up spot only minutes before the end when Pareja's Brun Porsche suddenly and cruelly expired. (Paul Skilleter)

Jaguar to second place before gaining the lead at around 9.15pm when the Nissan pitted for an unexpected pad change. This meant that two brothers (Alain and Michel Ferté) in identical cars were leading Le Mans! The first problems for Jaguar came at 10pm when A. Ferté stopped and had the water topped up. Seven laps later he was back again, but it was a relatively minor problem requiring the replacement of the swirl pot that had a pinhole leak in it. While doing this the front screen was replaced, the original being cracked and scarred by the stones flung up at the chicanes. Over eight minutes were lost and the car slipped to sixth place, requiring one more rapid stop to tighten up the new swirl pot.

Despite the frantic pace there had been only two

retirements after six hours, one because of an accident. At midnight, the No. 4 Jaguar driven by Davy Jones was slowing with a sticking throttle, a problem that could not be sorted until the end of his stint. A lap was lost and the car was now eighth but the others were second (No. 3), fourth (No. 2) and 11th (No. 1). Just after 1.30am the leading Nissan, despite having had the gearbox changed, stopped for good, out on the circuit. There was still another Nissan leading however and the Brun/ Repsol Porsche was third so the pressure was not abating. Another Nissan pad change promoted No. 3 Jaguar driven by Price Cobb into the lead although Lammers spoilt the show a little when he pitted with bodywork damage caused by being punted off at the first Mulsanne chicane. A real

The winning car (1090) of John Nielsen, Price Cobb and Martin Brundle passes the pits. Note that the big central roof intake vent of the XJR-9 has now gone. (Paul Skilleter)

dice now ensued between Cobb and his old IMSA rival Chip Robinson in the Nissan, continuing after the driver changes with Nielsen and Daly. Eventually Nielsen pulled out a 30-second gap on the Nissan, the latter marginally slowed by electronic problems. Just before the 13th hour Jaguar No. 4 was in with a damaged nose that lost it two laps, but worse still was the arrival of No. 2 driven by Franz Konrad who had missed his braking point at the first Mulsanne chicane, fortunately skimming over the gravel trap. Nevertheless a new nose, windscreen and door were needed and nearly five laps were lost.

As the early morning progressed No. 4 was back in for a new radiator underpanel, the original having suffered in the earlier incident. Now Jaguar No. 3 led by a lap from the Nissan with the Brun Porsche next who, in turn, was two laps ahead of the much delayed but fast recovering No. 1 car driven by Alain Ferté, with No. 2 seventh and No. 4 10th. Having climbed back to fifth after nearly 15 hours at an unabated pace Alain Ferté pitted No. 1 with a water pump belt detached. Sadly the engine was cooked and after 80 minutes the poor TWR crew had to give up and it was withdrawn, their first retirement. Co-driver Martin Brundle was then drafted into No. 3, allowing a much needed break for Nielsen and Price Cobb while Salazar was stood down. As Brundle charged on Salazar replaced Michel Ferté in No. 4 but then stopped for more bodywork repairs and at 8pm it was placed ninth with No. 2 now back to fifth. By 10am, the Brun Porsche had lost time with a flat battery, and the second-placed Nissan was out with a leaking bag-tank after two hours in the pits, leaving No. 3 Jaguar that apparently had no fourth gear and poor brakes ever further in the lead. Much time was spent keeping the Jaguar radiators free of circuit debris and muck and Brundle had a brake caliper problem, losing a lap to the second-placed Porsche. Jaguar No. 4 then succumbed to engine troubles having sounded rough for a little while and it was withdrawn at 12.25am. Elsewhere the Stuck/Bell/Jelinski Joest Porsche had soldiered on with a variety of problems including very heavy pad wear and now occupied fifth, but the Brun 962C with an unwell Larrauri at the wheel was only a lap behind the leading Jaguar. Lammers in No. 2 was a further two laps behind but at this pace could not catch the Porsche. Another Porsche doing well was the Alpha Team entry driven by Needell/Sears/Reid that was disputing fourth place with Hoshino's Nissan.

All seemed set but there were more tears when the Nissan developed transmission problems and lost ground rapidly with less than two hours to go. At 3.5pm Nielsen and Lammers followed each other around but TWR were still worried as the second-placed Porsche was still close and the leading Jaguar had gearbox woes. But it was not the Jaguars who had to worry as after making a final stop at 3.30pm, the Brun Porsche driven by Jesus Pareja expired in a cloud of smoke and steam only 15 minutes from the end. This was a savage and very sad end to a fantastic drive, and everybody else moved up a slot leaving Jaguar with a 1, 2 victory, their seventh win since 1951. The Alpha Team Porsche was third, the quasi-works

Joest Porsche fourth with the Nissan fifth and the surviving Toyota of Lees/Ogawa/Sekiya sixth.

1990 results

1st John Nielsen/Price Cobb/Martin Brundle Jaguar XJR-12 (1090) 359 laps, 3,033.788 miles (4,882.400km), 126.782mph (204.036kph).
2nd Jan Lammers/Andy Wallace/Franz Konrad Jaguar XJR-12 (290) 355 laps.

At the finish, only four cars were able to cross the line as the crowds swarmed across the track, many of them British of course.

The remaining WSPC rounds brought little joy with Mercedes-Benz winning all the races, five in total, while TWR racked up two thirds and several top six finishes with the XJR-11. During the year Mercedes had made use of two future F1 stars, Heinz-Harald Frentzen and Michael Schumacher, although ironically, neither would drive for them in F1.

Opposite: The final pit stop and John Nielsen leaves the pits in 1090, with Tom Walkinshaw looking on in short-sleeved shirt. The Jaguar won despite having gearbox problems, a common fault on all the XJRs caused by the huge torque of the V12 engines and the ultra high speeds at Le Mans. (Sutton)

Victory number seven. Price Cobb, Martin Brundle and John Nielsen enjoy their triumph along with Tom Walkinshaw and Jaguar chairman Sir John Egan. (Sutton)

Chapter 22

1991 – Second best

FISA's 3.5-litre 750kg formula for sports car racing had not proved to be popular, with only Peugeot, Mazda, Jaguar and Mercedes committing to the new cars in 1991, although Toyota joined the series at the end of the year.

The old C1 turbo cars were allowed to race on, but were subject to a punitive fuel consumption limit (51 litres per 100km, or a total of 2,550 litres/561gal for Le Mans). Additionally they had to weigh a minimum of 1,000kg (2,205lb) which caused much protest from Porsche customers, so FISA relented slightly, dropping the minimum weight to 950kg (2,095lb) for the sprint races, although Le Mans would be kept to the higher figure. Not content with this the new cars (they were essentially two-seater F1 devices) would benefit from shorter sprint races (430km/267 miles) that would allow them to cover the distance with only two refuelling stops and they were also able to use the specially blended F1 high octane fuel. The other cars had to use pump grade fuel. Of no particular note, the series was now renamed Sportscar World Championship (SWC).

For 1991, TWR had a new car for the shorter championship rounds, the XJR-14 using a 3.5-litre HB Cosworth V8, rebadged Jaguar, an obvious choice given that Ford now owned Jaguar. Their main rivals Mercedes, or Sauber if you prefer, were running a new and very complex V12 car that was not user friendly. Peugeot's existing 905 was still underdeveloped while Mazda had managed to persuade FISA on a minimum weight of 830kg (1,830lb) which was to prove decisive at

Le Mans for their small but very potent rotary-engined cars. Designed by Nigel Stroud the 787B with carbon fibre discs was a very good car indeed.

The season started with the two non-championship American rounds at Daytona and Sebring where TWR ran their 7.0 V12 XJR-12s, but one did not start after a practice accident and the other retired having been second quickest in practice. A Joest Porsche won. Sebring at least produced a fifth place, but once again the second Jaguar non-started after colliding with another car during qualifying. The first round proper at Suzuka produced just 15 cars with TWR's new XJR-14 dominating practice despite a dispute over wing heights that was to characterise the season. Both cars easily led the race until they retired and Peugeot scored a lucky win with a Mercedes second and a Porsche 962 third. Monza was a triumph with the TWR cars quickest in qualifying and finishing 1, 2 in the race. Silverstone was almost as good with a repeat qualifying performance and a 1, 3 finish, Brundle having been delayed with a broken throttle cable. Mercedes were second, albeit a lap behind.

Le Mans was now back in the championship fold, but concern grew about the durability of the new F1-type cars over 24 hours and the effect of the unfair weight limits imposed upon the Category 2 cars (XJR-12, 962C etc.). Unlike previous years the race was now between just two categories, the new 3.5-litre cars designated Group 1/C1 and all the rest including the Jaguar, Mercedes and

Porsche entries, designated Group 1/C2. Both Jaguar and Mercedes declined to actually race their 3.5-litre machines although both attended qualifying. Instead, TWR presented a 7.4-litre version of the XJR-12 to overcome the weight penalty and Sauber arrived with a warmed over version of their 1990 Le Mans car that had not been used since. Jeff Wilson, TWR's chief mechanic, recollected that extra sheets of alumimium were bolted to the floor of the car to make the 1991 1,000kg minimum weight limit, the 1988 winning car having weighed only 894kg (1,971lb).

Porsche was back again with the faithful old 962 still reasonably competitive, but this year there were only 15 of them! Mazda had two 787Bs and one 787 and Peugeot two of their 905 evolution models. The rest of the varied grid featured assorted cars using Cosworth, Porsche and even Ferrari engines, but they were not really in contention except by default. For the third year running TWR entered four cars, and these were:

No. 33 Derek Warwick/John Nielsen/Andy Wallace
    Jaguar XJR-12 (891).
No. 34 Teo Fabi/Bob Wollek/Kenny Acheson
    Jaguar XJR-12 (991).
No. 35 Davy Jones/Raul Boesel/Michel Ferté
    Jaguar XJR-12 (990).
No. 36 David Leslie/Mauro Martini/Jeff Krosnoff
    Jaguar XJR-12 (190).

Unlike previous years the Jaguars were now using Goodyear tyres.

The complete TWR Silk Cut Jaguar line up including the XJR-14s – Nos 3 (591) and 4 (691). Andy Wallace used No. 4 in qualifying only, the other car not being run. (LAT Photographic)

Once again TWR had a number of new drivers on hand together with some returnees, notably Derek Warwick and Raul Boesel. Fabi was ex-F1 and Indycar racing, sometime F1 driver Acheson had come over from Sauber while Italian Mauro Martini and American Jeff Krosnoff both hailed from Japanese F3000 racing. The other 'new' face belonged to long-time Porsche ace and Le Mans veteran Frenchman Bob Wollek.

Regardless of practice times the 10 3.5-litre machines were given the top 10 positions on the grid, while the actual quickest car, Schlesser's Sauber, was placed 11th! Only Peugeot amongst the serious contenders was racing its 3.5-litre car, the rest being mainly private Spice-Cosworth entries. The following is a list of the actual quickest times per manufacturer:

The Suntec XJR-12 (190) was driven (from left) by Mauro Martini, Jeff Krosnoff and David Leslie. Tragically, Krosnoff, a promising Indycar driver, died in a crash on the Toronto street circuit in 1996 when his car struck a lamp post. (LAT Photographic)

Jean-Louis Schlesser 5.0T Sauber-Mercedes C11 (03). 3min 31.270sec.
Andy Wallace 3.5 Jaguar XJR-14 (691). 3min 31.912sec (Not raced).
Phillipe Alliot 3.5 Peugeot 905 (EV14). 3min 35.058sec.
Oscar Larrauri Porsche 3.2T 962 (177). 3min 36.114sec.
Davy Jones Jaguar XJR-12 (990). 3min 43.496sec (Warwick 3min 47.875sec, Teo Fabi 3min 49.748sec, Jeff Krosnoff 3min 49.867sec).
Volker Weidler 1.3R Mazda 787B (002). 3min 43.503sec.

The relatively slow times recorded by the XJR-12s was caused by intermittent rain during qualifying and they never got a dry run. Instead they

concentrated on set-up, and finished 11th, 18th, 21st and 22nd on times but 18th, 24th, 26th and 27th on the grid thanks to the nonsense over the 3.5-litre cars. Bob Wollek survived a burst tyre approaching Indianapolis that spoilt Andy Wallace's pole position attempt in the XJR-14, but fortunately the car was not damaged.

Race day dawned dry and the sun had even put in an appearance when, at 4pm, the grid was unleashed. Concerns about the slower 3.5-litre cars, and some of them were very slow, getting in the way of the quicker C2 cars proved correct and the first few laps were quite lively. The Peugeots of Alliot and Rosberg established themselves at the front followed by Schlesser's Mercedes and the Porsches of Larrauri, Schneider and Stuck. Alas the Jaguars with their 7.4-litre engines and 1,000kg weight could not run on the pace and stay within the crippling fuel limits and were losing five to six seconds a lap to the quicker C2 cars. As expected, the Peugeot challenge faded, but even earlier than seems reasonable with the Rosberg car misfiring

and losing 11 laps while sorting out the problem, and the Alliot car caught fire in the pits, but was quickly extinguished. Ultimately both retired, one on lap 22, the other on lap 68. This left the two Mercedes, driven by Schumacher and Mass, in front followed by a Porsche, the third Mercedes and then Nielsen's Jaguar. The other XJR-12s were eighth, 13th and 24th. The lowest-placed Jaguar, driven by Martini, had stopped at the first chicane with fuel pump switch failure, but the Italian managed to coax it back to the pits for repairs. Nearly an hour was lost in total and the car was now out of contention. At 7pm the unfortunate Martini damaged the front suspension when he ran over the curbs at a chicane which necessitated a total front-end suspension rebuild. This took over two hours and the car did not run again until 9.23pm having dropped 52 laps.

Not long after, at around 9.25pm, Warwick spun into the gravel trap at Indianapolis in the leading Jaguar, losing third place and four minutes while it was retrieved. So at 10pm Mercedes led from

No. 190 before it was crashed twice at Tertre Rouge and had its front suspension rebuilt during the race. Probably to everybody's relief the car finally retired on lap 183 with gearbox failure. (LAT Photographic)

Porsche, Mercedes, Mazda, Porsche, Jaguar, Porsche, Jaguar, Jaguar and Mazda. As the night wore on the second Sauber was in trouble with handling problems, frightening Jonathan Palmer as it wandered about at speed caused by undertray damage but Schumacher in the 'junior' car set the race's fastest lap (3min 35.5sec) despite the fuel limitations. In the early hours TWR nearly lost Warwick when he had a loose fuel pump plug, (TWR certainly seemed to have a problem with fuel pumps over the years) stopping at Arnage but advice over the radio got him underway again, the delay losing him 13 minutes and slipping from sixth to ninth. Ominously, by half distance, the Weidler/Herbert/Gachot Mazda had overtaken the lead Jaguar and now Mercedes ran 1, 2 with Mazda

third and Jaguar holding down fourth, fifth and ninth.

Then trouble struck Mercedes again when their second-placed car suffering gearbox trouble losing 13 minutes and, one lap later, another 20 as the reluctant car wilted under the strain. It dropped to ninth. Andy Wallace driving Jaguar No. 33 added to this car's previous delays when he went off at the first chicane (5.22am) and spent three laps escaping while Martini crashed the No. 36 car at Tertre Rouge (5.50am) the Italian having an exciting time it seems. The poor car was patched up and carried on, while Acheson pitted with frontal damage to No. 34, having 'terminated Bugs Bunny' somewhere out on the course. Mercedes continued to lead but their No. 1 car was

Now using 7.4-litre engines the XJR-12s were all handicapped by the punitive fuel and minimum weight regulations and were unable to use their full speed. Derek Warwick, John Nielsen and Andy Wallace finished fourth in chassis 891. (LAT Photographic)

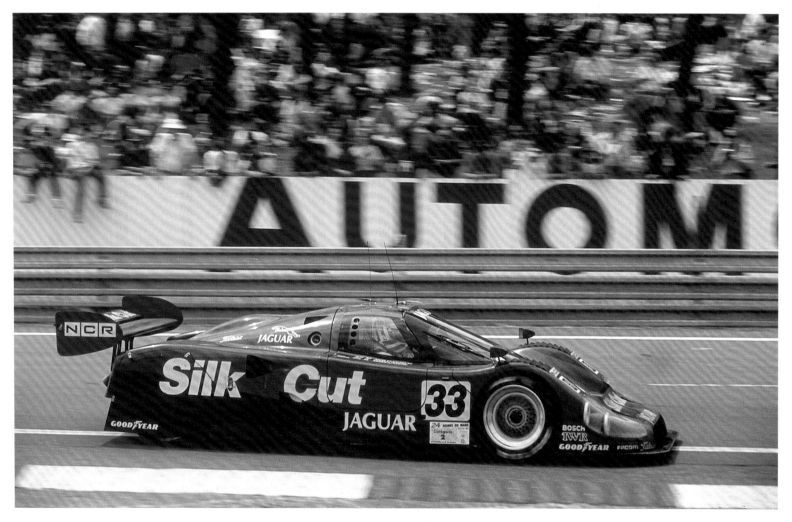

overheating with the Mazda and No. 35 Jaguar scrapping over second place. In reality the Mazda, not hobbled by the Jaguar's inadequate fuel allowance, was quicker and indeed was lapping faster than the leader. At 7.30am the second Mercedes was retired and then TWR suffered another familiar problem when No. 34's exhaust broke and Krosnoff crashed the Martini Jaguar at Tertre Rouge, again! Yet another marathon repair job was achieved by the TWR mechanics but then the car stopped for good on Mulsanne with no drive, a relief perhaps to all concerned.

With 18 hours gone the No. 1 Mercedes was leading the Mazda by three laps with the Nos 35 and 34 Jaguars third and fourth, one and two laps down on the Japanese car respectively. The junior Mercedes was fifth with the remaining Jaguar 6th and the first Porsche back in 8th. Before midday Schumacher stopped the fifth-placed Mercedes with overheating, the car requiring a new water pump drive belt and it lost a place to the No. 33 Jaguar. All eyes were on the leading Mercedes as a result and at around 12.50am Alain Ferté was radioed to return to the pits, his car's on-board telemetry indicating another water pump drive failure. After much frantic activity and general dismay the car resumed at 1.28pm but by now the Mazda and all the Jaguars were long gone, and one lap later the Mercedes was out, the overheating having destroyed the engine and its ancillaries. Meanwhile the Mazda cruised serenely on, never having missed a beat despite being driven so hard for so long and the Jaguars just could not catch it and stay within their fuel allocation. So it was that the rotary-engined Japanese car won, Johnny Herbert driving the final stint and crossing the line ahead of the three TWR Jaguars, the remaining Sauber and another Mazda. Afterwards an exhausted Herbert collapsed in his father's arms.

Teo Fabi, Kenny Acheson and long-time Porsche racer Bob Wollek drove their XJR-12 (991) to third place having suffered another perennial XJR Le Mans problem of a broken exhaust en route, as well as body damage. (LAT Photographic)

1991 results

1st Volker Weidler/Johnny Herbert/Bertrand Gachot
Mazda 787B (002). 362 laps, 3,059.140 miles
(4923.200km), 127.464mph (205.133kph).

The second-placed XJR-12 (990) of Davey Jones, Raul Boesel and Michel Ferté was two laps adrift of the winning Mazda at the end, a frustrating and infuriating situation when the Jaguar was at least seven seconds a lap faster without the fuel restrictions. (LAT Photographic)

2nd Davy Jones/Raul Boesel/Michel Ferté Jaguar XJR-12 (990). 360 laps.
3rd Teo Fabi/Bob Wollek/Kenny Acheson Jaguar XJR-12 (991). 358 laps.
4th Derek Warwick/John Nielsen/Andy Wallace Jaguar XJR-12 (891). 356 laps.

Mazda's achievement was undeniable, but reliability and speed apart, it was the lenient weight limit that they had negotiated with FISA that really won them the race. The Jaguars, Saubers and Porsches had to be a minimum of 170kg (374lb) heavier, a huge disadvantage both in terms of fuel consumption and wear and tear. Porsche suffered most with engine, transmission and suspension breakages and their best car could only finish seventh. This was the last Le Mans appearance of the Tony Southgate-designed XJR in its various guises (Southgate had left TWR and joined Toyota in 1991) although it raced in its final 12D form at

Daytona (second) and Sebring (fourth) in 1992 and again at Daytona in 1993 where all three cars retired, one after leading.

As for the rest of 1991, TWR won with the XJR-14 at the Nürburgring (1, 2), finished third and fifth at Magny Cours, sixth at Mexico and second and third at Autopolis, the mysterious purpose-built facility in Japan that was never used again. Subsequently the XJR-14 that Teo Fabi had used was rebuilt into the Joest-entered Porsche WSC95 that won Le Mans in 1996/97! TWR won the Team Championship, Teo Fabi and Derek Warwick finished first and second in the Drivers' Championship and Jaguar won the Manufacturers' title. This was a fitting end to nearly seven seasons of sports car racing and almost the end of Jaguar participation by Tom Walkinshaw, the Scottish team having won three championships and three drivers' titles (1987, 1988 and 1991). One last attempt at Le Mans awaited, but that was two years away.

Chapter 23

1993/95 – A cat's tale

The end of the Sportscar World Championship in 1992 (Peugeot were the final winners) produced a regulatory vacuum. A new GT class had been mooted for 1993 but arguments over what constituted a GT car ended in dissaray. Cost was a major factor, as it seemed, and indeed it was, unlikely that any manufacturer would want to fund an expensive development programme for racing. This was all the more so when the decline of recent international championships was taken into account with the associated loss of sponsors, TV coverage and general prestige.

Nevertheless there was no shortage of potential vehicles for a GT series as Chevrolet, Ferrari, Honda, Jaguar, Lamborghini, Lotus, McLaren, Porsche, Venturi and the reborn Bugatti all had suitable cars. Ultimately there was no championship and all the races except Spa (that ran a GT-only event) opted for a mix of the outgoing sports prototypes and the new GT cars. Another variation on a theme was the proposed World Sports Cars, which were to be kit car open two-seaters with no ground effects, using production-based atmospheric engines only. For 1993 however the status quo was that there was no status quo.

It was no surprise therefore that the series (sic) comprised just five events and two of these were the long established American races at Daytona and Sebring, plus of course Le Mans. The two brave outsiders were Spa and Suzuka, the Japanese final round held on 29 August 1993. Daytona kicked off the season in January and the GT class,

designated 'Invitational' was won by Porsche whose 911 Carrera 2 dominated the category. Sebring produced a similar result with a brand-new twin-turbo 911S LM which was effectively a works car driven by Stuck/Rohrl/Haywood winning the GT class by 12 laps from a Corvette. There was now a three-month gap to the next race at Le Mans on 19/20 June, although a pre-qualifying session took place in May. Before this however a significant announcement was made by TWR that they were going to race three XJ220s at Le Mans. These were purpose-built carbon fibre racing versions of Jaguar's 3.5T V6 road supercar and were known as

After the special works Porsche 911 Turbo S LM of Stuck/Rohrl retired there was no other car to touch the TWR XJ220Cs. David Brabham, John Nielsen and David Coulthard won their class in chassis 002 with ease despite some very lengthy pit stops. Here they are followed by the No. 51 car (001) of Hahne/Percy/Leslie that lasted only six laps in the race before retiring with head gasket failure. (Sutton)

The Paul Belmondo, Jay Cochran, Andreas Fuchs car (003) was crashed twice, once in practice and again in the race, both times by Fuchs. If the Jaguar had not retired due to the subsequent overheating problems caused by the second shunt, they, rather than the No. 50 XJ220C would probably have won the GT class as Brabham had lost 73 minutes changing a fuel tank. (LAT Photographic)

XJ220Cs. Long-time TWR driver Win Percy debuted the car at Silverstone on 9 May winning the BRDC National GT race convincingly from various Porsche and Aston Martin derivatives. Meanwhile in Italy, on 16 May, Paulo Cutrera won an Italian Supercar GT round at Vallelunga with another TWR-prepared XJ220. Three days later at Le Mans the pre-qualifying session proved how serious Porsche were about GT racing with their factory-backed 911 turbo lapping in 4min 04.67sec driven by Hans Stuck. TWR brought along two XJ220s and David Brabham recorded 4min 16.92sec and Jay Cochran 4min 20.44sec, but they were concentrating on development and set-up rather than going for fast times.

The French classic attracted a reasonable entry despite the appalling state of affairs surrounding sports car racing, proving once again that it could stand on its own given the chance to escape political control. Outright victory would come from one of the Peugeot, Toyota or Porsche prototypes that were still allowed to race here. The French concern were fielding three works cars, Toyota five

cars (three works and two private) and Porsche, five of their now positively antediluvian privately entered 962 models. The GT class was much more healthy however with four Porsche Carrera 2s, seven Carrera RSRs and the works-backed Turbo S LM, a total of 12 911 models. Safety in numbers as ever. Ranged against them was an esoteric range of machinery comprising five Venturi 500LMs, two Lotus Esprit turbos, a lone Ferrari and of course the three TWR Jaguars. A Russian-entered 3.5T MiG M100 provided some novelty interest, but it was very slow and did not qualify. The TWR Jaguar entries were:

No. 50 John Nielsen/David Brabham/David
   Coulthard Jaguar XJ220C (002).
No. 51 Armin Hahne/Win Percy/David Leslie
   Jaguar XJ220C (001).
No. 52 Paul Belmondo/Jay Cochran/Andreas Fuchs
   Jaguar XJ220C (003).

The cars were running in IMSA trim so they could use wider rims although they were racing without the road spec catalytic converters but with restrictors that limited power to 500bhp. Driver pairings reflected a typical TWR mix of touring and sports car drivers, four of them (Nielsen, Percy, Brabham and Leslie) being throwbacks to the XJR days. Brabham, the youngest son of triple F1 World Champion Jack, had also raced in F1 with an uncompetitive car in 1990. David Coulthard had progressed up the greasy pole from F3 to F3000, German Armin Hahne was one of TWR's touring car racers and fellow countryman Fuchs was best known for Porsche Carrera and Supercup racing. Paul Belmondo was another F3000 candidate and Jay Cochran had made his name in American sports car racing.

Qualifying revealed the huge gap between the outgoing Category 1 and 2 prototypes and the new Category 4 GT cars. The front cover of British motorsport magazine *Autosport* proclaimed 'Real cars are back!' Real or not they made up nearly half of the entry even if they were rather pedestrian by previous standards. Main contenders in this class rested with the Porsche and Jaguar entries, the best times for each being:

Hans-Joachim Stuck 3.6T Porsche 911S LM 4min 06.51sec.

David Brabham 3.5T Jaguar XJ220C (001) 4min 07.88sec (Paul Belmondo 4min 10.50sec, Armin Hahne 4min 11.71sec).
Marc Duez 3.0T Venturi 500LM 4min 21.77sec.
Richard Piper 2.1T Lotus Esprit Turbo 4min 31.44sec.

David Brabham set his time despite the Jaguar falling off its jacks and on to his foot! A packet of frozen peas was applied to the injured part to help the swelling, but he remained in some pain for the rest of the weekend. Andreas Fuchs crashed the third TWR car on Wednesday evening, losing it under braking at 190mph (306kph) for the first Mulsanne chicane. Poor Fuchs could not understand what had happened as the car spun round and hit the barriers hard. Fortunately although badly frightened he escaped injury and the Jaguar was repairable. Already the exhaust problem was causing trouble when the car's first qualifying times were disallowed after it was realised by race steward Alan Bertaut that they were not using catalytic converters. Discussions between the interested parties including Walkinshaw and IMSA technical chief Amos Johnson, who took Walkinshaw's side in stating that when raced, IMSA spec cars did not require 'cats', resulted in

The profile of the No. 50 XJ220C reveals its almost standard lines apart from that rear wing, although it was very different from the road car in reality. (LAT Photographic)

stalemate. Bertaut disagreed (he and Walkinshaw had a history of dissent) and the cars were allowed to race under appeal. The lone Ferrari was way off the pace and crashed in the warm-up, while the best of the non-turbo Porsches recorded 4min 22.96sec, so the Stuck car and the Jaguars were obviously going to dominate, mishaps apart. For comparitive purposes the fastest time in qualifying was 3min 24.94sec set by Alliot's Peugeot 905B.

Right from the start Stuck's turbo Porsche took the lead in the GT class, leading for over an hour before pitting with a sticking throttle. He lost five laps but after six hours the car had regained nearly two of them when co-driver Walter Rohrl hit the back of an unsighted car approaching the first Mulsanne chicane. This split the oil tank and the car's engine seized, leaving the No. 50 TWR Jaguar in charge of the class. TWR had already lost the Hahne/Percy/Leslie car with head gasket failure on lap six, Hahne joking that he thought it was a 24-minute race rather than 24 hours. The other XJ220C took up station behind No. 50 but not without drama, all three drivers spinning the car, followed by the remaining Porsche RSR and Carrera brigade.

By 2.55am on Sunday morning the leading Jaguar pitted for 73 minutes while a leaking fuel

John Nielsen, David Brabham and a very youthful looking David Coulthard celebrate their class win, but that was before the 'entente cordiale' kicked in. (Sutton)

tank was replaced, losing its class lead to the other XJ220C. Just after half distance the hapless Fuchs had a tyre blowout further back up the road from his practice shunt, and the car spun right round, which he survived. The now thoroughly rattled German could only say: 'it was exactly the same'. Back in the pits the team could hear the stationary car revving furiously over the radio link as Fuchs sat mesmerised from his experience, saying 'I have crashed'. He finally got the car back to the pits with minimal damage to the bodywork, but the engine had suffered and shortly after Belmondo had taken over the overheating car was out. The No. 50 Jaguar had briefly lost its class lead thanks to the aforementioned lengthy pit stop to one of the Porsches but it was soon back in front and stayed there to the end. David Coulthard driving in his first Le Mans, told *Autosport* afterwards that 'Before I came here I had the usual single-seater attitude that they are the best and that's where the world is, but my eyes have been opened. I underestimated just how difficult Le Mans is. I've now got a lot more respect for all the guys who race here.'

1993 result

15th (1st GT) John Nielsen/David Brabham/David Coulthard Jaguar XJ220C (001) 306 laps.

They were two laps ahead of their nearest class pursuer, the 3.8 Porsche Carrera RSR of Gouhier/Barth/Dupuy.

Alas the exhaust controversy would not go away and the Jaguar was subsequently disqualified. According to the ACO the cars were excluded because although TWR had appealed to the organising club it had failed to lodge its appeal with the *Federation Francais du Sport* in time. So there! TWR's Roger Silman was quoted in *Autosport:* 'We believe that we followed the appeal procedure as it's laid out. Since the race, we received no communication from Le Mans whatsoever. We're completely baffled as to what's going on and Tom [Walkinshaw] is simply not going to accept the ACO's decision.' Happily, TWR and Jaguar had proved the point and being disqualified over something that conferred little or no

advantage did not diminish the achievement. Thereafter TWR raced the 003 chassis at Elkhart Lake winning the International GT class and finishing 10th overall, but that was the last hurrah for 1993.

During 1994 there were no Jaguars competing in the championship, a great pity as a well-sorted XJ220 would surely have been a winner. For 1995 British team Chamberlain Engineering ran an XJ220 with no real success in some rounds of what was now titled the Global Endurance Series, yet another change of name. A new addition was the legendary McLaren F1 road car in racing mode which quickly became the vehicle of choice in the category. It had already won six of the seven preceding rounds before Le Mans. Originally Hugh Chamberlain had intended to enter two XJ220s for Le Mans, but the one car (pre-production chassis

No. 4) that they took to pre-qualifying on 30 April suffered terminal electrical problems and did not qualify, ending their bid. Two did make it however, these being the special carbon fibre cars built by TWR in 1992/93 entered by PC Automotive with additional support from XK Engineering. They were chassis 003 driven by Win Percy (the same car he had driven in 1993) and Tiff Needell in chassis 001, recording 4min 03.23sec and 4min 03.63sec respectively nearly five seconds quicker than their 1993 race qualification time. By comparison the best McLaren recorded 3min 58.78sec, but the fastest GT-1 car was Ferte's Ferrari F40LM with 3min 55.51sec. For the actual race the two Jaguars started in the following order:

No. 57 Richard Piper/Tiff Needell/James Weaver
Jaguar XJ220C (003).

The PC Automotive team and their two ex-TWR Jaguar XJ220Cs – Nos 58 (001) and 57 (003) – face the cameras at Le Mans 1995. The drivers are left to right, Olindo Iacobelli, Bernard Thuner, Win Percy, Tiff Needell, Richard Piper and James Weaver. Sadly, both cars retired and the enormous financial outlay and associated costs ended in financial meltdown for the team and its principals. (Win Percy)

Win Percy in 001 leads a long stream of cars down the hill as he turns into the beginning of the Esses. This car was crashed by Iacobelli and was subsequently withdrawn due to very wayward handling, a legacy of the accident damage. (LAT Photographic)

No. 58 Bernard Thuner/Olindo Iacobelli/Win Percy Jaguar XJ220C (001).

Both cars had strength in depth with Needell, Weaver, Thuner and former TWR man Win Percy backing up the lesser known Piper and Italian Olindo Iacobelli. Also present was a lone Lister Storm driven by Geoff Lees, Rupert Keegan and

Dominic Chappell powered by a Jaguar V12.

The best GT times were now dipping below the four-minute mark and for the first time there was almost the probability of one of these winning the race, the old prototype machines being few in number and no longer of the first rank. Apart from the seven McLaren F1 GTRs there were three Ferrari F40s, two Nissan Skylines, three Honda NSXs, three Calloway Corvettes, eight Porsche 911 GT2s, two Porsche 993s, one Toyota Supra, three Venturi 600s, two Marcos LM600s, the single Lister and, of course, the two Jaguars. The fastest times of the leading contenders representing each marque were as follows:

Fabio Mancini Ferrari F40-GTE (9001) 3min 55.15sec.
JJ Lehto McLaren F1 GTR (001R) 3min 57.18sec.
Jean-Marc Gounon Venturi 600SLM 3min 57.64sec
Dominique Dupuy Porsche 911RSR GTI 4min 02.91sec.
Tiff Needell Jaguar XJ220C (003) 4min 08.67sec (Win Percy 4min 09.45sec).
Almo Coppelli Calloway Corvette (02/95) 4min 09.19sec.

The Jaguars were not as fast in official qualifying as they had been in April, apparently running low boost for reliability purposes, but overall they were about midway in the GT class. The single Lister Storm recorded a worthy 4min 09.21sec, driven by Geoff Lees.

Unhappily for Jaguar Le Mans 1995 was not a vintage year. Rupert Keegan, sometime forgotten F1 driver, retired the Lister on lap 40 with gearbox failure, but the two XJ220Cs were going well initially. Wet weather during the night caused many crashes and Win Percy described the Jaguars as 'animals' in the slippery conditions. Win had made a decision to turn down the boost in the No. 58 car in deference to the dreadful weather, but this was a mistake as it lost ground to the other XJ220C. Nevertheless by midnight the Needell/Weaver/Piper car was running fourth with the other in ninth until Iacobelli hit the wall at the Porsche Curves. He came back to the pits and Win Percy took over, but found the car wandering all over the

road. Finally, after three more stops the car was withdrawn on lap 123 as it was too dangerous and obviously in serious structural trouble. Sadly the leading Jaguar broke its crankshaft less than an hour later on lap 135 and that was the end of the dream.

So they had acquitted themselves well enough, but the true potential of this car in carbon fibre form was never realised in competition. This was the last time in the present era that Jaguar raced at Le Mans, 45 years after they first appeared at the

Sarthe with three XK120s. The latter-day Lawrence Pearce Lister concern tried again in 1996 and were much faster, finishing 19th, returned in 1997 faster still (3min 49.563sec) but retired both cars. These machines however were far more Lister than Jaguar, and fall outside this book's terms of reference.

Sadly another, era ended in 1995 with the death of F. R. W. 'Lofty' England in May, one of the few surviving links with that first Le Mans attempt and the many triumphs that followed.

A night pit stop for the Piper/Needell/Weaver car (003) that briefly held fourth place before retiring with a broken crankshaft on lap 135. This was the last Jaguar to race at Le Mans in the 20th century, and the last as this book was written. (LAT Photographic)

Chapter 24

Reflections

When Jaguar first raced at Le Mans in 1950 the Second World War was only five years distant, and much of Europe was still under repair, albeit somewhat more rapidly and effectively than the chaotic mess in the UK.

British motoring journalists of the day were only too keen to cover foreign motor races like Le Mans as it guaranteed them an escape from the endless rationing, dreadful food and punitive restrictions imposed by the post-war Labour government. One famous motoring scribbler described it as 'Fortress Britain', so Jaguar's involvement at a world famous event like Le Mans was certain of a good British press.

The first post-war Le Mans in 1949 had been won by a 2-litre Ferrari, and a year later, when three XK120s were entered, the main opposition comprised thinly disguised 4.5-litre Talbot Lago grand prix cars and various Ferraris. However, as Jaguar quickly realised following their better-than-expected performance, a purpose-built car utilising the XK engine could win and so it turned out. The C-type victory of 1951 further enhanced Jaguar's already considerable reputation and the associated sales successes, especially in America.

With their second Le Mans victory in 1953 and the advent of the D-type one year later, Jaguar's racing had provided them with a perfect marketing tool for their production cars which was always the main priority. Their immediate counterparts at Aston Martin, Ferrari and more latterly Maserati, also made road cars, but these were virtually bespoke and certainly not series production cars in the volumes that Jaguar produced. These companies also built and sold some of their racing models to private entrants, but only Jaguar (and later Porsche) made competitive production versions, that could be bought off the shelf, in considerable numbers. A total of five Le Mans victories between 1950 and 1957 was unmatched by any other manufacturer and proved just how good Jaguar really were. How proud were the owners of XK140s and XK150s that bore the small enamel badge on the boot lid proclaiming those Le Mans wins. For Lyons and Heynes the goals had been more than achieved.

By contrast the Italians were first and foremost racing car manufacturers, while Aston Martin's priorities were probably half and half, and only viable due to David Brown's relatively deep pockets. After 1959 they too stopped official participation in sports car racing, unable to afford any new designs, leaving only their outdated and obsolete front-engined F1 project that expired in late 1960. They did reappear with the Project 212, 214 and 215 GT/Prototype cars in 1962/63 but these were only active and competitive briefly, victims of the new mid-engined era which began in 1963. Mercedes-Benz, who had won Le Mans in 1952 and then nearly everything they entered in F1 and sports car racing in 1954/55 bar Le Mans 1955, took a similar view to Jaguar, and quit, preferring to concentrate on their production facilities and future passenger vehicle investment. Only Porsche managed to satisfactorily combine volume production and racing with permanent factory involvement, possibly because their product base was very narrowly defined. Development and evolution rather than revolution meant that there was enough money to fund both spheres.

After their official withdrawal Jaguar continued in racing via private entrants at Le Mans and elsewhere. They offered factory preparation and assistance but the various 3-litre engines produced between 1958 and 1960 and the one-off E2A were never sufficiently developed and suffered accordingly. Even when the production E-type was launched in 1961, the chance to produce a proper racing version for the very prestigious GT category was squandered. They could have dominated GT racing for two years, had they been so inclined.

One low-drag coupé was produced but despite internal enthusiasm for the project, this was not fully pursued. The 1963 'lightweight' E-type was a more serious attempt, but in reality it was still half-hearted and hobbled by lack of funding and factory development. Too little, too late. Motor racing had begun to metamorphose into something more focused, more specialised, more competitive and more scientific. Jaguar had been away too long and needed all-new cars, engines and faces to make up the lost ground, but the will to do so and the huge investment required was lacking. The now legendary XJ13 was yet another example. Developed piecemeal and very slowly, it was never going to race in time and was ultimately used for testing and finally publicity purposes only.

However as already noted elsewhere, Jaguar were unable to escape the pull of racing, their close involvement with Briggs Cunningham proving very successful in American racing during the late 1950s and early 1960s. So it was entirely appropriate that the Americans should provide the catalyst for a reborn racing reputation. In stark contrast BL's Broadspeed V12 XJC debacle of 1976/77 is best forgotten. Ironically it was the obsolete V12 E-type raced successfully in the States by Group 44 (Bob Tullius) and Joe Huffaker in 1975 that would lead to the Trans Am XJS and ultimately the Group 44 Lee Dykstra-designed XJR-5. To begin with the *raison d'être* was driven by the need to boost flagging sales, and it succeeded. This in turn led to the 1984/85 Le Mans entries that pre-empted Jaguar's official return via TWR back into championship sports car racing. TWR had already won many races and the European Touring Car Championship with the XJS, but the possibility of winning Le Mans again must surely have been encouraged by the efforts of Group 44.

The belt and braces, experience is all, 'that's the way we do it' world of the 1950s had long since disappeared over the pale horizon. Now it was necessary to be at the forefront of innovation and technology, anything less and you were left behind very quickly. Unlike Porsche, who had kept their factory competition department alive and continued racing and winning all those years, Jaguar had no such infrastructure. It was necessary to employ a specialist racing team instead, and TWR was the best and most obvious choice. They had a successful track record, brilliant designer (Tony Southgate), knew all about the Jaguar V12 engine, enjoyed state-of-the-art facilities and employed some of the very best drivers. Even so it took three years to finally end Porsche's domination at Le Mans, such was the grip that the German company had on sports car racing. TWR Jaguars won twice at Le Mans, and would have won more but for bad luck and unfavourable fuel and weight regulations. Unlike their Browns Lane predecessors they also won the Sports Car Championship or its equivalent three times, something that was never of course a priority for Lyons and Heynes more than three decades earlier. These achievements, starting from scratch against such formidable opposition can never be overstated. TWR and all involved deserve far greater recognition for their efforts than they have ever received.

There is a common thread running through the long history of Jaguar racing, and specifically at Le Mans. It is the use of production-based engines and the fact that all seven Le Mans victories from 1951 to 1990 used just two basic engines, the XK twin-cam six, and the single-cam V12 originally designed for production use that arrived in 1971. Admittedly, the V12 underwent a complete transformation, but it was still the same basic design that powered the Series 3 E-type. Wally Hassan had a hand in both, and it is a wonderful achievement that these two road car engines should be able to take on and defeat the very best of all the pukka racing engines of their respective eras. The final attempts that were limited to the GT class by the XJ220s in 1993 and 1995 were thwarted by regulatory inconsistency and in the last instance by lack of funding. Even so they still acquitted themselves well, or as a famous American driver once remarked of another occasion, 'Not too shabby'.

For many however it is the memory, or even the suggestion imprinted upon the mind by countless filmic and photographic images, of the lithe, beautifully curved dark green C-types and D-types racing into the twilight over the French countryside long ago, that lingers on.

Drivers

The following is an alphabetical list of drivers, nationalities and the years that they raced Jaguar and Jaguar-powered cars at Le Mans:

Kenneth Acheson (GB) 1991
Tony Adamowicz (USA) 1984
Jim Adams (USA) 1985
Claude Ballot-Lena (F) 1984/85
Don Beauman (GB) 1955
Paul Belmondo (F) 1993
Clemente Biondetti (I) 1951
Peter Blond (GB) 1959
Raul Boesel (BR) 1987/88, 1991
Peter Bolton (GB) 1956
David Brabham (AUS) 1993
Gianfranco Brancatelli (I) 1986
Jean-Pierre Brousselet or Brussin 'Mary' (F) 1957/58
Martin Brundle (GB) 1987/88, 1990
Ivor Bueb (GB) 1955/56/57/58/59
'Doc' Bundy (USA) 1984
Maurice Charles (GB) 1958, 1962
Eddie Cheever (USA) 1986/87
Johnny Claes (B) 1954/55
Peter Clark (GB) 1950
Price Cobb (USA) 1988/89/90
Jay Cochran (USA) 1993
Kevin Cogan (USA) 1988
David Coulthard (GB) 1993
John Coundley (GB) 1962 (Did not drive in the race as car retired early.)
Briggs Cunningham (USA) 1962/63
Derek Daly (IRL) 1988/89
Norman Dewis (GB) 1955

Claude Dubois (B) 1958
Johnny Dumfries (GB) 1988
Teo Fabi (I) 1991
Jack Fairman (GB) 1951, 1956, 1958
Alain Ferté (F) 1989/90
Michel Ferté (F) 1989/90/91
Paul Frère (B) 1956/57
Andreas Fuchs (D) 1993
Andrew Gilbert-Scott (GB) 1989
Masten Gregory (USA) 1957/58/59 (Did not drive in the 1958 race as car retired early.)
Bob Grossman (USA) 1963
André Guelfi (F) 1958
Dan Gurney (USA) 1960
Bert Hadley (GB) 1950
Armin Hahne (D) 1993
Nick Haines (GB) 1950
Bruce Halford (GB) 1958/59/60
Duncan Hamilton (GB) 1952/53/54/55, 1957/58
Walt Hansgen (USA) 1960/63
Mike Hawthorn (GB) 1955/56
Hurley Haywood (USA) 1985/86
Hans Heyer (D) 1986
Olindo Iacobelli (I) 1995
Leslie Johnson (GB) 1950/51 (Did not drive in the 1951 race as car retired early.)
Davy Jones (USA) 1988/89/90/91
Franz Konrad (A) 1990
Jeff Krosnoff (USA) 1991
Jan Lammers (NL) 1987/88/89/90
Roger Laurent (B) 1953/54
John Lawrence (GB) 1957/58/59 (Did not drive in the 1958 race as car retired early.)

Robert Lawrie (GB) 1951
David Leslie (GB) 1990/91, 1993 (Did not drive in the 1993 race as car retired early.)
Peter Lindner (D) 1964
Jean Lucas (F) 1957
Peter Lumsden (GB) 1962/63/64
John Marshall (GB) 1950
Mauro Martini (I) 1991
Stirling Moss (GB) 1951/52/53/54
Brian Naylor (GB) 1958
Tiff Needell (GB) 1995
John Nielsen (DK) 1987/88/89/90/91, 1993
Peter Nöcker (D) 1964
Augie Pabst (USA) 1963
Win Percy (GB) 1986/87, 1993, 1995 (Did not drive in the 1993 race as car retired early.)
Larry Perkins (AUS) 1988
Henri Pescarolo (F) 1988
Richard Piper (GB) 1995
Brian Redman (GB) 1984/85/86
Paul Richards (USA) 1963
'Chip' Robinson (USA) 1985
Tony Rolt (GB) 1952/53/54/55
Freddy Rouselle (B) 1956/57/58
Eliseo Salazar (RCH) 1989/90
Roy Salvadori (GB) 1962/63
Ninian Sanderson (GB) 1956/57/58
Peter Sargent 1962/63/64
Jean-Louis Schlesser (F) 1986
Bill Spear (USA) 1955
Ian Stewart (GB) 1952/53
Danny Sullivan (USA) 1988

Jacques Swaters (B) 1954/55/56
Patrick Tambay (F) 1989
Bernard Thuner (CH) 1995
Desmond Titterington (GB) 1956 (Did not drive in the race as co-driver Paul Frère crashed on lap two.)
Charles de Tornaco (B) 1953
Bob Tullius (USA) 1984/85
Peter Walker (GB) 1951/52/53/54
Andy Wallace (GB) 1988/89/90/91
Ivan Waller (GB) 1951
Robert Walshaw (GB) 1956
Phil Walters (USA) 1955
Derek Warwick (GB) 1986, 1991
John Watson (GB) 1984, 1987/88
James Weaver (GB) 1995
Ken Wharton (GB) 1954, 1956 (He did not drive in the 1956 race as co-driver Jack Fairman retired on lap two due to accident damage.)
Graham Whitehead (GB) 1955
Peter Whitehead (GB) 1950/51/52/53/54/55
Bob Wollek (F) 1991
John Young (GB) 1958 (Did not drive in the race as car retired early.)

A total of 106 drivers practised and nine apparently did not race due to early race retirements. One Jaguar driver died (Brousselet in 1958). Of the total, 16 were works Jaguar drivers during the 1950s, and 40 were employed by TWR. Reserve drivers are not included.

Le Mans Jaguars

Listed below by year are the Jaguar and Jaguar-powered entries for the period 1950–95 with drivers, chassis numbers and results.

1950

No. 15 Haines/Clark Jaguar XK120 660041 12th
No. 16 P. Whitehead/Marshall Jaguar XK120 660042 15th
No. 17 Johnson/Hadley Jaguar XK120 660040 Retired

1951

No. 20 Walker/P. Whitehead Jaguar C-type XKC003 1st
No. 21 Lawrie/Waller Jaguar XK120 660449 11th
No. 22 Moss/Fairman Jaguar C-type XKC002 Retired
No. 23 Johnson/Biondetti Jaguar C-type XKC001 Retired

1952

No. 17 Moss/Walker Jaguar C-type XKC011 Retired
No. 18 Rolt/Hamilton Jaguar C-type XKC001 Retired
No. 19 P. Whitehead/Stewart Jaguar C-type XKC002 Retired

1953

No. 17 Moss/Walker Jaguar C-type XKC053 2nd
No. 18 Rolt/Hamilton Jaguar C-type XKC051 1st

No. 19 P. Whitehead/Stewart Jaguar C-type XKC052 4th
No. 20 Laurent/de Tornaco Jaguar C-type XKC047/012 9th

1954

No. 12 Moss/Walker Jaguar D-type XKC403 Retired
No. 14 Rolt/Hamilton Jaguar D-type XKC402 2nd
No. 15 P. Whitehead/Wharton Jaguar D-type XKC404 Retired
No. 16 Laurent/Swaters Jaguar C-type XKC047 4th
The No. 16 Belgian-entered C-type was an amalgam of two cars after it was crashed en route to Le Mans and rebuilt using Jaguar's own XKC012 as a donor vehicle.

1955

No. 6 Hawthorn/Bueb Jaguar D-type XKD505 1st
No. 7 Rolt/Hamilton Jaguar D-type XKD506 Retired
No. 8 Beauman/Dewis Jaguar D-type XKD508 Retired
No. 9 Spear/Walters Jaguar D-type XKD507 Retired
No. 10 Claes/Swaters Jaguar D-type XKD503 3rd
No. 11 P. Whitehead/G. Whitehead Cooper-Jaguar MkII CJ/1/55 Retired

1956

No. 1 Hawthorn/Bueb Jaguar D-type XKD605 6th

No. 2 Frère/Titterington Jaguar D-type XKD603 (Replaced XKD606) Retired

No. 3 Fairman/Wharton Jaguar D-type XKD602 Retired

No. 4 Flockhart/Sanderson Jaguar D-type XKD501 1st

No. 5 Swaters/Rouselle Jaguar D-type XKD573 4th

No. 6 Walshaw/Bolton Jaguar XK140 FHC S804231 Disqualified

1957

No. 3 Flockhart/Bueb Jaguar D-type XKD606 1st

No. 4 Hamilton/Gregory Jaguar D-type XKD601 6th

No. 15 Sanderson/Lawrence Jaguar D-type XKD603 2nd

No. 16 Frère/Rouselle Jaguar D-type XKD573 4th

No. 17 Lucas/Brousselet ('Mary') Jaguar D-type XKD513 3rd

1958

No. 6 Fairman/Gregory Jaguar D-type XKD603 Retired

No. 7 Sanderson/Lawrence Jaguar D-type XKD504 Retired

No. 8 Hamilton/Bueb Jaguar D-type XKD601 Retired

No. 9 Dubois/Rouselle Lister-Jaguar BHL105 Retired

No. 10 Halford/Naylor Lister-Jaguar BHL5 15th

No. 11 Brousselet ('Mary')/Guelfi Jaguar D-type XKD513 Retired (Brousselet killed in accident.)

No. 57 Charles/Young Jaguar D-type XKD502 Retired

1959

No. 1 Bueb/Halford Lister-Jaguar BHL2.59 Retired

No. 2 Hansgen/Blond Lister-Jaguar BHL3.59 Retired

No. 3 Ireland/Gregory Jaguar D-type XKD603 Retired

No. 4 Flockhart/Lawrence Tojeiro-Jaguar TAD 1/59 Retired

1960

No. 5 Flockhart/Halford Jaguar D-type XKD606 Retired

No. 6 Gurney/Hansgen Jaguar E-type E2A Retired

1962

No. 8 Charles/Coundley Jaguar E-type 860458 Retired

No. 9 Sargent/Lumsden Jaguar E-type 850009 5th

No. 10 Salvadori/Cunningham Jaguar E-type 860630 4th

1963

No. 14 Hansgen/Pabst Jaguar 'lightweight' E-type 850664 Retired

No. 15 Grossman/Cunningham Jaguar 'lightweight' E-type 850659 9th

No. 16 Salvadori/Richards Jaguar 'lightweight' E-type 850665 Retired (Destroyed in accident and written off.)

No. 17 Sargent/Lumsden Lister-Jaguar Retired

1964

No. 16 Lindner/Nöcker Jaguar 'lightweight' E-type 850662 Retired

No. 17 Sargent/Lumsden Jaguar 'lightweight' E-type 850663 Retired

1984

No. 40 Adamowicz/Watson/Ballot-Lena Group 44 Jaguar XJR-5 008 Retired

No. 44 Tullius/Redman/Bundy Jaguar Group 44 XJR-5 Jaguar XJR-5 006 Retired

1985

No. 40 Redman/Adams/Haywood Group 44 Jaguar XJR-5 006 Retired

No. 44 Tullius/Robinson/Ballot-Lena Group 44 Jaguar XJR-5 008 13th

1986

No. 51 Warwick/Cheever/Schlesser TWR Jaguar XJR-6 286 Retired

No. 52 Heyer/Haywood/Redman TWR Jaguar
XJR-6 186 Retired

No. 53 Brancatelli/Percy/Haywood TWR Jaguar
XJR-6 Retired

1987

No. 4 Cheever/Boesel/Lammers TWR Jaguar XJR-
8LM 387 5th

No. 5 Watson/Percy/Lammers TWR Jaguar XJR-
8LM 286 Retired

No. 6 Brundle/Nielsen TWR Jaguar XJR-8LM 186
Retired

1988

No. 1 Brundle/Nielsen TWR Jaguar XJR-9LM 588
Retired

No. 2 Lammers/Dumfries/Wallace TWR Jaguar
XJR-9LM 488 1st

No. 3 Boesel/Watson/Pescarolo TWR Jaguar
XJR9-LM 287 Retired

No. 21 Sullivan/Jones/Cobb TWR Jaguar XJR9-
LM 186 16th

No. 22 Daly/Perkins/Cogan TWR Jaguar XJR9-
LM 188 4th

1989

No. 1 Lammers/Tambay/Gilbert-Scott TWR Jaguar
XJR9-LM 588 4th

No. 2 Nielsen/Wallace/Cobb TWR Jaguar XJR9-
LM 688 Retired

No. 3 Jones/Daly TWR Jaguar XJR-9LM 288
Retired

No. 4 A. Ferté/M. Ferté/Salazar TWR Jaguar
XJR9-LM 287 8th

1990

No. 1 Brundle/A. Ferté/Leslie TWR Jaguar XJR-
12 990 Retired

No. 2 Lammers/Wallace/Konrad TWR Jaguar
XJR-12 290 2nd

No. 3 Nielsen/Cobb/Brundle TWR Jaguar XJR-12
1090 1st

No. 4 Jones/M. Ferté/Salazar TWR Jaguar XJR-12
190 Retired

1991

No. 33 Warwick/Nielsen/Wallace TWR Jaguar
XJR-12 891 4th

No. 34 Fabi/Wollek/Acheson TWR Jaguar XJR-12
991 3rd

No. 35 Jones/Boesel/M. Ferté TWR Jaguar XJR-12
990 2nd

No. 36 Leslie/Martini/Krosnoff TWR Jaguar XJR-
12 190 Retired

1993

No. 50 Nielsen/Brabham/Coulthard TWR Jaguar
XJ220C 002 15th (1st GT)
(Subsequently disqualified.)

No. 51 Hahne/Percy/Leslie TWR Jaguar XJ220C
001 Retired

No. 52 Belmondo/Cochran/Fuchs TWR Jaguar
XJ220C 003 Retired

1995

No. 57 Piper/Needell/Weaver Jaguar XJ220C 003
Retired

No. 58 Thuner/Iacobelli/Percy Jaguar XJ220C 001
Retired

Jaguar and Jaguar-powered cars made 89 starts
spread over 24 races that produced seven wins
(1951, 1953, 1955/56/57, 1988 and 1990); five
second places (1953/54, 1957, 1990 and 1991);
three third places (1955, 1957 and 1991); eight
fourth places (1953/54, 1956/57, 1962, 1988/89 and
1991); two fifth places (1962 and 1987); two sixth
places (1956/57) and ten other finishes outside the
first six including the 1993 disqualification. A total
of 37 finishes out of 89 starts gives a survival rate of
41.57 per cent.

Jaguar, in its original 1950s factory guise, entered
six Le Mans as a works team and won three (1951,
1953 and 1955) with two won by Ecurie Ecosse
(1956/57). TWR also entered six Le Mans,
excluding their one-off GT class attempt in 1993,
and won two races (1988 and 1990).

Bibliography

Bamsey, Ian and Saward, Joe *Jaguar V12 Race Cars*, Osprey Publishing Limited 1986

Clarke, R. M. *Le Mans 'The Porsche & Jaguar Years' 1983–1991* Brooklands Books Ltd

Clausager, Anders Ditlev *Le Mans*, Arthur Barker Limited 1982

Clausager, Anders Ditlev and Clarke R. M. *Le Mans 'The Jaguar Years' 1949–1957* Brooklands Books Ltd

Clausager, Anders Ditlev and Clarke R. M. *Le Mans 'The Ferrari Years' 1958–1965* Brooklands Books Ltd

Edwards, Robert *Archie and the Listers,* Patrick Stephens Limited 1995

Finn, Joel E. *Ferrari Testa Rossa V12,* Osprey Publishing Limited 1980

Frère, Paul (translated by Louis Klemantaski) *Starting Grid to Chequered Flag,* B. T. Batsford Ltd 1962

Gauld, Graham *Ecurie Ecosse A Social History of Motor Racing from the Fifties to the Nineties,* Graham Gauld Public Relations Ltd 1992

Hamilton, Duncan and Scott, Lionel *Touch Wood,* Barrie & Rockliff 1960

Hawthorn, Mike and Wilkins Gordon, *Challenge Me the Race,* William Kimber and Co. Limited 1958

Hodges, David *The Le Mans 24 Hour Race,* Temple Press Books Limited 1963

Ireland, Innes *All Arms and Elbows,* Pelham Books Ltd 1967

Jaguar at Le Mans 1954–1958 Random Films Ltd

Ludvigsen, Karl *Mercedes-Benz Quicksilver Century,* Transport Bookman Publications 1995

Moss, Stirling and Nye, Doug *Stirling Moss My Cars, Career,* Patrick Stephens Limited 1987

Nixon, Chris *Mon Ami Mate The Bright Brief Lives of Mike Hawthorn & Peter Collins,* Transport Bookman Publications 1991

Nixon, Chris and Wyer, John *Racing with the David Brown Aston Martins Volume One,* Transport Bookman Publications 1980

Nye, Doug *Powered by Jaguar,* Motor Racing Publications Ltd 1980

Orsini, Luigi *Mille Miglia Una Corsa Italiana,* Edizioni Abiemme 1990

Pascal, Dominique *British Cars at Le Mans,* Haynes Publishing 1990

Pascal, Dominique *Ferraris at Le Mans,* Haynes Publishing Group 1986

Porter, Philip *Jaguar E-type The Definitive History,* Haynes Publishing 1989

Porter, Philip *Jaguar Sports Racing Cars C-type, D-type, XKSS, Lightweight E-type,* Bay View Books Ltd 1995

Skilleter, Paul *Jaguar Sports Cars,* Haynes Publishing 1975

Small, Steve *Grand Prix Who's Who 3rd Edition,* Travel Publishing Ltd 2000

The Le Mans 24-Hour Race 1949–1973 (Translated and adapted by D. B. Tubbs) Automobile Year/Christian Moity, Edita S.A. 1974

Whyte, Andrew *Jaguar Sports Racing & Works Competition Cars to 1953,* Haynes Publishing 1982

Whyte, Andrew *Jaguar Sports Racing & Works Competition Cars from 1954,* Haynes Publishing 1987

Wilkinson, 'Wilkie' and Jones, Chris *'Wilkie' The Motor Racing Legend,* Nelson & Saunders 1987

Wimpffen, János L. *Time and Two Seats Five Decades of Long Distance Racing* Books 1 and 2 Motorsport Research Group 1999

It should be noted that the excellent Brooklands Books compilations comprise period race reports from: *Autocar, Autosport, Car & Driver, Modern Motor, Motor, Motor Sport, Motor Trend, Road & Track, Sporting Motorist* and *Wheels.*

Additional issues of *Autosport* and *Motor Sport* were used for reference purposes regarding the later Le Mans races.

Index